Information Management Technology

A librarian's guide

Information Management Technology

A librarian's guide

Paul F. Burton

Lecturer
Department of Information Science
University of Strathclyde

J. Howard Petrie

Principal Administrator – Systems Development
European Patent Office
Munich

CHAPMAN AND HALL

University and Professional Division

LONDON • NEW YORK • TOKYO • MELBOURNE • MADRAS

UK	Chapman and Hall, 2–6 Boundary Row, London SE1 8HN
USA	Van Nostrand Reinhold, 115 5th Avenue, New York NY10003
JAPAN	Chapman and Hall Japan, Thomson Publishing Japan, Hirakawacho Nemoto Building, 7F, 1–7–11 Hirakawa-cho, Chiyoda-ku, Tokyo 102
AUSTRALIA	Chapman and Hall Australia, Thomas Nelson Australia, 480 La Trobe Street, PO Box 4725, Melbourne 3000
INDIA	Chapman and Hall India, R. Seshadri, 32 Second Main Road, CIT East, Madras 600 035

First edition 1991
Previously published in 1986 as *The librarian's guide to microcomputers for information management*

© 1991 Paul F. Burton and J. Howard Petrie

Typeset in 10½/12½pt Times by
Scarborough Typesetting Services, Scarborough
Printed in Great Britain by
T. J. Press (Padstow) Ltd, Padstow, Cornwall

ISBN 0 412 34130 1
     0 442 31275 4 (USA)

British Library Cataloguing in Publication Data
Burton, Paul F. (Paul Frederick) *1947–*
   Information Management Technology
   A librarian's guide
   1. Libraries. Applications of microcomputer systems
   I. Title.   II. Petrie, J. Howard.   III. Burton, Paul F.
   (Paul Frederick) *1947–*, Librarian's guide to microcomputers for information management
   025.00285416

      ISBN 0–412–34130–1

Library of Congress Cataloging-in-Publication Data
Burton, Paul F.
   Information Management Technology
   A librarian's guide
   Paul F. Burton, J. Howard Petrie. – 1st ed.
      p.   cm.
   Includes bibliographical references and index.
   ISBN 0–412–34130–1
   1. Microcomputers – Library applications.
   2. Information services – Automation – Management.
   3. Libraries – Automation – Management.
   4. Information technology.   5. Information retrieval.
   I. Petrie, J. Howard.   II. Title.
   Z678.93.M53B87   1990
   025′.00285′416 – dc20   90–42752
                                                                       CIP

Contents

Preface

Once again the wide-ranging and rapid developments in microcomputer technology of the last few years have meant that a detailed revision of *The librarian's guide to microcomputers for information management* was required, if it was to fulfil its objectives of providing a single source of information on the process of automating with a microcomputer.

For this new edition, we have taken into account not only the developments in hardware, but also the growing sophistication and power of software, and the growing sophistication of library and information service managers. The latter are more and more familiar with the use, or at least the principles, of microcomputers, and it no longer seems necessary to spell out certain details. We have, where relevant, indicated sources of more detailed information, particularly of practical applications, and so we hope that the changes we have made will ensure that this book remains of value to practitioner and student alike.

ACKNOWLEDGEMENTS

We remain, as always, grateful to those who have written or spoken about their experiences with microcomputers and have described applications. We would also like to thank the referees who commented on a first draft of the book, and provided useful suggestions and amendments. Mandy and Lindesay once again patiently accepted our absence during the writing of this edition.

In the course of this book, numerous software, hardware and other commercial products are mentioned by name. This does not imply any form of recommendation or endorsement by either the authors or the publisher. Rather than attempt any conversion of prices which might result in a misleading impression, prices have been retained as sterling or US dollars, where appropriate.

Electronics for microcomputers | 1

1.1 MILLIONS OF MICROCOMPUTERS

There are microcomputers in homes in North America, Western Europe and elsewhere. Very inexpensive machines cost only a few hundred dollars and they can be bought in stores, supermarkets and by mail-order. The number and sizes of microcomputer magazines have rocketed; *Byte*, which is perhaps the best known worldwide, regularly tops 400 pages per issue. Other magazines, such as *PC Magazine (USA)* have specialized in particular sectors, in this case in IBM and so-called IBM-compatible microcomputers. This particular magazine appears approximately twice a month, generating around 10 000 pages a year. Microcomputers feature heavily in the press in many other countries, even though those publications from the USA are widely distributed abroad. In addition to the specialist press, it is common for national daily newspapers to carry regular sections on information processing.

The microcomputer industry is dominated by the United States. However, other countries have begun to play an increasingly important role. Japan is strong in certain products, such as portable computers, optical disks, printers, scanners and integrated circuits. Other Far Eastern countries, such as Taiwan and South Korea, have also made their mark, particularly in producing inexpensive machines. In relation to the size of its markets, the microcomputer industry in Europe is relatively underdeveloped.

The list of available software and the bibliography at the end of this book show that information retrieval and library applications are not being left behind. These applications will be described in this book, in addition to some of the general-purpose software now in production. The microcomputers used may not cost very much more than the inexpensive machines used at home, such has been the rate of progress. However, the range of programs available has grown and we are demanding more powerful machines to run them. The manufacturers continue to supply them, with increasing value for money. More powerful machines can perform several tasks and serve more than one user simultaneously. It is also now commonplace to join together individual microcomputers, printers, etc., into networks.

It is sometimes difficult to define, therefore, how microcomputers differ from their larger relations, particularly the minicomputer and the so-called engineering workstations. They are certainly at the cheap end of the market and their availability has been brought about by the development of integrated circuits. These have been used to produce a range of electronic devices or 'chips' at low cost, so enabling computers to be marketed at the extremely low prices we see today.

The development of integrated circuits led to the birth of large numbers of new companies, and the success of the microcomputer led even the giant IBM to begin to produce its own machines, a move which did much to make the microcomputer industry come of age. Since then, IBM has been the leading force in microcomputers, although other companies, such as Apple, have produced innovations which have contributed to their success. The introduction of the IBM PC (personal computer), with its Intel microprocessor, led many other companies to produce machines which were very similar, in addition to optional extras and spare parts for the same machines. This 'standardization' created a huge industry which is still growing and which has led to the favourable prices seen today.

Microcomputers are not the answer to all our computer problems, although they are taking on many more tasks today than would have been thought possible even five years ago. For very small organizations, they may serve most of the immediate needs, and when joined together into networks, they can be quite powerful systems. However, in larger organizations, they are likely to be connected to mini- and mainframe computers, acting as terminals to these more powerful machines, as well as being used as computers in their own right. Larger computers have also benefited from developments in microelectronics and there is often a range of hardware and software providing a solution to a particular need.

The storage and retrieval of information are of interest to us all, and are not the sole domains of librarians or information specialists. The microcomputer has given us the chance to improve the control of information in libraries, information services and a wide range of other occupations. For instance, real estate agents can retrieve more exact details of property for sale and can even show an image of a property on the screen. Car dealers can locate vehicles more in line with a customer's requirements using databases of stock and forthcoming production from the factory.

The contents of this book will, it is hoped, provide insight into how microcomputers work (Chapters 1–3), their application to information retrieval and other library automation problems (Chapters 4–7), acquisition of hardware and software (Chapters 8 and 9) and, once obtained, how to make them work successfully (Chapter 10). First of all, we shall look at the electronics that is the basis of all computers.

1.2 FROM VALVES TO SEMICONDUCTORS

Early computers contained vacuum tubes (American) or thermionic valves (British), just as old-fashioned radios did. There were other, bulky components and the resulting hardware was extremely large, consumed large amounts of electricity and was unreliable. The invention of the transistor changed both computers and other electronic machines, since here was a device that could do the same job and, at the same time, was smaller, more reliable, consumed less power and produced less heat than the valve.

Transistors are built from materials called semiconductors, which have properties which make them neither good conductors nor good insulators. Silicon and germanium crystals are most frequently used to make transistor devices.

The trick comes in altering the properties of the semiconductor by introducing a very small amount of an impurity. The process is called **doping** and it interferes with the conducting properties of the semiconductor. There are two basic ways of doing this. One, the n-type, is formed by adding an impurity which produces an excess of electrons (these are the basis of the conduction of electricity). The other (p-type) produces a deficiency of electrons. By putting the two together, a p–n junction is formed which can form the basis of a device called a **diode** which will conduct a greater current in one direction than in the other (Figure 1.1). It will be explained that computers work with the binary system (i.e. with ones and zeros). These two numbers can be represented in the computer by the states of various electronic devices, and the numbers can be manipulated with the aid of other circuits and devices, such as the diode.

By putting three pieces of doped semiconductor together, transistors are formed which can be made to have various electrical properties. For instance, the n–p–n transistor, formed by sandwiching a piece of p-type semiconductor between two pieces of n-type, can be made to amplify a current (Figure 1.2). This particular property is used, for instance, in audio amplifiers, but the transistor effect is also used in computers.

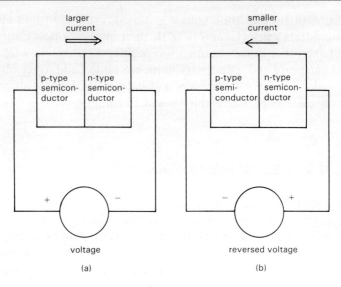

Figure 1.1 A diode formed from a p–n junction conducts a greater current in one direction (a) than in the other (b).

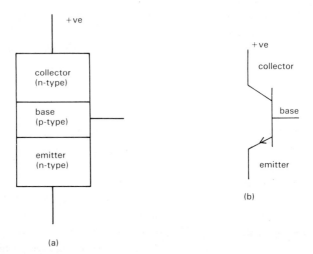

Figure 1.2 Arrangement of semiconductor materials (a) in an n–p–n transistor and (b) its symbol used in diagrams.

1.3 THE MANUFACTURE OF INTEGRATED CIRCUITS

The first transistors were individual devices with wires joining them to other electronic components such as resistors, capacitors and other transistors. It became clear that the production of electronic circuits could be made more efficient if transistors, other devices and the circuits connecting them could be built up together (integration). At first, only a few circuits could be used to make electronic devices in this way. Numbers of circuits increased as techniques became more advanced. Today it is possible to build a whole computer on a single chip of silicon crystal. A photolithographic process is used to dope minute areas of the silicon and so gradually build up the required circuits. The chips are very small and the whole process must be very accurately controlled.

The individual chips, together with other electronic components, are held in printed circuit boards (PCBs). These are made of an insulating material into which the chips are placed. The connections between the electronic components are achieved by laying down the circuits onto the surface of the PCB. This is much easier than using individual pieces of wire! Most microcomputers have a master PCB, often called a **mother-board**. Other PCBs may be attached directly to the mother-board or connected to it via **slots** provided in the machine.

Many of the integrated circuits in use today employ silicon as the basic semiconducting material. Selected natural sand, especially free from impurities such as iron, is the raw material used in the production of modern integrated circuits. The process begins by heating the purified material until it becomes molten. A small flawless crystal of silicon is then dipped into the molten silicon and, as the crystal is withdrawn, molten silicon attaches itself to the crystal and it begins to grow. This process, which is known as **seeding**, creates a large crystal with the same atomic arrangement as the original small seed crystal. The enlarged crystal is then sliced into individual disks or wafers which, after polishing, are about a quarter of a millimetre thick. Each wafer is large enough to produce around a hundred integrated circuits.

The aim of the manufacturing process is to build up a series of selectively doped areas of silicon which are connected together by metal wiring. The surface of the wafer is first oxidized to form silicon dioxide and is then coated with a layer of a light-sensitive material called a **photoresist**. The treated wafer is then exposed to ultraviolet light which is shone onto its surface through a mask, thus exposing only part of the photoresist (Figure 1.3). The process can be likened to the way in which photographic negatives are turned into prints in a darkroom. Figure 1.4 shows how the mask is used to create an identical pattern in the photoresist. The ultraviolet light hardens the photoresist and the

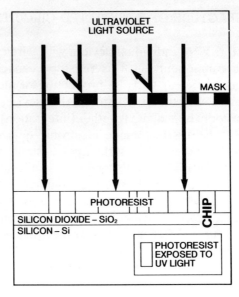

Figure 1.3 Chip surface covered with photoresist and exposed to ultraviolet light. (Reproduced courtesy of IBM.)

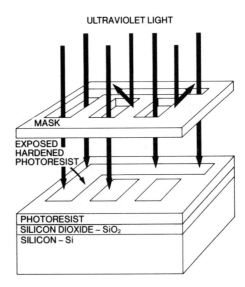

Figure 1.4 Photoresist exposure pattern governed by pattern of mask. (Reproduced courtesy of IBM.)

unexposed areas have the protective coating washed away (Figure 1.5). The wafer is then etched with acid which removes the silicon dioxide but leaves the pure silicon untouched (Figure 1.6) and then the remaining photoresist is removed (Figure 1.7). The dopant is then introduced into the pure silicon. Figure 1.8 shows the dopant diffusing into the silicon where the surface is exposed, thus reflecting the design of the mask. It is not possible to lay down all the circuits at once and hence the process is repeated a number of times. The silicon dioxide layer is refreshed as shown in Figure 1.9 before restarting the operation.

Once the devices are built into the silicon, they have to be connected together. Contact holes are etched into the surface and an aluminium–copper alloy is sprayed on. A photoetching process then removes the unwanted alloy, leaving the required wiring pattern (Figure 1.10). A typical wafer may be subjected to ten or more sequences of work patterns and all must be precisely aligned. The finished wafer is then sealed and connectors made to the outside world. After testing, wafers are broken into separate **chips** which are embedded into a substrate containing pin connectors to allow easy connection to other devices.

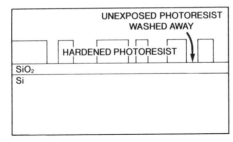

Figure 1.5 Unexposed photoresist washed away. (Reproduced courtesy of IBM.)

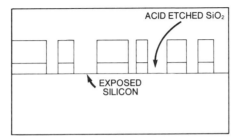

Figure 1.6 Exposed silicon dioxide acid-etched away. (Reproduced courtesy of IBM.)

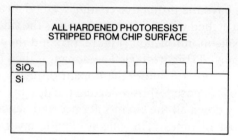

Figure 1.7 Hardened photoresist stripped from surface: chip ready to receive dopant. (Reproduced courtesy of IBM.)

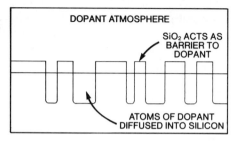

Figure 1.8 Introduction of dopant into silicon. (Reproduced courtesy of IBM.)

1.4 SCALE OF INTEGRATION

There are integrated circuits to perform many different tasks, such as storing or processing data. Single-chip computers, in which all the various functions are integrated, are also available. The number of logic units which can be stored in a single chip has increased rapidly since they first went into production and this is reflected in the terms used for the scale of integration. The term used today for the highest density is VLSI (very large scale integration), where several million circuits can be laid down on one chip. Small- and medium-scales have been, and continue to be, used for some devices. The term ULSI (ultra-large scale integration) has also been used for these million-plus densely packed chips. Devices which contain up to several million circuits on one chip are now in regular production.

Some chips are termed 'general purpose' in that they can be used in a wide range of applications (e.g. storage devices) but others are specially built, for example as controlling devices for washing machines. There are also chips which are general purpose but which can be customized to

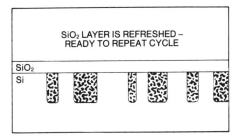

Figure 1.9 Silicon dioxide layer refreshed. Chip is ready to be retreated. (Reproduced courtesy of IBM.)

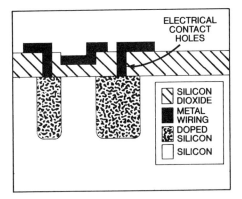

Figure 1.10 Addition of connectors and wiring to create a finished transistor. (Reproduced courtesy of IBM.)

a particular application. Most microcomputer designers would try to use general-purpose chips to reduce costs: volume production leads to very low prices. Indeed, the cost of the chips represents only a small fraction of the total cost of a microcomputer.

1.5 BINARY DIGITS

At the heart of every computer is a large number of electronic circuits that manipulate electric currents and voltages. Very early on, it was realized that an electric current was easy to regard as a two-state system; for example, a light is either on or off, a voltage might be present or not. If, by convention, one of these states represents a **zero** (0) and the other a **one** (1), there begins to be the basis of a number-processing system. Figure 1.11 illustrates the principle.

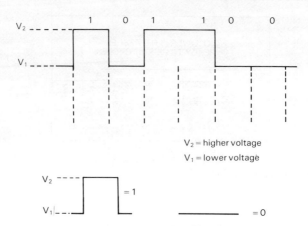

Figure 1.11   Convention for representing binary numbers with voltages.

The decimal system is used as the basis of the western counting system; it is convenient because we have ten fingers. Ones and zeros on their own can form a counting system just as the digits zero to nine do in the decimal system; it is just a different convention. (If mathematics is your weak point don't give up – understanding is reasonably easy.) The binary equivalents of the decimal numbers one to ten are shown in Table 1.1. Starting from zero, decimal zero and one are the same as binary. However, decimal two becomes binary 10 (not ten). This is because in binary we are dealing with a base of two, and not ten as in decimal.

Each **binary** dig**it** is known as a **bit** and eight bits together provide a

Table 1.1   Decimal numbers from 0 to 10 and binary equivalents

Binary	Decimal
0	0
1	1
10	2
11	3
100	4
101	5
110	6
111	7
1000	8
1001	9
1010	10

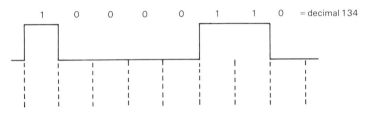

Figure 1.12 Representation of the decimal number 134 by binary pulses.

range of numbers between zero (00000000) and 255 (11111111). Such a group of eight bits is often referred to as a **byte**. This is significant in computing, as will be explained below. Conversion of binary to decimal is easy when it is remembered that each binary digit represents a power of 2. But first look at decimal numbers. The number 134 is:

$$(1 \times 10^2) + (3 \times 10^1) + (4 \times 10^0)$$
$$\text{i.e. } 100 + 30 + 4 = 134$$

Similarly, the eight-bit binary number (10000110) is:

$$
\begin{array}{cccccccc}
1 & 0 & 0 & 0 & 0 & 1 & 1 & 0 \\
\end{array}
$$
$$(1 \times 2^7) + (0 \times 2^6) + (0 \times 2^5) + (0 \times 2^4) + (0 \times 2^3) + (1 \times 2^2) + (1 \times 2^1) + (0 \times 2^0)$$
$$
\begin{array}{cccccccc}
128 & + & 0 & + & 0 & + & 0 & + & 0 & + & 4 & + & 2 & + & 0 & = 134
\end{array}
$$

The transmission of ones and zeros through electronic circuits is often achieved by means of voltage pulses. These can be produced by a generator that produces a sudden change in voltage for a specified length of time. A series of pulses representing the number 134 would be as shown in Figure 1.12, where the presence of a pulse is, by convention, a one, and the absence of a pulse, a zero. These pulses may, for instance, be sent down a single wire one after another (**serially**) or simultaneously down eight wires side-by-side (**in parallel**).

1.6 REPRESENTATION OF DATA

In the early days, computers were used by mathematicians to process numbers. It was necessary to store different sorts of numbers, but it was found useful to store letters and symbols as well, so conventions for storing different types of data were devised.

Each symbol or character was given an equivalent code, and numerous early conventions developed into the ASCII (American Standard Code for Information Interchange) code. Here the significance of the byte comes in, as the following examples show (note that eight bits equals one byte):

The letter A is represented by 01000001   = 65
The letter B is represented by 01000010   = 66
The symbol % is represented by 00100101   = 37

The size of the byte provides 256 possibilities (numbers in the range 0–255) so that this number of symbols can be stored, which is sufficient for most applications. Sometimes, however, it is not enough, and extra symbols, e.g. for a non-Roman alphabet, can be stored by a more complex arrangement of multiple bytes. Computer programmers use the octal (base 8) and hexadecimal (base 16) systems. Thus the letter 'A' would be represented by 41 (hexadecimal) and 101 (octal). We leave the reader to work out the conversion for the letter 'B'! In order to be able to write down all hexadecimal numbers as two single symbols, the letters 'A' to 'F' are used to represent decimal 10 to 15. It is not necessary to understand octal and hexadecimal to read the rest of this book. However, anyone who thinks this sort of thing is fun might make a good programmer!

1.7 COMPUTER DEVICES

It is not hard to imagine that computers have complex transistor circuitry; one has only to look at an audio amplifier which also has electronic circuits to manipulate voltages and currents, but for a different purpose. However, the individual circuits are themselves quite simple. A common operation in computing is to add two numbers together and a simple circuit can be built to carry this out. As an example, take the decimal numbers *1* and *2* and add them together:

in decimal $2 + 1 = 3$
in binary $10 + 01 = 11$

An adding device can be constructed with input and output (result) lines as shown in Figure 1.13. The two numbers to be added together are sent as pulses along wires into the adding device. Pairs of digits from the two numbers are added together in separate circuits and a 'one' can be carried from a less significant to a more significant pair. The result is sent out by the adding device along the output lines.

Adders are built into chips, along with devices to perform all the operations needed in a computer. It is not really necessary to know how these are arranged in order to understand how a computer operates. For this level of detail the reader should turn to a basic book on computer

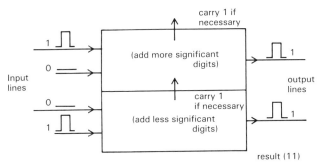

Figure 1.13   An adding device to add together two (two-digit) binary numbers.

hardware, *The Ladybird Book of Computers* being an excellent example! The whole computer is built of many circuits, each performing different functions and integrated on chips of silicon.

In Chapter 2 a description is given of the essential building blocks of a computer system and the way in which they are put together.

2 | Microcomputers: the building blocks

2.1 ARRANGEMENT OF CHIPS IN A MICROCOMPUTER

An outline of the main components of a microcomputer is shown in Figure 2.1. The processing of data is carried out by a central processing unit (CPU) which is sometimes called a microprocessor unit (MPU). Adding devices, similar to the one shown in Figure 1.13, are part of the CPU. Instructions and data are read in by the CPU and processed data come out. The operation of the CPU is determined by a set of machine instructions (ADD is one); there are usually around a hundred of them. Processing is carried out according to a program which is a sequence of machine instructions designed to carry out a particular task.

The program is stored in memory, and the immediate memory which feeds the CPU is one of two basic types (Figure 2.1):

1. ROM (read only memory)
2. RAM (random access memory or read/write memory)

The main difference between RAM and ROM is that the content of the memory in the former can be changed whereas in ROM it cannot. Memory is discussed in detail later in the chapter. The microcomputer also has, among other things, a clock device which synchronizes all the various high-speed operations, so that they do not get out of step. It also has interface chips that are used to connect the microcomputer to other devices such as printers and visual display terminals.

The transmission of data between individual chips is carried out by means of a number of **buses**. A bus is a group of lines joining together individual electronic components and is often one of three types:

1. Address bus: for the direction of data to and from individual locations;

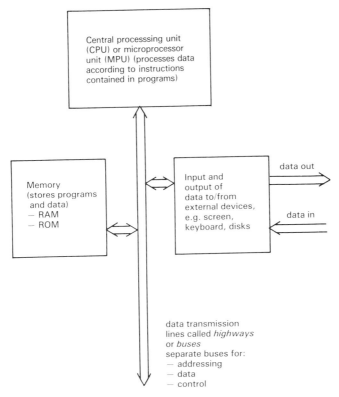

Figure 2.1 The main components of a microcomputer.

2. Data bus: for transmission of data (most frequently from CPU to memory and vice versa);

3. Control bus: for controlling the operation of the various devices that make up the microprocessor.

In some microcomputers one bus can carry different traffic, e.g. both data and address signals, without getting them mixed up. The term **bus** is used because it is a common highway to which individual devices of the microcomputer connect. Data are moved around these devices as if by bus.

The CPU receives program instructions and data from the memory and transmits results back to it. In this case the address bus is used by the CPU to select particular locations in memory to which data are to be written and from which program instructions and data are to be read. The data bus carries data and instructions from one component of the microcomputer to another. A usual route is between the CPU and

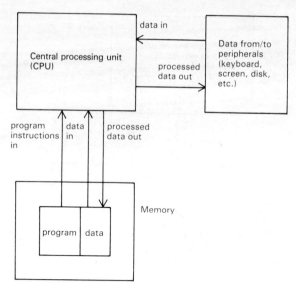

Figure 2.2   Flow of program instructions and data in a microcomputer.

memory. The control bus carries the signals required to organize the operation of the microcomputer. An outline of the flow of instructions and data is shown in Figure 2.2.

Microcomputers generally provide vacant slots in their equipment so that additional equipment can be connected. It might be required to add more RAM, for instance. This can be done by fitting a printed circuit board containing the RAM into one of the vacant slots which connect the RAM to the bus. The design of buses depends on the manufacturer. For instance, IBM PS/2 machines generally use the **micro-channel** bus, a design different from that used by previous IBM machines. A group of other manufacturers uses an alternative design of bus called EISA, although some manufacturers use the IBM design.

2.1.1 Categorization of microprocessor units

A particular microcomputer is, perhaps above all, characterized by the manufacturer, and the type, of its CPU. A manufacturer of machines tends to stick to the CPUs from one producer. For instance, IBM uses Intel products whereas Apple uses Motorola.

Microprocessors are often categorized by their size, i.e. as 8-bit, 16-bit or 32-bit. This refers to the size of a normal machine instruction that the CPU can process. The size occupied by such an instruction is often known as the word length. For example, the Motorola MC68000 16-bit

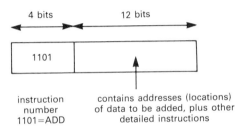

Figure 2.3 Format of the ADD instruction stored in a 16-bit word (Motorola MC68000 microprocessor).

microprocessor has a word length of 16 bits, although the micro-processor can deal with 'long words' of 32 bits.

The instruction to add together two numbers in the MC68000 is stored in a 16-bit word, as shown in Figure 2.3. The four bits on the left contain the instruction number, which is binary 1101 for the 'ADD' instruction. The rest of the word contains details of where to find the data and other details of how to execute the instruction. This explanation is very oversimplified and the reader interested in further detail is advised to consult a book on computer hardware. A large word size provides room to store larger numbers, giving scope for more instructions, and a larger range of addresses and other instruction information. It is, therefore, usually associated with more powerful microprocessors, although RISC processors (section 2.1.5) provide increased power through other means. The size of the word often coincides with the size of the data bus. Normally a 16-bit CPU will have a 16-bit data bus (i.e. 16 lines joined to it) but this is not necessarily the case. The 16-bit Intel 8088 CPU has an 8-bit data bus so that it can fit in with other chips made for 8-bit machines. In theory, therefore, it takes longer to process data with the 8088 than it does with a 16-bit data bus as is found in the Intel 8086. A summary of Intel CPUs is shown in Table 2.1. Figure 2.4 shows the transmission of data along an 8-bit data bus from memory to CPU.

The size of the microprocessor is not the only factor to determine its power. The speed of operation, i.e. the time taken to process a simple instruction, is important. This is usually quoted as a frequency (mega-hertz, MHz, i.e. a million cycles per second). Microprocessors with several tens of MHz are in use.

Some microprocessors are designed to operate with a co-processor. These additional processors are built to carry out particular tasks, such as handling arithmetic operations or the processing needed to display information graphically, and hence relieve the main processor of these burdens. The Intel 80486 processor has such a processor already built into it.

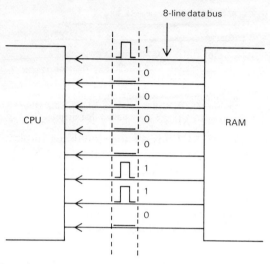

Figure 2.4 Transfer of data from RAM memory to the microprocessor unit along an eight-bit data bus. Example shows binary 10000110 (134) transmitted from RAM to CPU.

Another important factor is the size of the address bus, which will determine the size of memory that can be addressed, although some microprocessors support the ability to specify (in a program) a memory size larger than that actually physically available (virtual memory). A number of microprocessors also provide the required hardware arrangement to support several users and/or programs operating simultaneously. It is difficult, therefore, to compare the power of processors on just a few factors. Perhaps the most critical point will be how the system builder has put the chips together into a working machine.

Table 2.1   Intel microprocessor family

	Address bus (bits)	Data bus (bits)
8080	16	8
8086	20	16
8088	20	8
80286	24	16
80386	32	32
80386SX	32	16
80486	32	32

2.1.2 Early microprocessors

One of the first microprocessors was the Intel 4004 which was introduced in 1971 and had a 4-bit data bus. However, until the development of the 8-bit processor, the general-purpose microcomputer was not feasible. The Intel 8080 was one of the devices which helped to bring about the general-purpose microcomputer. Other manufacturers of 8-bit processors included Motorola (MC6800) and MOS Technology (6500/2), but probably the most successful 8-bit chip was the Zilog Z-80. It powered many of the successful 8-bit microcomputers and is still in use for some specialized purposes (for instance controlling the operation of printers).

2.1.3 Intel microprocessors

Intel is, without doubt, one of the most important producers of microprocessors. A major reason was the adoption by IBM of microprocessors from this company for the IBM PC in the early part of the last decade. In addition, the open and flexible nature of the design of the IBM PC allowed other manufacturers to copy ('clone') the design. The IBM PC design with Intel CPUs became the model for machines produced by many manufacturers.

Intel has a family of CPUs, ranging from 8 to 32 bits. A summary of the popular CPUs produced by Intel is given in Table 2.1. A feature of them is that more recent ones are compatible with earlier, less powerful, types. The 16-bit 8086 and its sister chip the 8088 are still in production. The Intel 8086 will support a 20-bit address bus and a 16-bit data bus, but 16 bits of the address bus are shared with the data bus. Thus this chip can address 2^{20} or 1 048 576 locations (one megabyte) and process a simple instruction of 16 bits. The 8088 is essentially the same as the 8086, except that the data bus is only 8 bits, instead of 16 in the 8086. The 8088 is therefore usable with the less expensive chips developed for earlier 8-bit machines.

The size of the address bus in the 8086 restricted the memory to one megabyte. The 80286 increased the address bus to 24 bits, thus giving an addressing capacity of 16 megabytes (2^{24}). The 80286 was used in the IBM PC AT microcomputer, and is still being used in microcomputers manufactured today.

The introduction of the Intel 80386 CPU has led to further progress up the power league. This chip can handle a 32-bit word, and supports a 32-bit address bus and a 32-bit data bus. It can thus address 2^{32} (over 4 billion) locations. Intel also introduced the 80386SX chip which supports a 16-bit data bus and thus allows this chip to be used with 16-bit support chips. An 80486 chip is now in production that contains circuitry to carry out some functions which were previously performed by separate chips, e.g. it contains a mathematics processor and a cache controller and memory (section 2.1.6).

2.1.4 Motorola microprocessors

A range of microcomputers employing Motorola 16- and 32-bit CPUs is available. They are used notably in the Apple Macintosh and Atari machines. The Motorola MC68000 has a 24-bit address bus which can address over 16 million locations. This microprocessor, introduced in 1979, was the first of a family of 16-bit offerings from Motorola, and it powered the original Apple Macintosh machine. Since then, the more powerful 68020, 68030 and 68040 32-bit processors have appeared.

2.1.5 Other microprocessors

Intel and Motorola microprocessors are not the only microprocessors available. For instance, some of the Intel designs are made under licence by other companies. Other designs are also available and some of them are based on quite different principles. Inmos devised what it called a transputer, a device to process instructions in a parallel fashion, so as to provide increased computing power. Another development is the reduced instruction set computer (RISC) which provides extra power through simplification of the microprocessor by reducing the number of different machine instructions available. Microcomputers are available with RISC microprocessors.

In another area, computers which were formerly outside the micro-computer range, e.g. the so-called 'workstations', are now overlapping microcomputers in terms of price and power. These machines were originally developed for applications such as computer-aided design and other engineering applications. The power of the microcomputer is growing to an extent that it is difficult to define such a machine, except on the basis of price.

2.1.6 Central memory

The microprocessor can operate very quickly: in order, therefore, for the CPU to operate efficiently, it needs to be able to read instructions and data from memory quickly, and to write processed data just as quickly back into memory. If this can be done, the CPU will not be waiting to process data and instructions, but will be operating at

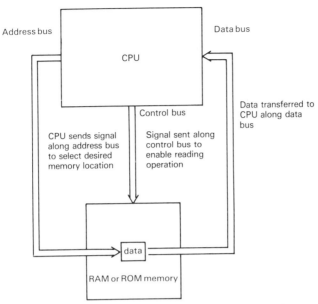

Figure 2.5 Retrieval of data from memory and transfer to CPU.

maximum efficiency. Bearing in mind that the CPU operates sequentially, i.e. it processes instructions one at a time, it needs a 'fast' storage device to back it up. The two major devices, ROM and RAM, are both integrated circuits. Both devices are directly addressable in that the CPU can get almost immediate access to any byte. Figure 2.5 shows how this is carried out.

Data which are to be permanently stored in directly addressable, fast-access storage can be placed in ROM. Data are written into ROM by special equipment and, once written, they are stored permanently, i.e. they remain even when the machine is switched off. ROMs are often used for storing programs that will not need to be changed and that need to be used frequently. Operating systems (see Chapter 3) are sometimes placed in ROM on machines that do not have disk drives and in portable machines. The major advantage is that a program in ROM is always ready for use, with the disadvantage that the memory space cannot be used for anything else, should this be required, without changing the ROM. Variants of ROMs include PROMs (programmable read-only memories) and EPROMs (erasable PROMs) which offer some flexibility over ROMs but do not get over the problem of the CPU not being able to write data to them. In some machines, ROMs can be easily exchanged, allowing new programs to be loaded when required.

Random access memory (RAM) is the most important type of central memory in general-purpose microcomputers. The operation of reading data from RAM is essentially the same as reading from ROM. The main differences are that RAM can be written to by the CPU, and when the power is switched off the data are lost. The number of bits of data which can be stored on a single RAM is growing as technology develops.

The two basic types of RAM are called static (SRAM) and dynamic (DRAM). The former is more expensive to buy but is faster in operation. The state of the memory also does not need to be refreshed periodically, as does dynamic RAM. So-called CMOS RAM is used in small amounts for storing essential data which need to be kept when the machine is switched off, e.g. the date and time. This is because it needs very little power and so can be maintained by battery. Dynamic RAM chips containing several megabits are on the market. A number of RAMs are used together to provide the required storage capacity: several megabytes is not uncommon in some 16- and 32-bit machines. The manufacture of these high-density chips is problematical and sometimes partially occupied chips are used: these are higher-capacity devices that are used at a lower capacity because some of the storage locations are not correctly formed.

The performance of RAMs is measured in terms of the access time. This is typically around 100 nanoseconds (10^{-9}) for DRAMs. However, RAMs have to recover after being read, this time being almost as large as the access time. SRAMs recover more quickly than DRAMS, in addition to not needing the periodic refreshing. A typical access time for an SRAM is less than 50 nanoseconds.

The range of storage locations that a CPU can address is sometimes called the address space. A 20-bit address bus can address 2^{20} (1 048 576) memory locations (bytes). It is possible to address more than this by switching between different groups of memory locations using a technique called **bank-switching**. The address space itself can be made up of different physical devices as, for instance, shown in Figure 2.6 in which part is ROM and part RAM.

Matching the speed of operation of the processor and the memory is becoming more difficult as processor speeds increase. In some micro-computers, it is necessary to insert so-called **wait states** when the microcomputer is communicating with the memory. The processor has to idle to allow the memory to catch up. There are ways of improving this situation. One way is to employ a **cache** memory. This is a small amount of very fast RAM which sits between the processor and the RAM and directly feeds the processor. Data are shuffled backwards and forwards between the cache and the main RAM when processor time is available. If the required program statements and data are already in the cache, the machine can operate with **zero wait states**. If data have to be transferred from the RAM, the processor must wait. Another technique to speed up

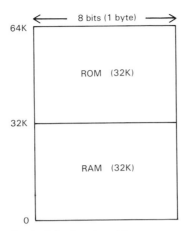

Figure 2.6 Different physical devices in address space.

transfer of data to and from memory is to **interleave** the RAM memory. This means that it is possible for the microprocessor to obtain access to data in one part of the RAM whilst another part is recovering from being read.

Some microprocessors support the use of **virtual memory**. This is a technique which enables programs to be written which are larger than the available physical memory. The computer organizes a large program into **pages** or **segments**. Only those segments that are currently being used and those that have recently been used are kept in the memory. The rest are stored on disk until they are needed. Unused segments are 'swapped out' to make room for those segments needed by the program that is currently running.

2.1.7 The 'stored program' concept

A computer program is a set of instructions to the microcomputer designed to carry out a desired operation. Without a program, or software as it is also known, the microcomputer is useless. The operation of a program will be dealt with in this section and an explanation of programming languages will be given in Chapter 3. Programs are usually written in so-called high-level languages, which are fairly easily manipulated by human beings. The machine language understood by the CPU is essentially different and is much more restrictive. High-level languages, such as Cobol or C, must be translated into machine language by the computer before a program can be executed.

The translated program, of machine instructions and data, is stored in RAM or ROM (see Figure 2.7). The hundred or so different machine

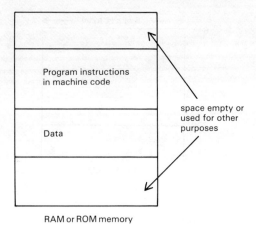

Figure 2.7   Storage of program and data in RAM or ROM.

instructions will be sufficient to carry out the full range of microcomputer operations, including:

1. data transfer (e.g. moving data from one location to another)
2. data manipulation (adding, Boolean logic, etc.)
3. transfer of control (e.g. branching to another instruction)
4. input/output (e.g. bringing data from external devices)
5. machine control

Each instruction type has a unique number and a sample program in machine language is described later in this chapter. Figure 2.3 showed an example of an ADD instruction in the MC68000.

The execution of a program is controlled by a program counter (PC) which, at the start of execution, points to the first instruction (see Figure 2.8). Instructions are processed one after another, and after the execution of one instruction by the CPU, the PC points to the following one unless the previous one involved a branch to a different part of the program.

Instructions from the program are processed until the program is interrupted or the 'stop' instruction is reached. The data to be processed are usually stored in a different part of the memory from the program.

The microprocessor operates in three steps:

1. fetch the instruction from memory
2. decode the instruction
3. execute the instruction

Signals are placed on the various buses to fetch the instruction. Decoding is carried out in the CPU and execution employs the necessary circuits

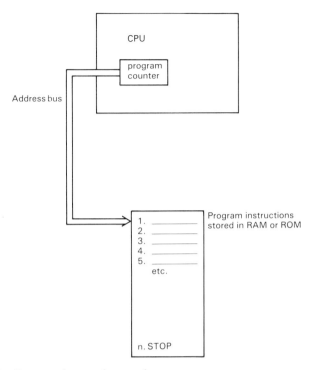

Figure 2.8 Program instructions and program counter.

within the CPU to carry out the instruction, together with any reading and writing of data. The procedure followed in order to carry out a simple instruction is shown in Figure 2.9, in which the program counter (PC) is pointing to the first instruction (Instr. 1). The first operation is to fetch this instruction from memory and store it in the CPU. It is shown in the top box of the CPU in Figure 2.9. The instruction is then decoded and executed. In this particular case, Instr. 1 is an instruction to read data from memory into the CPU. The instruction contains the memory address of the required data. The CPU sends out this address along the address bus to locate the required data which are then transferred (Data 4 in Figure 2.9) along the data bus into the CPU. Subsequent instructions would be likely to process Data 4 in some way.

2.1.8 Assembly languages

An assembly language is a symbolic version of a machine language. In such a program, the word ADD rather than the numerical equivalent would be used. Programs are sometimes written in the machine language; if this is necessary, the symbolic or assembly language version

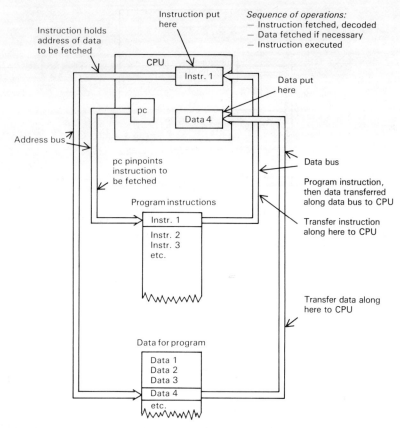

Figure 2.9   Processing of a simple (one-byte) instruction.

is normally used because programs can be written more quickly. Assembly languages are used when a high-level language would place too many restrictions on the programmer and/or the language would not be able to express what was required. For instance, it might be required to write a program which occupied the smallest possible amount of memory or which operated with the minimum number of machine instructions. Use of the machine language gives the programmer more control over these factors than does a high-level language, even though the program would probably take longer to write. Assembly languages are normally only used by programming experts, but an example will be given as an aid to understanding how a microcomputer operates.

An 8-bit CPU, such as the Motorola MC6800, has a number of storage locations called registers or accumulators in the CPU itself. The MC6800 has two registers into which data are loaded from memory: they are called A and B. Larger CPUs have more storage registers than this.

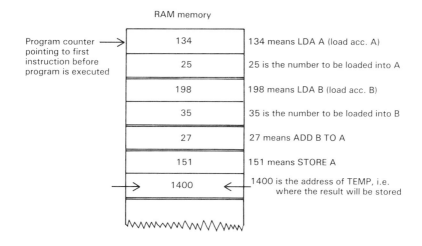

RAM memory

Program counter pointing to first instruction before program is executed →

134	134 means LDA A (load acc. A)
25	25 is the number to be loaded into A
198	198 means LDA B (load acc. B)
35	35 is the number to be loaded into B
27	27 means ADD B TO A
151	151 means STORE A
1400	1400 is the address of TEMP, i.e. where the result will be stored

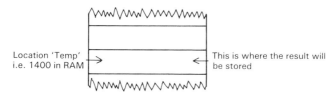

Location 'Temp' i.e. 1400 in RAM — This is where the result will be stored

Figure 2.10 Machine instructions for program to add two numbers.

The following simple assembly language program loads a number (25) into A and a second number (35) into B. It then adds the two together and stores the result in a location called TEMP, which is in RAM. The program comprises four mnemonic instructions as follows:

    LDA A #25   (this means load 25 into A)
    LDA B #35   (load 35 into B)
    ABA   (add contents of B into A)
    STA A TEMP   (store contents of A in TEMP)

The instructions are translated into numerical machine instructions by an assembler and are stored in RAM. The program is then ready to execute as shown in Figure 2.10. The numbers in the boxes are the translated instructions and data. The assembly language instruction:

    LDA A #25

is stored in the RAM as two 8-bit numbers, 134 and 25. The CPU knows that the 134 means 'load into accumulator A': it also knows that the next box of eight bits (one byte) contains the data to be loaded into accumulator A. A similar consideration applies to the second instruction. 198 means 'load into accumulator B' and the content of the next byte (35) is loaded. The CPU similarly knows that 27 means 'add accumulator B into accumulator A'. This instruction occupies only eight bits as there are no data to fetch from memory. A two-byte instruction such as 'LDA A #25' will involve at least two fetches from memory with this 8-bit CPU. A 16-bit CPU, with a 16-bit word length, would probably cut this down to one.

An assembly language usually allows the programmer to use symbolic names for storage locations. The location 'TEMP' in the program is an example. The assembler assigns a unique location for TEMP; in Figure 2.10 it is shown as location 1400.

It is reasonable to ask at this stage how adding together, or comparing the sizes of, two numbers can be relevant to, say, an information retrieval system. Such a system would probably be programmed in a high-level language, such as COBOL. Statements such as:

IF WORDA = WORDB THEN DO. . .ETC.

might be used to compare two strings of characters, such as a search term entered into an information retrieval system and a word in a document title stored in a record in the computer. An information retrieval system would comprise thousands of instructions like the one above and all the statements would be translated into machine instructions by a special program called a compiler. A single high-level language statement would generate a number of machine instructions, the exact number varying from one high-level language statement to another. In the sample statement just shown, it is very likely that one of the machine instructions generated by the compiler would be to compare two numbers to see whether they were equal. It was shown in Chapter 1 how individual characters are stored as numbers, so an English word can be regarded as a string of numbers. All high-level language program statements are reduced to a series of simple machine instructions in a similar way. This is essential if the microprocessor is to be able to carry them out.

2.2 MAGNETIC STORAGE DEVICES

2.2.1 Storage on magnetic peripherals

Something more than RAMs or ROMs is required for the permanent storage of significant quantities of data. The main task of both these devices is to service the CPU. In addition, they can store only limited amounts of the data required for immediate or frequent processing. Magnetic disks and tapes are the main media for storing data permanently, although optical storage devices are now becoming increasingly available (see section 2.3). Such peripheral devices are connected to the microcomputer bus via a controller and a cable.

The CPU can process a single instruction in much less than a microsecond. It takes significantly longer to read data from disk or tape into RAM, and hence some strategy is needed to manage data or programs so that those most likely to be needed are most readily available. The use of caching and virtual memory techniques have just been described. There are also techniques which can be used to handle files of data to speed up access, and these are described in Chapter 3.

Data coming from peripheral devices, such as magnetic tapes or disks, can be fed via the CPU into the RAM memory as shown in Figure 2.11. There is, however, a method that bypasses the CPU and feeds data directly into the RAM. This usually involves another chip but has the advantage of freeing the CPU from this task. The technique is called **direct memory access**.

Important criteria for judging the performance of peripheral storage devices include:

1. the total storage capacity
2. the cost per byte stored
3. the time required to access data and the transfer rate into the microcomputer
4. the ability to exchange the storage medium
5. the ability to reuse the medium

The ideal medium should have a large capacity, be inexpensive, be able to retrieve data and transfer them to the central memory quickly, and be flexibly designed so that the medium can be removed from the unit and replaced by another. In practice, there are compromises to be made. Different media have their relative advantages and disadvantages.

2.2.2 Magnetic tape

Magnetic tapes are used to store large quantities of data. However, because data have to be written onto the tape, or read from it, in a serial fashion, they are mainly used for archival purposes or for transporting files to other locations. Standard audio cassette recorders were widely used on home computers because they were inexpensive. However, their use was mostly as a substitute for the more expensive floppy disk drives, now reasonably inexpensive. Reel-to-reel recorders, similar to those used with larger computers, are available but they are expensive

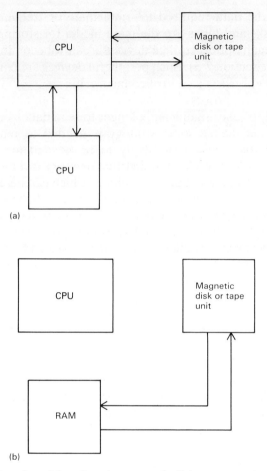

Figure 2.11   Transfer of data from/to magnetic disk or tape unit and RAM: (a) transfer via CPU; (b) transfer by direct memory access.

and are rarely used with microcomputers. So-called magnetic tape streamers are used for 'backing-up' disk drives. Data are written in a continuous 'stream' to the tape. They employ various designs of magnetic cassettes and cartridges.

A fairly recent development in the consumer electronics field is digital audio tape (DAT). It is used for recording and playing back hi-fi music, and is also beginning to be seen in the microcomputer world. Because it is a digital device it is used for making back-up copies of files stored on magnetic disk. It has a storage capacity greater than 1 gigabyte (10^9).

The time taken to transfer data from a magnetic tape to a microcomputer depends on the time taken to locate the required data on the tape and the actual speed of transfer once located. This can be several seconds or, more likely, minutes, depending on where the data are on the tape. The speed of operation and the capacity of reel-to-reel drives are much greater than cassette tapes. The average access time for DAT is as low as 20 seconds. Hence, given its large capacity, there may be more of a role for this new medium than just as a back-up device.

2.2.3 Magnetic disks

Magnetic disks are, without doubt, the most important medium for bulk data storage in microcomputers. A magnetic disk is a film of magnetic material on a disk substrate. The whole disk is rotated, and read/write heads are used to read data from the disk and to write data onto it. The magnetic material is essentially the same as that used for magnetic tapes but the set-up of the device enables data to be accessed much more quickly (in the order of milliseconds). There are two main types:

1. diskettes (also known as floppy disks because the older designs are flexible)
2. hard disks (so-called because the disks are rigid)

Without the diskette, data processing on microcomputers would have been severely retarded. They come in different diameters: the main ones being $5\frac{1}{4}$ and $3\frac{1}{2}$ inch. The original floppy disks were 8 inch and single-sided, i.e. data were recorded on one side only. These disks are no longer in widespread use. Disk drives are now available which will record data on both sides and, with improving technology, more and more data can be stored on the disk surface. One $5\frac{1}{4}$ inch disk can hold up to several million characters. The cost of diskette drives depends on the capacity but around $100 per unit is typical.

The $3\frac{1}{2}$ inch disk has been widely adopted and is destined to become the dominant size for the next few years. It is used, among others, by Apple and by IBM for the PS/2 personal computers. Present capacities are above one 1 Mb and the disks have a rigid plastic cover and hence cannot strictly be called floppy.

The sub-$3\frac{1}{2}$ inch market remains fluid. These tiny disks are used in some portable computers where the drives have the advantage of being lighter in weight than those for larger disks.

Floppy disks can be either hard- or soft-sectored. Hard-sectored disks have physical holes in the disk itself that mark the beginning of each sector. Soft-sectored disks have just one hole in the disk to mark the beginning of the first sector; the remaining sectors are specified by software. The latter method is the normal method used today (see Figure 2.12). A device called a RAM disk is sometimes used; this technique uses part of the RAM memory in effect as a disk. It is not a substitute for a

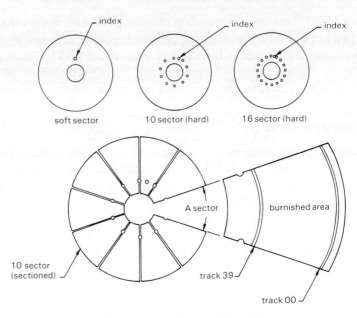

Figure 2.12 Sectors and tracks for floppy disks. (Reproduced courtesy of Verbatim Corporation.)

floppy disk drive because the data are not retained after the machine has been switched off.

Rigid, or hard, disks have been an essential part of large computers for a long time, and more recently, have been adapted for use with microcomputers. A disk is made up of a series of individual rigid disks, arranged one above another, and spinning about a vertical axis. Some disk drives allow this arrangment of disks or disk pack to be removed and exchanged for another. A series of magnetic reading heads, which is usually movable and arranged like a comb, is used to read and write data (see Figure 2.13).

IBM developed and popularized a disk drive known as the Winchester, in which the whole disk pack was hermetically sealed, and this design has become the basis for the Winchester disks available on microcomputers. Most Winchester disks cannot be removed from the drive, although some can. The design of the Winchester has produced a less expensive product, with a lighter read/write head travelling closer to the surface of the disk. These disk drives have been incorporated into microcomputers at astonishingly low prices. Drives with capacities of almost a gigabyte are available, although 20–40 Mb is the range of capacities most commonly seen. Microcomputers with Winchester disks are now widely available for as little as $1500.

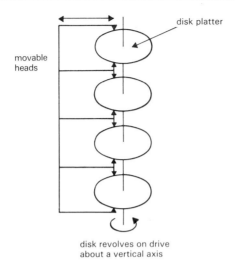

Figure 2.13 Outline of the operation of a disk drive.

Removable magnetic disk storage can be of the Winchester type or the cartridge type, the latter being somewhat like a large floppy diskette. The Bernouilli Box is an example of this cartridge approach to removable magnetic storage.

Despite the developments, the great majority of disk drives are of the fixed type. The large capacity of these Winchester drives is problematical when backing-up files. They can be copied to floppy disks but a large number of disks are needed as their capacity is so much smaller. Some Winchesters have a built-in magnetic tape streamer unit to which the whole disk can be copied. Another alternative is to have a second Winchester drive. The answer will depend on the application and the budget available.

In order to arrange data on a disk, the surface is divided into a number of tracks, each being that part of the disk which the head can read without moving. Data on disks with more than one **platter** can be organized using the concept of a cylinder. This is a device for reading or writing a group of tracks together, so as to maximize the speed at which data can be transferred. A cylinder comprises the tracks which can be written without moving the heads (see Figure 2.14).

Each circular track on a hard disk is divided into sectors, which is usually the amount of data written at one time. Because it takes a certain length of time to read or write a sector, adjacent sectors on a particular track are sometimes not used during a particular sequential write operation. Data may be written to every other or every third sector instead. If this interleaving technique were not used and sectors were

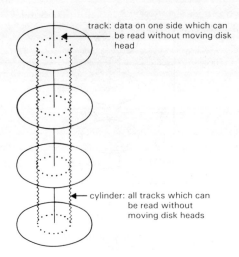

Figure 2.14   Tracks and cylinders on rigid (hard) disks.

written physically adjacent, the disk may have already spun past the place where the next sector was to have been written before the equipment was ready to write that particular sector. This slows down the rate at which data are written to the disk. An interleave factor of 2 : 1 means that data are written to every other sector. A higher interleave factor does not mean that areas of the disk are left empty; the sectors left empty are filled later.

No disk is manufactured perfectly and fortunately this is recognized by the computer. For instance, bad sectors can be marked and avoided. Problems also occur over a period of time, due to wear. For instance, the

Table 2.2   Comparison of the attributes of floppy disk and Winchester disk magnetic storage media

Floppy disks	*Winchester disks*
Comparatively high disk failure rate	Comparatively low disk failure rate
Lower disk capacity	Higher disk capacity
Lower total cost for drive	Higher total cost for drive
Disk exchangeable	Disk usually not exchangeable
Back-up easy to another floppy-disk	Back-up to floppy clumsy, to another Winchester is expensive, to video tape is error-prone, to tape streamer
Lower data access speed and transfer speed	Higher data access speed and transfer speed

alignment may change so that the tracks are not exactly in the same place relative to the read/write head. On some drives, the head is automatically parked when the drive is switched off. On others the head comes to rest on the disk surface causing friction wear. A hard disk is one of the parts of a microcomputer most likely to cause trouble. However, with good housekeeping, the effects of such problems can be minimized.

In the past, it was a question of whether a microcomputer had a hard disk drive, as well as a diskette drive. The former is now an essential part of a microcomputer, with diskettes being used for transferring files, making back-ups etc. A comparison of the two types of disk is shown in Table 2.2.

2.3 OPTICAL DISKS

A range of peripheral devices, which use optical processes to store and retrieve data, has become available at prices which make it practicable to link these devices to microcomputers. Most of them use a spinning disk and hence the mode of operation is not unlike that of a magnetic disk, although there are some fundamental differences. There are also other formats, notably optical tape and optical card systems, the latter storing several megabytes of data on a card no bigger than a credit card. Their availability opens up some exciting new ways to use microcomputers.

Some of the optical disks in use with microcomputers were developed for, or derived from, products developed for specific purposes not connected with microcomputers. It is therefore difficult to categorize them. Using the recording mechanism as a basis, optical disks can be broadly grouped into three categories:

1. read-only media
2. write once, read many (times) media (WORM)
3. erasable and rewritable media

2.3.1 Read-only optical disks

Read-only disks are prepared in a factory. The data are recorded in the disk surface by a mass-production process. Once the disk has been made, no more data can be added to it: it can only be read. Broadly speaking, there are two types of read-only disks:

1. videodisks
2. compact disks

Videodisks were introduced to compete with videotape in the consumer market, but they were never a serious competitor because of the inability to record as required. However, because it is possible to locate individual video frames quickly on a disk, the equipment is being used in a range of interactive situations, such as industrial training, education and at points of sale in retail stores. Although the storage mechanism is best suited to television images, a technique has also been developed to store digital data on the videodisk.

Compact disks (CD) were developed by Philips and Sony for the storage and playback of audio material, and have proved to be extremely successful in this respect. Versions of the CD have been introduced which store digital data, the best known being the CD-ROM.

2.3.1.1 Videodisks

The permanent storage of moving visual images and accompanying recorded sound on disk has been a goal of researchers for many years. Early systems used a process similar to that employed for the recording of gramophone records. However, the use of lasers to record video information on a disk and playback afterwards has provided the most satisfactory solution.

The production of videodisks is somewhat similar to the production of audio disks. Once a master disk has been produced, copies can be made inexpensively by a stamping process. A copy can then be placed onto a turntable and read by a read head, again in a similar way to the audio disk. There are, however, some important differences, as will be outlined below.

When the systems were developed, there were two methods of recording which seemed to be viable: capacitance and optical. In the former, a signal recorded on a circular disk is read by measuring the change in capacitance betwen an electrode and the surface of the disk. The video high density (VHD) system, developed by the Victor Company of Japan, uses the capacitance effect. However, the optical videodisk is the preferred technology. The data (images, etc.) to be transferred onto a master disk are first encoded on videotape. The data then modulate a laser beam, which is focused onto a master disk coated with a thin film of material which is sensitive to light (photoresist). After recording, the exposed areas of photoresist are etched away to leave the data encoded in the surface of the disk. A metal coating is then applied to the master and a number of sub-masters are produced from which copies are taken. Data are read from the disk by means of a low-power laser beam, which is shone onto the disk and the modulated reflected light reads back the contents into a detector.

A number of companies manufacture optical videodisk systems, but perhaps the best known is the Laservision system. It employs a 12 inch diameter disk and the data are encoded in the surface of the disk in a series of small, variable-length holes in the disk surface (pits). The videodisk can hold up to 54 000 television frames on one side of a disk, together with sound and control data. Two methods of recording, constant angular velocity (CAV) and constant linear velocity (CLV) are employed. In the former, the disk always spins at the same angular velocity and hence the density of storage is lower on the outer than on the inner parts of the disk. The speed of rotation is chosen to enable a single TV frame to be read many times, in order to give a 'freeze frame' image on a TV screen.

The other method of recording, CLV, allows more data to be stored on the outer parts of the disk and the drive spins faster when this part of the disk is being read. This mode is superior to CAV for the continuous viewing of sequentially organized images, e.g. a film or movie, because more images can be stored on the disk. Stills and sound can also be recorded. If used to store digital data, the composite video frames have the digital data encoded in the lines of the signal. In theory up to one gigabyte can be stored in this way. It is possible to store the digital data in the tracks reserved for sound, thus allowing video and digital data to recorded on the same disk.

The videodisk player can locate an individual frame on a disk in a matter of seconds. It is this possibility which brings in the microcomputer as a controlling device. Each of the 54 000 frames is numbered and the microcomputer can be used to store indexes to the content of the disk. Images can be of textual material as well as diagrams, still photographs and movies. For instance, if still photographs were stored, each could be described using a variety of indexing terms, such as name of photographer, date, description of scene. Using an information retrieval system, the descriptions of the photographs could be searched, and the corresponding image(s) located on the disk and displayed. Videodisk players can contain inbuilt microcomputers to provide the access to individual frames. However, more sophistication is likely to be achieved by attaching the videodisk player to a separate general-purpose microcomputer, with the display of frames under the control of the latter, rather than the player itself. The potential for use of the videodisk in computer-assisted learning has already been recognized and the microcomputer is beginning to play an increasingly important role in the operation of sophisticated image retrieval and presentation systems. However, the number of interactive videos available for educational purposes is not large as the cost of production is still quite high.

2.3.1.2 Compact disks

The compact disk (CD) was designed to provide high-fidelity sound in the home, using a digital recording technique. Since its introduction, the CD has become popular at an extremely rapid rate and playing equipment and disks are now widely available.

The compact disk is mass-produced in a similar way to a videodisk. There are three stages to the manufacturing process: pre-mastering, mastering and replication (Figure 2.15). In the pre-mastering process, the database is converted to a CD-ROM master tape. This is then fed into a minicomputer which drives the mastering process. The minicomputer controls a CD master code cutter which produces a glass master disk. The disk is covered with photoresist and a laser beam in the code cutter is shone onto it to create a pattern according to the data to be encoded. After treatment by an etching process, the photoresist exposes a series of pits (holes) and lands (no holes) which correspond to the stored data.

The glass master is subjected to a complex duplication process in order

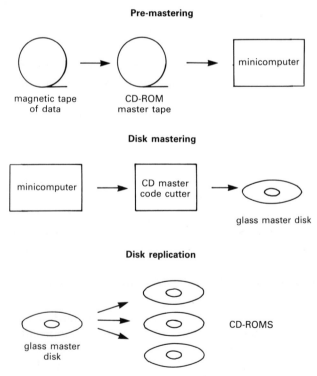

Figure 2.15 CD-ROM production process. (Reproduced courtesy of Sony Corporation.)

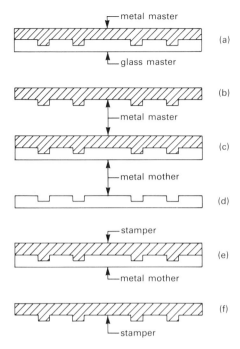

Figure 2.16 Production of CD-ROM stamper from glass master. (Reproduced courtesy of Sony Corporation.)

to produce a stamper. Figure 2.16 shows the successive steps. A metal master is first made from the glass master: (a) and (b). The metal master is then used to produce a metal mother: (c) and (d). Finally the stamper is made from the metal mother: (e) and (f). The CDs themselves are produced from the stamper by an injection moulding process, using a transparent poly-carbonate resin. Each CD copy is subjected to a final treatment with the addition of reflective and protective layers (Figure 2.17).

CDs have a diameter of 12 cm (4.72 in). The reading device in the player (a laser) shines light through the coating and does not physically touch the surface of the disk as it spins. Dust and minor scratches are said not to affect the performance of the disk. It is a CLV device which leads to a greater storage capacity than a CAV arrangement, but access times are relatively slow.

The use of a digital recording technique meant that it was relatively easy to modify the hardware to store computer data, and hence use the compact disk as a mass storage peripheral with microcomputers. This version of the compact disk is called a compact disk read-only memory (CD-ROM). Currently the normal CD-ROM can store over 500 Mb of data.

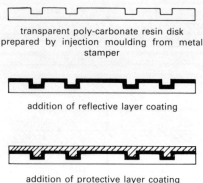

transparent poly-carbonate resin disk
prepared by injection moulding from metal
stamper

addition of reflective layer coating

addition of protective layer coating

Figure 2.17   CD-ROM final disk treatment. (Reproduced courtesy of Sony Corporation.)

CD-ROM drives were originally available in similar housings to CD audio players. More recently, they have been produced in the same sizes as full- and half-height floppy disk drives. In addition, it is possible to store and use the disk in a caddy, which eliminates the need to handle the disks themselves and protects them from dust.

It is now possible to store audio data, character data and images on a CD-ROM. However, other forms of compact disk are available which can also handle these different data. CD-I (compact disk-interactive) is a variant which is designed to be included in proprietary systems aimed at specific markets, such as computer-based training and in the home. It is designed to provide a variety of qualities of sound, in addition to data and video images.

Compact disk-video (CD-V) is aimed at the consumer electronics market, holding six minutes of video and audio. The low capacity of the compact disk was thought to prevent it from storing large amounts of video. However, a technique developed by General Electric (digital video-interactive, or DV-I) incorporates a fast operating data compression/decompression technique and stores the differences between adjacent video frames. DV-I was acquired by Intel in 1989 and, in addition to video, can store still photographs, stereo audio and data. Its advantage over CD-I is that it can be used with any microcomputer system.

Yet a further variant of CD-ROM is CD-ROM-XA. CD-I, as mentioned above, is designed for specific hardware and a particular operating system. CD-ROM-XA looks as if it will be a variation of CD-I for IBM-compatible microcomputers. How all these developments fare remains to be seen. Hopefully, wide compatibility between the CD variants will be possible or one will emerge as the winner. In addition, prices will need to come down further, hopefully to the levels prevailing for CD audio systems.

2.3.2 WORMs and erasable optical disks

Videodisks and compact disks were originally developed for the entertainment industry and have only subsequently been used for the storage of digital data. A third category of optical disks comprises types of equipment which have been developed especially for use as mass-storage devices for computers.

Digital optical disks fall largely into two categories, i.e. write once, read many times optical disks (WORM) and erasable (rewritable) disks. Digital optical disk drives are available from a range of suppliers and are already being used for a number of applications. The costs of these drives have, until fairly recently, been fairly expensive for use with microcomputers, although prices have fallen and, no doubt, will continue to fall.

It is clearly an advantage to be able to write data onto an optical disk as required. A number of manufacturers, IBM included, have produced such disks. WORM drives for microcomputers are usually the same size as full-height $5\frac{1}{4}$ inch diskette drives with the medium being contained in an exchangeable cartridge. Capacities range from over 200 to around 500 Mb per side. This can mean, therefore, that over a gigabyte per cartridge can be stored. Access times are between 50 and over 100 milliseconds and hence are slow compared with the best magnetic disks, but are faster than CD-ROMs. The cartridge designs are far from standardized which leads to a large degree of incompatibility in the WORM market. Prices of the drives range from $3000 to around $6000, with the cartridges being over $100 dollars each.

The recording mechanism is not the same in all drives. One type uses a tellurium alloy, the laser recording mechanism burning a pit in the material to write. A lower-powered laser beam is used to read the data, and the changes in the level of the reflected light are detected. Another type of recording mechanism uses a medium which changes the phase of reflected light.

The ultimate flexibility comes with the erasable optical disk. These disk drives have been produced by a number of manufacturers for microcomputers. There are two technologies which are most promising:

1. Magneto-optic materials: laser light is used to heat the already magnetized material so that a magnetic field applied to the material can change the direction of magnetization. This change can only be applied when the material has passed its Curie point. The magnetic orientation cannot change after the material cools below this point.

The stored data are read by reflecting laser light from the surface of the disk. Using the so-called Kerr effect, the polarity of the light is affected by the direction of the magnetization. The data are read by measuring the polarity of the reflected light;

2. Phase-change materials: these can exist either in crystalline or amorphous states, the optical properties of the materials being different. The state can be changed by heating the material with a laser.

Erasable disks are new to the market with prices currently around $5000 for a storage capacity of 500 Mb. Access times are similar to those for WORMs. There is, however, a better chance that the format of the erasable drive will be standardized. Cartridge prices are currently over $200.

2.3.3 Potential uses of optical disks

For the user, it would be invaluable to have a single, mass-produced and standardized drive to handle read-only (including CD-ROM) WORM and erasable disks. This dream seems to be very remote at the present time.

With the exception of the CD-ROM, the economics of using microcomputer optical disks are not clear at the present time. Several hundred megabytes can be stored on a microcomputer magnetic disk. In addition, the access speeds are faster and prices are lower than optical disks. However, the potential storage capacity of optical disks is likely to be much higher than that of magnetic disks and they are easily removed from the drive. Mass-produced disks (CD-ROMs), which are used in electronic publishing, are already in a unique position. No doubt, there will be important developments in the next five years.

The CD-ROM is having a growing impact on the information dissemination process, by allowing a wide range of optical publications to be produced. Many bibliographic databases are available on optical disk and a growing number of optical products containing primary publications are appearing. They are discussed in more detail in Chapter 4.

The optical disk has the potential to replace microfiche in many applications and could be valuable as a mass storage device for office management systems. 'Juke-boxes' are available which hold the disk cartridges in a store and from which a chosen disk can be retrieved rapidly and inserted automatically into the drive. This enables enormous quantities of data to be held. A number of document storage and retrieval systems exist which use optical disks and juke-boxes for mass storage but they are still mainly above the microcomputer price range.

These so-called **document image processing** systems are being used by banks, building societies, etc., for the storage and retrieval of facsimile images of documents, but such systems are only starting to become available in the microcomputer domain. However, it is very likely that this will become an important microcomputer application in the future.

2.4 DISPLAYS

Display units are the devices that are used to show the information entered into and/or retrieved from the computer. They are sometimes known as visual display units (VDU), visual display terminals (VDT) or simply as screens or monitors. The most frequently used technology employs a cathode-ray tube and operates rather like a television set. However, other technologies, such as the liquid crystal display (LCD), have advantages and are increasingly being used. The most obvious application of LCDs is in the portable computer when the size, weight and large power consumption of the cathode-ray tube make it unsuitable.

2.4.1 Cathode-ray tube displays

A cathode-ray tube monitor works in a similar way to a television set. A stream of electrons, corresponding to the image to be built up, is fired from an electron gun onto a phosphor-coated screen and controlled by electromagnets. When an electron hits a particular point on the screen, it excites the phosphor which glows momentarily. When it has covered the whole screen, the beam then repeats the process. Monochromatic screens have one electron gun, the colour being determined by the type of phosphor used. It is possible to vary the intensity of the display to produce a number of levels of brightness: for example with a white phosphor, various shades of grey will be produced.

Colour displays have three guns and three different phosphors which glow red, green and blue, respectively. They also have a so-called **shadow-mask** or grid which contains the three points of phosphor corresponding to a particular point or dot on the screen.

There are two important frequencies in a cathode-ray tube mechanism: the vertical scanning frequency determines the number of frames a monitor shows per second. It is measured in hertz (Hz; cycles per second). A frequency of 50 Hz means that the image is **refreshed** or renewed 50 times a second. The other important frequency is the horizontal frequency which is related to the resolution of the screen. A technique called **interlacing** is sometimes used to achieve a higher resolution for a particular horizontal frequency. Only every other line is scanned on the first scan. Those not scanned on the first scan are scanned on the second. This means that the image is only refreshed at half the rate. It is possible to use phosphors which 'persist' longer so that the image is held steady and the picture does not flicker. Interlacing is not frequently used for microcomputer displays. The resolution is often specified by the number of dots or picture elements (pixels) on the screen. For example, 640 × 480 means 640 dots horizontally and 480 dots vertically.

Cathode-ray tubes are made in a range of sizes. The stated size in inches is the diagonal distance across the screen. Larger screens can be useful for applications such as desktop publishing, when whole pages need to be displayed on the screen. Another important factor is the ability to display graphics. Early microcomputer monitors could only display a fixed set of characters. Graphical images could be constructed by using characters, such as horizontal, vertical and diagonal lines. Modern displays can control whether individual dots are on, or not, and what colour they are. The term **all points addressable** is sometimes used for graphics screens.

The display standards used for IBM microcomputers have improved over time. The VGA (video graphics array) is the display standard used with IBM PS/2 machines and with many 'compatibles'. The resolution of VGA can be varied, depending on the number of individual colours required. The more colour data there are to be stored, the less memory space there is available for storing the 'dot' data. Some cathode-ray tube displays are made to operate to only one standard. However, so-called **multi-sync** monitors can be operated at a range of frequencies which allows them to be used with different standards. They are usually more expensive than mono-sync monitors.

2.4.2 Liquid crystal displays

The major disadvantage of the CRT is that it is bulky. In contrast, the liquid crystal display is extremely compact and light in weight. It is commonly found in portable microcomputers. An LCD display consists of a matrix of crystals sandwiched between two polarizers. The particular crystals used twist the polarity of the light which arrives at the front surface of the screen. The arrangement of the two polarizers and the crystal ensures that the light is reflected back. However, when a voltage is applied to the crystal, it no longer twists the polarity of the incident light. The light is no longer reflected at the rear polarizer and the particular crystal appears dark.

LCD displays are thus dependent on incident light. The screen needs to be adjusted to the best position to enable the reflected light which has travelled through the crystal to be seen, but not the glare reflected from the front of the screen. The quality of the display is improved by using backlighting. The back-lit display depends on an artificial light source coming from the rear of the display. However, it consumes more power, which can be an important factor in a portable computer operating on batteries. LCDs are usually only monochrome displays, but colour versions are available.

A version of the LCD display is used in connection with an overhead projector to project a computer display onto a screen. This is a fairly inexpensive method of projecting an image of a computer screen onto a large screen for lectures and demonstrations.

2.4.3 Other display technologies

Gas plasma displays are used with some of the more expensive portable computers. The display consists of a matrix of pockets of particular gas mixtures (usually inert gases). A matrix of electrodes is connected to the gas pockets. A gas pocket glows when a voltage is applied to it. The gas plasma display does not need backlighting because the light is produced by the gas itself; however, relatively high voltages are needed.

Electroluminescent displays use a film of material which emits light in the presence of an electric field. These displays are not widely used today in microcomputers.

2.5 PRINTERS

The development of microcomputer printer technology during the 1980s was perhaps as remarkable as the developments in the microcomputer itself. Both the prices and the quality of the output have improved dramatically. The dot-matrix printer is still the most popular printer, although the laser, inkjet, thermal and other technologies have been increasingly used.

2.5.1 Dot-matrix printers

Dot-matrix printers are the mainstay of the microcomputer printing industry. In the simplest models, a print-head with a column of nine pins is arranged so that each pin can independently be released to strike an inked ribbon. A dot is thus made on the paper held behind the ribbon. Each pin is held away from the paper by an electromagnet but it is also spring-loaded. Releasing the electromagnet allows the spring to recoil.

Turning on the electromagnet makes the pin return to its original position, ready for firing again. As the print-head moves horizontally along the paper, a row of characters is printed. The paper is then fed through, to allow the next line to be printed.

The data relating to the shape of each character (the set of dots required to print it) are stored in the printer. The printer itself has a small computer to control its operation and carry out the printing according to the instructions received from the microcomputer. The characters themselves are usually stored in ROM. Different typefaces, styles and founts can be stored and printed. The printer itself may have a range of founts, fount cartridges may be plugged into the printer, or the founts may be in RAM memory obtained by **down-loading** from the microcomputer.

The data to be printed and the accompanying instructions are sent to the printer as ASCII characters. Certain sequences of characters, called escape sequences, are recognized as instructions, rather than as data to be printed. These instruct the printer to go to the next line, next page, etc. Standardization is important so that the microcomputer sends the character sequence required to obtain the desired result. Fortunately, the schemes designed by some manufacturers have been adopted by others. It is said that printer A emulates printer B. In a similar way, a particular software package will provide a **driver** for printer B so that the software can be used on all printers which provide a printer B emulation. The driver produces the correct character sequence for the printer to ensure that the page is printed as required. In practice, there are a large number of different printers on the market and hence each software package must have a large number of drivers. This situation is changing with the availability of printer drivers which are already installed in a windowing system, such as Microsoft Windows. They can be used by a program which runs under the windowing system (Chapter 3 discusses software). This eliminates the need for the software producer to develop a driver.

Dot-matrix printers have been improved in a number of ways with time. Many of them can print graphically. The printing is not limited by the fixed character set stored in the ROM, but rather by character shape data sent directly from the microcomputer. This mode of operation is more flexible, but the printing speed is slower.

The quality of the output has also been improved. One way has been to print the dots closer together, by forming the character with more than one pass of the print-head. The paper can be moved vertically less than a full line at a time. Some dot-matrix printers can also print proportionally spaced characters. They can also store more than one set of characters. Even with these developments, the quality of the output from dot-matrix printers was not satisfactory for printing business letters. Printers with more pins were introduced. The 24-pin version is the most widely used, having an arrangement of three parallel columns of eight pins. The quality of printing provided is called 'near-letter quality' or NLQ. Most of these NLQ machines provide at least two printing speeds, a fast draft quality and the slower NLQ speed. Some nine-pin printers also claim to print NLQ quality.

The prices of dot-matrix printers vary from the low hundreds to several thousand dollars. The more expensive printers usually provide better quality, faster printing speeds, longer life, superior paper handling, envelope handling and quieter operation than cheaper models. Colour printing is also possible.

2.5.2 Page printers

Laser printers have become an essential element in some microcomputer applications. This type of printer originated in the 1970s when it was introduced to cope with long print runs on large central computers. Apple, with the Laserwriter, and Hewlett Packard, with the LaserJet, brought the laser printer to the microcomputer world.

The laser printer is called a page printer because it prints a whole page at once. A beam of laser light is modulated so that, at a particular point in time, it shines, or not, to show whether a particular bit is set. The beam is reflected onto a photosensitive drum which rotates so that the image is built up. In this way the data to be printed are transformed into a dot pattern on the drum. Toner is then transferred to the drum in a similar way to that of a photocopier. The image is then transferred from the drum to the paper, the toner being fused by passing the paper through heated rollers. There are other mechanisms for transferring the image to the photosensitive drum. Notable ones are the LED (light-emitting diode) and the liquid crystal. The laser is by far the most frequently used technique, however.

Like dot-matrix printers, laser printers also have a wide range of prices. As noted above, they have much in common with photocopy machines and can suffer from similar problems, such as paper jams. The printing speed is rated in pages per minute but this is usually the optimum speed which is usually obtained when printing multiple copies of the same page. Printing of different pages, in particular when a page contains a lot of graphical data, can take an extremely long time and is much longer than the optimum rating given by the manufacturer. This is because the printer must receive a lot of data and it requires time to organize the page for printing.

The resolution of the printer is usually given in dots per inch (dpi) in the horizontal and vertical directions. The usual resolution is 300×300 dpi but higher resolutions are available.

2.5.2.1 Typefaces, typestyles and founts

The laser printer has become an essential part of the move towards producing better quality documents with the microcomputer. During the second half of the 1980s, the increase in the use of desktop publishing techniques was marked (Chapter 6). An important development has been the increasing availability of different typefaces, typestyles and founts. Some laser printers have several megabytes of RAM memory and a fast microprocessor. Some even have a hard disk drive to improve performance. This memory is used, among other things, to store the page image and the different founts. The founts can be:

1. resident in the printer
2. down-loaded from the microcomputer (onto the RAM of the printer)
3. held in cartridges (they are physically plugged into the printer)

Some founts are merely an assembly of dots, others are stored as 'fount outlines' which are described mathematically and can be scaled to the required size.

2.5.2.2 PostScript and other page description languages

PostScript is one among a number of page description languages which can be used with laser printers. If PostScript is used, pages are sent to the printer in PostScript format. The printer itself contains an interpreter (Chapter 3) which creates the facsimile page from the data sent in the PostScript language. Very few of us will ever need to understand the language itself. A page containing, say, text and graphics, might be prepared on a screen and then the image can be automatically stored as a PostScript file by the software.

PostScript can handle outline founts: founts normally have to be stored in the printer or sent to it. PostScript can generate the different size founts mathematically as required from outline founts. This has the advantage that only the PostScript outline is stored and the required fount is then created when required. To store all the possible founts on the hard disk on the microcomputer would require a large capacity. The problem is that the founts themselves need to be generated and this takes time and slows down the printer. In addition, PostScript printers are normally more expensive to buy than other similar printers. PostScript 'clones' are available which are less expensive but there is always the possibility of incompatibility. PostScript can also handle colour data.

Colour page printers are coming onto the market but they are currently highly priced. It is now possible to buy printers which will print a four-colour image (yellow, cyan, magenta and black) at 300 dpi. Laser printers with add-in cards can also print grey-scale images.

2.5.3 Other printer technologies

Daisywheel printers were the original answer to the quality problem associated with dot-matrix printers. They are impact printers which operate very much in the same way as an electric typewriter. A hammer hits a particular petal on the daisywheel corresponding to the required character and the character image is then transferred to the paper.

Inkjet printers, offering an alternative to both the dot-matrix printer and the laser printer, are growing in popularity. They work by squirting the ink at the paper through very fine nozzles and are quiet in operation. The quality is excellent but the ink cartridges can be expensive.

Thermal printers are also quiet in operation and can be a solution in some cases. The image is transferred to the paper by a heat method. Some models work with specially treated paper, others with normal paper and a ribbon which can be relatively expensive. The printing speed is likely to be low. Thermal printers have, however, found a use where quiet operation and high-quality output are important.

2.6 OTHER PERIPHERAL DEVICES

A range of other peripheral devices has been introduced to the microcomputer market in the last few years. For instance, the ability to process images in the microcomputer has stimulated the development of low-cost scanning devices. Plotters, or pen recorders, are used to produce engineering drawings. Bar-code readers are used in libraries and supermarkets to capture item data.

A scanner works by capturing reflected light from an image recorded on paper. The variations in the signal are recorded as a bit pattern which can then be processed in a number of ways, such as optical character recognition (OCR). This technique is used to turn what is otherwise just a facsimile representation into recognized characters. There are three basic types of scanner. The least expensive is the hand-held type which is moved across the page by hand. Only a limited amount of the page can be read at one time, often only a line at a time. The other two systems handle the physical scanning automatically. The first of these holds the paper still and moves the scanning mechanism. It is sometimes called a flatbed scanner and looks rather like a photocopier with a glass platten. The second feeds the paper across the fixed scanning mechanism. Only the former can be used, therefore, for scanning pages of a book. Low-cost scanners create only black and white images but some machines can capture different shades of grey or colour data.

The type of scanner required depends very much on the output required and on the type of data being scanned. Machines tend to be designed to handle either graphics or text, although some can handle both. For images, the resolution of the image (300 dpi is common), and capture of grey-scale or colour data may be important. A large image requires a lot of memory in the computer. Hence a graphics scanner might provide software to manage the storage and editing of such images. For OCR, the success in recognizing the characters is important. There are basically two methods of doing this. The first is called the **matrix-matching** technique. It matches the character it has scanned with the fount images stored. This can be acceptable for fixed-width characters, such as those obtained from typewriters and many printers. The other method analyses the individual features of each character, such as the presence or absence of descenders and circles. This latter technique is more successful at recognizing a wider range of typefaces, styles and founts. Some systems also recognize words and compare them with a computer-stored dictionary.

The capture of video images in a microcomputer from TV, video and videocamera is also possible. Special image capture or **frame grabber** boards are used. Some of them have powerful processors and fast RAM, in order to capture images from live television or a video. In the fastest systems, one frame is 'grabbed' by the microcomputer before the next frame arrives.

The mouse has become an almost universal input and control device for microcomputers. It is essential for many programs which use a graphical user interface (GUI; see Chapter 3 for an explanation). A mouse is a pointing device which is linked to screen tools within a particular program. The tool might be a pointer which can be used to select a required function from a menu. The selection is done by pressing a button on top of the mouse itself. The exact use of the mouse will be dependent on the program being used. For example, a mouse can be used to make line drawings with a drawing package. The normal mouse used for IBM microcomputers has two buttons, only the left-hand one being normally used. The other button is reserved for special user functions. Mice for other systems can have more than two buttons. Examples of other pieces of equipment used for input include the graphics tablet, touch screen, light pen, roller ball and joystick. The

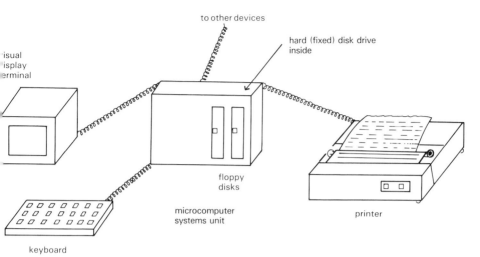

Figure 2.18 Peripherals attached to a microcomputer.

graphics tablet can be used to enter vector data, such as those used in engineering drawings, very accurately. Ignoring the peripherals which can be regarded as not being part of a normal microcomputer set-up, a diagram of a microcomputer is shown in Figure 2.18.

Bar-code readers are frequently used to simplify the issuing and discharge of books in a library and at supermarket check-outs. In a library, each book is given a unique number which is coded in vertical bars and placed in the book (see Figure 2.19). A wand, which can read the number by passing it across the bars, is connected to the microcomputer via one of its interfaces (see Figure 2.20).

Graph plotters used to be only available for mainframe computers. They can be obtained for microcomputers and can handle colour as well as black and white. They are used for printing engineering drawings, maps and other diagrams that are made with drawing packages.

Phototypesetters (also now known as image setters) can also be attached to microcomputers. They are relatively expensive ($25 000 and above) but are likely to come down in price. They produce film output which has a resolution of 1000 dpi and more. The film can then be used

Figure 2.19 An example of a bar-code label.

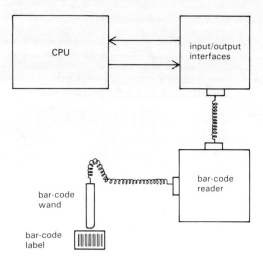

Figure 2.20   Connection of a bar-code reader to a microcomputer.

for printing. Some are PostScript-compatible and hence can use output files directly.

2.7 TELECOMMUNICATIONS AND NETWORKS

2.7.1 Telecommunication factors

Microcomputers communicate with other devices by means of inter-faces. The outward sign of these are sockets in the back of the machine. Behind the sockets are some integrated circuits designed to allow the microcomputer to communicate with the outside world in a standard way. Serial interfaces are most common; they transmit bits one after another, i.e. serially. A common standard serial interface is the RS232C which takes a 24-pin plug and is commonly used to connect many peripherals, e.g. printers and modems. Parallel interfaces are also available; they transmit a number of bits simultaneously. They are used, for instance, to connect to printers which also have a parallel interface; the Centronics parallel interface is a common example. Another interface is SCSI (small computer system interface), used to connect peripherals to the computer. Its advantage is that different peripherals, such as disk drives and printers, can be connected without modifying the microcomputer hardware or software, as long as the peripherals are SCSI devices.

It is possible to connect two microcomputers together using their

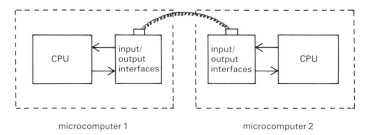

microcomputer 1   microcomputer 2

Figure 2.21 Hardware connections of two microcomputers through their interface ports.

interfaces. Correctly wired, and with the appropriate programs, data can be transferred from one machine to the other (see Figure 2.21). This is a perfectly feasible way of transferring data to a new machine when the floppy disks are incompatible. Often, no equipment other than the machines, plugs and cable is required.

To communicate with another computer at a distance (for instance to carry out an online search), it will be necessary to take into account the available communications links, the interface device (e.g. modem) and the communication protocol to be used. The types of line will include:

1. ordinary telephone lines
2. private data networks
3. public data networks

Whichever method is used will depend on the particular needs and constraints. Modems (modulator–demodulator) may be necessary to ensure the data can be sent in both directions and correctly interpreted at both ends of the line. The communication protocol (method) used by the large computer will have to be investigated since this is the way that the machine wishes to transmit its data. For instance, large IBM computers use the 3270 protocol with the system network architecture (SNA) for communicating to terminals. Programs can be obtained for microcomputers to make them behave like an IBM 3270 terminal.

There are two basic forms of data transmission:

1. asynchronous transmission (in which the transmitting and receiving devices are not in step)
2. synchronous transmission (in which the transmitting and receiving devices are in step)

Asynchronous transmission is a simple, low-cost method of transmitting data. It is the most frequently used method of communicating with computers over public networks. The microcomputer's interface is connected to a modem which is connected to the line, often via a normal telephone outlet.

A device called an acoustic coupler can be used in place of a modem. Its advantage is that it does not require any physical connection to the telephone, since communication is through the handset. The likelihood of data transmission errors is greater, however, and it is not recommended for constant use. The equipment for asynchronous transmission is shown in Figure 2.22. The microcomputer requires a software package which provides the necessary routines for the transmision and reception of data. The use of microcomputers for information retrieval from distant computers is covered in section 4.4.

The protocol of data transmission will also be dependent on the modem used. This device converts the data from the microcomputer into a form suitable for transmission to another device (e.g. a host computer). Factors to be considered in selecting a suitable modem include:

1. The mode of transmission (synchronous or asynchronous);
2. The speed of transmission and reception (bits per second);
3. Whether a 'smart' modem is necessary which may have its own microprocessor and ROM containing autodial, autoanswer, telephone number storage and inbuilt telecommunications software;
4. The compatibility of the modem with the standards used by the device at the other end of the line;
5. Whether both full-duplex (transmission simultaneously in both directions) or half-duplex (transmission in one direction at a time) are needed, or both;
6. Whether the modem is, or can be, part of the microcomputer or needs to be a separate physical device.

Synchronous transmission is a more efficient technique than asynchronous but requires more sophisticated timing equipment to ensure that the transmitting and receiving devices are kept in step. It is normally used with higher transmission speeds and frequently when a whole screen of data is transmitted from the large computer to the terminal.

Transmission of data over long distances can be expensive if normal long-distance telephone lines are used; the cost is no different from using the telephone for normal speech. To make data transmission more cost-effective, many countries have public data transmission services. Many of these use a technique called packet-switching in which data are sent from transmitter to receiver in small bundles or packets. It is not necessary to set up a fixed line between the two communicating parties and many callers can share the high-capacity networks. In many respects packet-switching is analogous to the motorway or freeway networks in which packets are like trucks sharing a busy route but ultimately going to

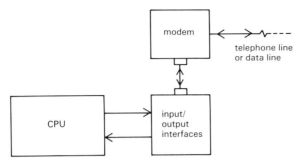

Figure 2.22 Data transmission via a modem and telephone or data lines.

different destinations. Connection to a network can be by a telephone call to a local node (entry point to the network) or possibly by a direct line to the mode (see Figure 2.23). The cost of using these networks is often based on the duration of the connection and on the volume of data transmitted, but they offer a cheaper and more reliable service than the telephone.

It is often necessary to connect together various computers and peripherals in a more permanent way. In that case a network of lines would be used. If all the equipment is reasonably close, a local-area network (LAN) can be used. If communication with distant computers is necessary, a wide-area network (WAN) can be constructed. Local-area networks (LANs) have been developed to link together microcomputers and other computers over relatively short distances, and are described below. Communication with computers outside the organization usually involves the use of some form of public network, although private lines can be obtained even for long distances.

2.7.2 Local-area networks

Multi-user microcomputers allow a number of operators to share the machine. The complexity of the operations which can be carried out depends on the size of the machine (RAM, disks, etc.), on the power of the CPU and on the operating system (Chapter 3). Although a powerful machine is likely to be needed at the centre, users can be equipped with inexpensive microcomputers or normal terminals. The equipment can be at some distance from the central processor, thus forming a crude sort of network.

At a more sophisticated level, local-area networks (LANs) are available. A LAN is a communications network which normally operates in a restricted area and provides data transmission speeds usually in excess of a million bits per second. A variety of equipment can

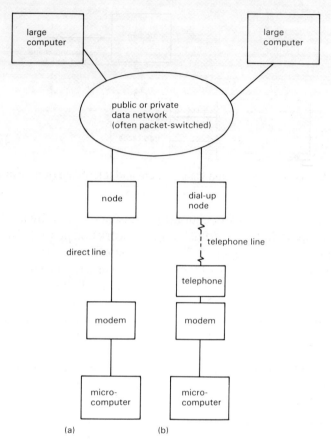

Figure 2.23 Connection of a microcomputer to a network: (a) direct line; (b) dial-up.

be attached to these networks, such as microcomputers, central disk stores and and printing facilities. There are different network configurations, the main ones being star, ring and bus configurations. They are shown in Figure 2.24.

A LAN is, therefore, a means of bringing together microcomputers and peripheral devices to create a more powerful computer system than the sum of the individual unconnected machines. One printer, for example, can serve a number of users. A database held on one machine can be accessible from another machine. The growth in the use of microcomputer LANs has increased rapidly in recent years. A number of LAN schemes exist of which the best known are probably Ethernet and the Token-Ring. The former has been used for a considerable number of years and was devised long before microcomputers became popular. The IBM Token-Ring scheme was introduced in the mid-1980s.

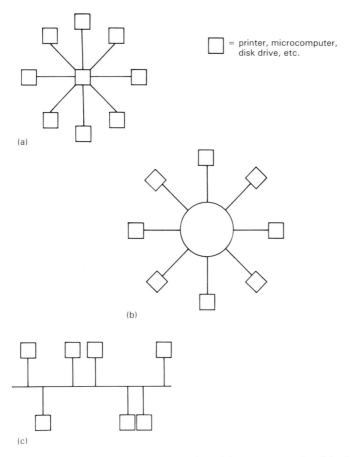

= printer, microcomputer, disk drive, etc.

Figure 2.24 Local-area network topologies: (a) star network; (b) ring network; (c) bus network.

System builders will need to be aware of the main reasons for joining microcomputers together: a LAN may not be the right answer in many cases. It may be more cost-effective to duplicate equipment, rather than sharing, e.g. printers, and duplications of databases may also be easier. Simple communication techniques, such as described earlier, or the use of a larger minicomputer may be more effective answers. However, the speed of transmission between machines in a LAN is high, they are flexible in use, and can also be used to connect to in-house mainframe computers. The LAN operating systems and application software are not expensive and can allow increased usage of machine resources. Databases can be made more widely available and more easily controlled. These are just some of the reasons for introducing a LAN.

3 | Software concepts

Programs are needed to make a microcomputer work. Fortunately, there is a large range of software available: the chances are that something can be found to solve a particular problem. Many microcomputer users will, therefore, never write a single program instruction. Had the programs of interest to them not been available, they would never have bought a microcomputer.

Programs written to satisfy a particular need are called applications programs. They are discussed in detail in Chapters 4, 5 and 6. This chapter deals with software other than applications programs and gives a brief glimpse at record and file structures. There is a range of software essential to the correct functioning of applications and to their development. It includes the following:

1. Operating systems, which manage the running of the machine and, increasingly, microcomputer networks;
2. Programming languages, for writing particular applications;
3. Systems software: a range of programs such as editors, to make life easier for the programmer and user;
4. Database management systems for handling structured data (described in Chapter 4).

All these tools are themselves programs and hence have to be written in one or more programming language.

3.1 OPERATING SYSTEMS

An operating system usually comprises a suite of programs to manage the operation of the microcomputer. The facilities offered by individual operating systems vary greatly. Some systems for large computers support a large number of users and computing tasks operating at the same time. Microcomputer operating systems are much more modest but no less important to the running of the machine. However, microcomputer operating systems are, in themselves, becoming more complicated, supporting more than one user and carrying out different tasks at the same time.

The elements of an operating system are normally held on disk and are loaded into RAM when required, although on some machines the system is permanently stored in ROM. The basic elements of an operating system include the following:

1. Supervision of, and support for, applications programs;
2. Device handlers: to allow the programmer easy access to the computer's subcomponents (e.g. disks, screen);
3. A file handler: to simplify the handling of files of data (e.g. to support different file organizations, the cataloguing of files, file protection and back-up systems);
4. A command interpreter: to accept and implement user commands (e.g. password management and other commands given by the user).

Simple microcomputer operating systems allow only one program to be run at a time. More sophisticated systems allow more than one program to be run concurrently (sometimes called multi-tasking) and more than one user to operate the computer at a time. The management of the programs for a number of users can be likened to the work of an air traffic controller at an airport who has to share the resources of the airport between the aircraft which are competing for runway, terminal, etc. Each program and user makes use of the resources of the computer (disks, interface ports, etc.) and each program in the machine will occupy part of the RAM or ROM. At a greater level of sophistication, the operating system will be able to swap parts of programs in and out of memory (to disk) in mid-operation (paging) in order to bring in another part of the program. Individual programs can also be completely swapped in or out of memory, in order to let them share the resources of the machine. A simple example of resource sharing is the running of a printing program in the background when the user is using another program.

The priorities for deciding which program to process at a particular time will need to be managed. A multi-user and multi-tasking operating system should allow the user to decide these priorities. There will be conflicting demands: two programs may want to use the disks simultaneously, for instance, and the order of priority will need to be decided by the operating system. An outline of the storage of programs and data in such a system is shown in Figure 3.1. The allocation of the memory to a particular program will be under the control of the operating system.

Virtual memory systems are used with some microcomputers. With such an arrangement, the amount of memory that a programmer can use

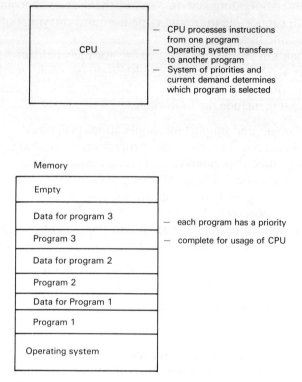

Figure 3.1   Operating system running several programs concurrently.

is not limited by the physical size of the central memory. The program occupies a certain amount of physical memory, the rest being stored on disk. However, it seems to the programmer as if the available RAM were much bigger. Often, virtual memory systems operate in conjunction with a paging system. The program and its data areas are divided into pages (a fixed amount of memory). Those pages of a program that are currently needed are stored in the physical memory available to the program. If another page is needed, it is brought in from disk and an unwanted page is put onto disk.

An operating system for a machine with disks will include a series of routines to handle the disk files. These are sometimes known as a DOS (disk operating system), although the term can refer to the whole operating system. Data or programs are stored in files, each of which is given a name. A DOS will provide tools for looking after these disk files, e.g. copying, renaming, cataloguing, storing them on disk and looking after their allocation to free space on the disk. A DOS will release free space after a file has been deleted and make it available to another file when needed. The operating system will also make available a number of methods of organizing, and obtaining access to, the data files stored on disk. Various methods of file organization techniques are available, and they are discussed later in this chapter.

An essential feature provided with an operating system is a general file editor. Some provide it through a Basic interpreter (see section 3.5) but the most useful is a general-purpose program that will simplify the task of input, editing and deletion of programs and data. Editors are mainly used for programming, in particular for the construction of the files containing the program statements. They are not recommended for the input of large amounts of data to files; for this a purpose-built input module is usually available with each applications program. Editors broadly fall into two categories, line and screen, the latter being easier to use because a whole section of the text can be viewed on the screen and the cursor can be used to make the required changes. Line editors show data a line at a time, and are preferred by some programmers because they have been available on large computers for many years.

Seemingly, as with many of the early developments in microcomputers, the outstanding operating system for 8-bit machines, CP/M, was developed in the proverbial garage. CP/M stands for control program monitor but it is most often referred to by its shortened name. Originally developed for the 8080 chip, its use became almost obligatory on machines using the Intel 8080/8085 and Zilog Z-80 MPUs. Its rapid spread was helped by the ease with which it could be adapted to individual manufacturers' machines. Other operating systems, such as those for the Apple II, were not available for other machines as CP/M was. It thus became the *de facto* standard and its supremacy was secured when the stream of applications software began to hit the market. CP/M was an operating system for single-user, single-program 8-bit machines. The move to 16-bit machines proved to be the demise of CP/M. However, some details of the system will be given to illustrate the operation of a simple operating system. With an address bus of 16 bits, the occupation of the 64 K address space is shown in Figure 3.2. This is sometimes called a memory map. The various components of the operating system which are stored in RAM took up about 8 K, leaving around 56 K for the applications program which occupied the transient program area (TPA). Considering that CP/M was in widespread use in the first half of the 1980s and that several megabytes of RAM can be required for the new generation of microcomputer operating systems, it shows just how much more powerful today's machines are.

Microsoft MS-DOS and the IBM version, PC-DOS are presently the dominant operating systems for IBM and 'compatible' computers. The adoption of the Microsoft product for the original IBM PC and the

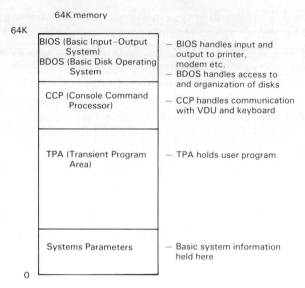

Figure 3.2   The occupation of 64 K of memory by the CP/M operating system.

ongoing relationship between the two companies has contributed greatly to this position. The large number of IBM PCs and clones manufactured and the vast array of available software encouraged other manufacturers to produce IBM-compatible machines, which also operate under MS-DOS. It is an operating system for a single user and a single task.

MS-DOS runs in 8088 mode which itself limits the memory to one megabyte because of the size of the address bus. The memory space above 640 K is reserved for the input and output routines. Extension schemes are used to increase the available memory, but are not ideal. MS-DOS can be adapted to share the resources of the machine between different applications but individual applications are not protected from one another. MS-DOS is said to run in 'real mode'. This means that one program can interfere with another by, for instance, writing data into a memory location used by another program. In addition the memory limitation of 640 K can be overcome, but with difficulty. To achieve this, DOS extenders and 'window' software use techniques such as bank switching and use of extra memory for RAM disks.

The limitations of MS-DOS and other operating systems of the same generation, the demands of resource-hungry programs, such as spreadsheets, and the availability of more powerful microprocessors have stimulated the development of multi-user, multi-tasking operating systems for microcomputers. OS/2 is an example.

OS/2 is planned by IBM and Microsoft to be the main operating system for IBM and 'compatible' machines for the 1990s. It is a multi-tasking operating system which runs in 'protected mode' on 80286, 80386 and 80486 microprocessors. This means that one applications program cannot interfere with the operation of another by, for example, writing into its address space. In addition to multi-tasking support for applications programs, OS/2 provides the following:

1. A built-in graphical interface called 'Presentation Manager';
2. A Communications Manager for networking. This includes support for LAN and connection to IBM mainframe computers;
3. A Database Manager;
4. A DOS 'compatibility box' to run DOS programs.

OS/2 can exploit the 80286 to achieve physical addressing of 16 megabytes and, with virtual memory, much more. A new version of OS/2 is planned to run in 80386 mode.

OS/2 is not the only operating system to raise the levels of service provided to the user. Apple Computer is continually improving the system for Macintosh machines. The Apple graphical user interface has had a profound impact on microcomputers since its introduction. Versions of the Unix operating system, first developed for minicomputers, are available for a range of microcomputers. IBM offers a version of Unix, called AIX. Microsoft offers Xenix which is also a version of Unix. The Pick operating system, with its inbuilt database management features, is also available for microcomputers. It is used for library systems for both microcomputers and minicomputers.

3.2 GRAPHICAL USER INTERFACES

Until the advent of the microcomputer, the numbers of persons directly exposed to computers was relatively small. Little thought was paid to the interface between the computer and the user. Despite this, research work by Xerox in the USA during the 1970s led to the development of the graphical user interface (GUI). They are also known as WIMPs (windows, icons, mice and pointers). Apple Computers developed a graphical user interface for the Lisa and the Macintosh computers in the first half of the 1980s. The development of the GUI is probably one of the most important achievements in computing from the user's point of view. It has had a profound effect on the way users interact with computers in general, not only in the microcomputer world.

A GUI presents information in a graphical form as well as text on the screen. Items such as files are displayed on the screen as icons – specifically designed pictographs which easily become familiar to the user. There are different designs for data files and for programs, for instance. Pictographs are used in sport, it being simple to recognize the particular sport depicted on a sign used by the roadside or on television. Another important aspect of a GUI is the 'window'. This helps the user to carry out more than one task at once by allowing each task to be seen through a window on the screen. A window can occupy the whole screen, or only part of it, thus enabling more than one window to be seen on the screen at once. One window can be partially or fully hidden behind another and then brought to the front when required. A large screen is useful if several windows need to be seen on the screen simultaneously. The third ingredient necessary to a GUI is a mouse or similar pointing device. This allows the user to manipulate the display in order to enter the required commands. Finally, the screen image contains drop-down or pull-down menus which can be manipulated with the mouse. Specific commands can be displayed in the menus, the required one being chosen by pointing at it with the mouse pointer and then 'clicking' on it with the mouse button. If the contents of a file are displayed in a window, it is possible to move (scroll) up or down using scroll bars. In some systems an image of a lift (elevator) is provided at the side of the window which can be moved by pointing at it with the mouse and dragging it up or down. This also has the effect of scrolling up or down the file. The same technique can also be used to move from left to right. To delete a file in the Apple Macintosh GUI, the icon can be 'dragged' with the mouse to the wastepaper ('trash') basket.

A simple example of how a particular command is carried out will be given in order to show the difference between giving an MS-DOS command to the computer and using a GUI. Everyone who has used the Microsoft DOS operating system will be familiar with the "C:>" prompt which appears when the machine is switched on. The computer waits for a command and provides little in the way of help to the user. The example is a simple command to copy a file from one disk drive to another. In MS-DOS this would be:

XCOPY A:FILE.TXT B:

The 'XCOPY' command copies a file called 'FILE.TXT' from disk drive A to drive B. In contrast, a GUI displays on the screen as icons the files stored on the two disks. One way of doing this is to show the icons of all the files stored on a disk drive in a single window. Each file stored on the disk is shown as an icon in the window. The icon for the file is a standardized pictograph, usually with a label, in this case the file name. The windows for both drives A and B are displayed simultaneously (side-by-side) on the screen. In order to copy a file, the mouse is used to move a screen pointer until it is over the icon corresponding to the file needing to be copied. One of the mouse buttons is then pressed and held down while the icon is 'dragged' from its own window to the window corresponding to the destination disk drive. On releasing the mouse button, the file is stored automatically on the second disk drive. An icon will then be shown in each window. In practice, the way this operation is carried out varies from one GUI to another. However, the aim is the same: to provide a more intuitive and easily learnt method of operating the computer.

One advantage of a GUI is that if programs are specially written to be used with it, the display and manipulation tools provided by the GUI can be used by the programmer. This means that different programs written for the same GUI look similar and thus it is easier to learn how to use them. They are said to have a similar 'look and feel'. The GUI also provides advantages to the software producer. Often standard screen and printer 'drivers' are provided for popular equipment, thus removing the need for the software developer to provide them. In addition, GUIs are providing an increasing range of founts for both screen and printer which the applications developer can also take advantage of.

GUIs are available for most microcomputers, the 'classical' example being that for the Apple Macintosh. For IBM machines, Microsoft introduced the 'Windows' GUI which runs in conjunction with MS-DOS and provides the interface to the user. 'Windows' can also transfer data between two applications programs. Digital Research devised the GEM system which also runs on IBM microcomputers. For OS/2 there is the fast-developing 'Presentation Manager'. An interesting development is the 'NewWave' GUI extension to Windows from Hewlett Packard. This allows, for example, documents to be constructed from data stored in a variety of individual packages, such as a spreadsheet, a wordprocessor and a database program. The interesting development is that the data are not transferred to a new file to make up the document. Rather, they are left under the control of the original applications program. Thus, if the data are updated, this can immediately be incorporated in the new version of the document.

Another example of a GUI for IBM machines is QuarterDeck's DesqView. This does not use a graphics screen but can display a graphical image in a window. However, it is also presently a popular way of introducing multi-tasking to the IBM microcomputer. There are several GUIs associated with Unix machines, e.g. 'Open Look' from Sun and AT&T, and 'Motif' from the Open Software Foundation, an alliance of several manufacturers, including DEC and IBM. Motif is similar to Presentation Manager in OS/2. Some of the Unix GUIs are based on the X-Windows system, developed at MIT in the USA.

3.3 NETWORK OPERATING SYSTEMS

A network operating system (NOS) provides the software tools to set up and control the operation of a local-area network. It provides the tools to allow equipment connected together in a network to work together. Microcomputers can be connected together on an equal basis (peer-to-peer) or one or more of the computers can be designated as a 'server'. In addition to being a normal microcomputer, a server provides its own resources to others in the network. Examples of joint tasks which can be carried out over the LAN include:

1. joint use of data;
2. joint use of programs;
3. sharing of equipment.

Data files stored on a server can normally be used by other machines over the network, as long as they are designated as 'common files' by the server. It is also possible to store common programs on the server and have them used by other microcomputers across the network. Programs not specially written for network usage can be employed but there may be unforeseen problems if the programs are used simultaneously by more than one user. An example might be if two users of the same files tried to alter the same record at the same time. Programs can be written to be 'network sensitive'. They then behave predictably and correctly according to a desired plan. Equipment, such as printers, can be shared by microcomputers on the network. For instance, it may be economical to provide only one laser printer and direct high-quality printing to it. LAN network operating systems also can provide electronic mail functions, although separate packages can be obtained for this.

There is a range of software packages to manage network functions. Apple has its AppleShare package which lets Macintoshes share files on an AppleTalk network. The basic tools to enable an application to interface to a LAN in the MS-DOS world is provided by 'NetBIOS'. This is called an API (applications program interface), and allows IBM microcomputers' programs access to LAN facilities. For instance, there are commands to send data to, or receive data from, other machines on the network. It is common for network operating systems for IBM machines to support NetBIOS functions. Currently, the most popular package is Novell's 'NetWare' which allows equipment to be connected in Token-Ring, Ethernet and other arrangements. IBM supplies its own PC LAN programs. OS/2 also provides support for LAN operation through its LAN Manager.

The decision on which operating system to use will be dependent on what the user wishes to do. The choice of a computer system needs to be approached along project management lines (see Chapter 10), the choice of the operating system being only one of the factors. Most machines will be supplied with at least one operating system. This is likely to be the best one to use, as more software packages are likely to have been written for the most widely available operating system. It is the ability to run the applications program that is probably the most important factor in deciding which operating system to use. However, the choice is getting wider and a particular operating system may provide features, e.g. multi-user operation, a favoured GUI or the availability of a particular programming language, which make it worth while to abandon the normal one. For users of MS-DOS, the move to OS/2 or an alternative presents some interesting challenges. In this area, it will very much depend on how much microcomputer expertise the user has, or is able to access.

3.4 SYSTEM UTILITIES

Early versions of operating systems were far from being perfect and the gaps in their provision of tools were partly filled by independent software houses. This was particularly true for the large market of users of IBM and 'compatible' machines. Packages are provided for tasks such as the following:

1. Backing-up hard disk files: this can be done using the operating system but back-up programs provide a wider range of options, such as partial restoring of files and data compression to reduce the number of diskettes needed for back-ups.
2. Defragmentation of disk files: when files are written to disk, the operating system normally tries to store the file on sectors which are adjacent. If it cannot, it finds sectors on different parts of the disk but keeps track of where they are. However, this slows the machine down and the problem gets worse as the disk fills up and if files are constantly updated. Disk defragmenters reorganize the files on the disk so that sectors which are logically adjacent are also, as far as possible, physically adjacent.
3. File-handling packages: they allow files to be managed with more powerful and more convenient tools than the normal operating system. They can, for instance, show the files in alphabetical, creation date, etc., order, rename files easily, display and list them in helpful ways, etc.
4. File recovery: some programs allow data to be recovered from disks which normally cannot be read (perhaps if the master index is damaged).

5. Desktop tools: some programs provide tools, such as a clock, calendar, electronic notepad, outliner (e.g. for developing contents lists of documents), time managers. They are on the borderline between system utilities and applications programs for use in the office. However, they are sometimes included in utility programs (PC Tools is an example of such a package for IBM machines).

This is only a taste of the many packages which are not strictly applications programs but rather help with the management of the computer itself.

3.5 COMPILERS, INTERPRETERS AND PROGRAMMING LANGUAGES

It was shown in Chapter 2 how a microcomputer was dependent on computer programs or software to make it work. A small program was written in an assembly language and an assembler was used to translate the program into machine code so that the program could be run. Assembly languages are important for some applications but their use should, in general, be restricted to those special applications when another language would not be satisfactory. Assembly language programs:

1. normally occupy less memory space than an equivalent program written in another language;
2. can be executed faster because there are likely to contain fewer instructions to do the same job;
3. can do some jobs that high-level languages cannot, such as handling unusual input or output devices or manipulating individual bits of data in special ways.

However, for most applications, one of the high-level languages will be sufficient. It is also possible to use more than one language for a single application: those parts requiring an assembly language can be written in one; the rest can be written in a more convenient high-level language. One reason for using a high-level language is ease of use. The four line assembly language program to add together two numbers (see section 2.1.8) could be reduced to one simple instruction such as:

$$TEMP = 25 + 35$$

In addition it will be possible to carry out complicated data manipulation operations with single instructions. For example, groups of similar pieces of data can all be processed at the same time by arranging them into lists or 'arrays' (each item being pigeonholed). There is a range of many different progam instructions in a particular language and their power can be augmented by using a database management system (Chapter 4). Some languages have specialist applications, e.g. for mathematicians or for processing strings of text, the latter being particularly useful for information retrieval applications.

Once a computer program has been written the steps to be taken to execute it are:

1. compilation (translation of the statements of the program into machine instructions);
2. linking (bringing together all the necessary parts of the final program);
3. loading (bringing the final program into memory ready to run);
4. execution (running the program).

The operation of a **compiler** is shown in Figure 3.3. The compiler sits in memory and operates as a program. The program to be compiled, which is often known as the source program, is treated as data by the compiler. The program statements are checked for syntax and logical errors and then, if no errors are apparent, each statement is translated into the equivalent machine code instructions. A complete source program may be written in more than one language and each part will need to be compiled separately. In addition, a number of 'subroutines' may be called in by various parts of the program (these are specific pieces of program designed to perform difficult or repetitive tasks). The linking stage brings all these individual parts together into a single object program which is loaded into RAM ready to be executed.

Interpreters provide an alternative method of executing a source program. A good analogy is the difference between the two methods by which humans are helped to communicate in international organizations when they cannot speak each other's language (Figure 3.4). Compilation uses a similar process to the translation of a document, which is then read by the other party. Interpreters work in the same way as a simultaneous interpreter in a meeting, translating 'on-the-fly'. The source program is loaded into memory and the individual source statements are translated into machine code as they are needed (Figure 3.5). The interpreter is kept in memory during the operation of the program.

Interpreters can be very useful for initial testing of programs because they are quicker and more flexible to use than compilers. Some interpreters have a built-in editor to simplify program alterations. For operational programs, a compiler is important in order to produce object programs that will be independent of the compiler and will execute more quickly.

Basic is traditionally the most popular language for microcomputers

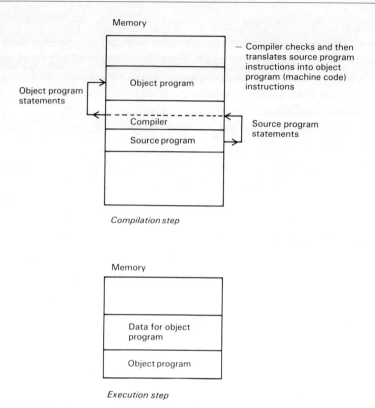

Figure 3.3   Use of memory for compilation and execution of a program.

amongst 'end-users', although not amongst professionals. It is usually available as an interpreter but compilers are also obtainable. It is simple to learn and use, and is a general-purpose language with some commands to manipulate strings of characters. Most, if not all, machines have a version of Basic available but there are a number of different dialects and only minimal standardization, which is important if programs are to be taken from one machine to another (portability). Basic has been criticized for being unsuitable for professional programmers and rather more suited to use in educational establishments, but it has been successfully applied in many fields of application. The power of the language varies considerably between the various versions. Other popular languages are Pascal and C.

Neither Basic nor Pascal are favourite languages for mini- and larger computer applications. One that is widely used, at least in the commercial and business world, is Cobol which is short for 'commercial and business oriented language'. There are versions available for microcomputers. PL/1, a language developed by IBM to satisfy a wide

Translation (analogous to compilation)

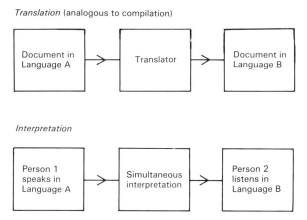

Interpretation

Figure 3.4 Similarity of computer program compilation and interpretation to document translation and interpretation of speech.

range of data processing needs, is also available for microcomputers. There are other languages in use, all of which have some advantages. Examples include Forth, Lisp (a list processing language) and Fortran (a language used mainly by scientists but also used for other purposes). The C language has grown in popularity. It was originally written for the PDP-11 minicomputer and operated under the Unix operating system. One advantage of C is that it is not tied to a particular brand of hardware: it is very easy to write programs in C which will run on a number of machines. A number of information retrieval systems for microcomputers has been written using C. It has been described as a fairly low-level language, but this can provide some of the advantages of an

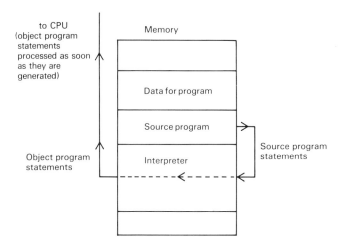

Figure 3.5 Execution of a program using an interpreter.

assembly language whilst still offering some powerful programming features.

'Object oriented programming languages' (OOPL) are increasingly being discussed. They have their origins in the 1960s and 1970s, and allow programmers to set up objects which model real world objects. The state of an object can be altered by performing operations on it: in contrast, traditional languages work with data and procedures. An example of an OOPL is 'Smalltalk' but object orientation has been built into other languages, such as C++.

It is likely that some of the languages in widespread use on larger machines will gain in popularity on microcomputers as the machines become more powerful, the languages more readily available and users more sophisticated. There are also programming languages built into some database management systems and they are discussed in Chapter 4.

3.6 THE ORGANIZATION OF DATA

Data stored in a microcomputer must be organized in a way that optimizes the performance of hardware and software for a particular application. How data are organized will, of course, depend on what is to be done: an information retrieval system may, for instance, need to locate individual items of data in seconds. In this case the data will have to be organized to make this possible. Data must also be physically stored on a device. Magnetic disks are the usual bulk storage devices used, magnetic tapes being less useful because of the time required to locate data. How data are placed on a device is known as the physical organization and this is limited by the physical layout of the device itself. On a disk, data will have to be stored in the sectors and tracks which have been laid out to hold them. This use of cylinders of data to improve retrieval speed (Figure 2.13) and the grouping of records into blocks to save space are two of a number of techniques of physical data organization techniques. Fortunately, many of the problems associated with physical organization of data are handled by operating systems.

Programmers are usually more concerned with logical organization. Figure 3.6 illustrates the difference between the two forms. A file of data will usually need to be logically organized so that each item has its correct place. From a programming point of view, item B may be logically next to item A. Physically, they may be separated but connected together by links or pointers so that the logical arrangement can be presented when required. This arrangement of data avoids having to sort all the items into the correct order every time new ones were added. The new data could, for instance, be put at the end and the pointers rearranged. It is

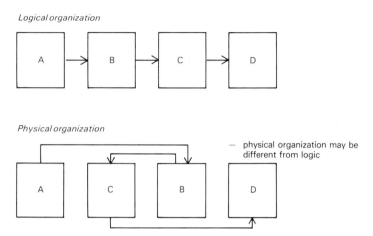

Figure 3.6 Logical and physical organization of data on a disk.

also useful if the same data were regularly used in two different sequences, such as in a thesaurus.

Database management systems can be used to provide complicated logical arrangements of data and they are discussed in Chapter 4. As might be expected, there are a number of conflicting terms to describe data storage concepts. Terms such as 'record', 'field', 'data element', 'key', 'item' and many others have been used in a variety of contexts. Within that of database management systems, the terminology is better controlled, but use of it requires a good understanding of a complicated subject.

In the library and information service fields, a number of computer systems have been developed which are commonly called information retrieval systems. They tend to employ a relatively simple arrangement of the data to be retrieved, together with some sophisticated indexes to provide fast access to the data. Data for a particular item can be grouped together into a record. An example is to build records to describe a set of documents. This set is commonly called a database, but it would be more accurate to call it a file. Each record contains a number of data elements (author, title, etc.). A place reserved for a data element is sometimes referred to as a field. There may be one or more occurrences of each data element (e.g. a document may have two or more authors) and each may be put in a separate field (see Figure 3.7). The indexes which are built to provide fast access are sometimes referred to as inverted indexes or inverted lists. The organization of data in information retrieval systems is dealt with in more depth in Chapter 4.

Various computer programs will need to access the data elements within a record and it is necessary to structure the data in a helpful and

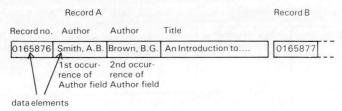

Figure 3.7 Arrangement of data elements into fields within a record.

unambiguous way. The computer thus needs to keep track of where each data element is within the record and how long it is. It is simpler to do this if each record has the same length (fixed-length records) and if each occurrence of a data element in different records has the same length (fixed-length fields). An example is shown in Figure 3.8.

Some data elements in a bibliographic database do have a fixed length, e.g. the date a record was created, but most do not. Placing variable-length data elements into fixed-length fields will mean wasting space if the field size is made larger than the longest occurrence of each data element. Otherwise some occurrences will not fit into the space provided and space is still wasted for very short occurrences.

Records containing variable-length fields will of necessity vary in length. An example is shown in Figure 3.9. One widely used record structure employs a directory to the record with an entry for each occurrence of a data element. The entry contains details of the type of element, its position in the record and its length. Each record is divided into a number of sections. When the record is created, its length is placed at the beginning of the record and this can be followed by a section containing fixed-length data elements, if required, in order to simplify access to them. A directory is constructed to point to each variable-length data element and then, finally, the variable-length data elements themselves appear. The example shown in Figure 3.9 is only one of many possible arrangements. The standard one used for the distribution of bibliographic databases has a similar structure to that just described.

The flexibility of variable-length records is bought at a price. A database of fixed-length records is easier to update since a new record can exactly take the place of an old one, although if new records need to

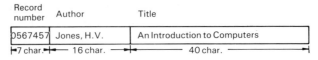

Figure 3.8 Arrangement of data in fixed-length fields.

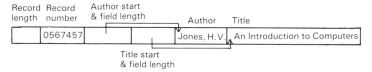

Figure 3.9 Arrangement of data in variable-length fields (note record number is in a fixed-length field).

be added at a particular place in the sequence, space will need to be made available. Techniques that allow sophisticated logical and physical arrangements may be needed for updating a file of variable-length records or the file may need to be copied, at the same time creating the necessary space. This problem is considered later in the chapter.

The examples shown in Figures 3.8 and 3.9 are extremely simple data structures. The record structure can become more complicated if some data elements occur more than once. A bibliographic record for a document containing two authors is an example. Single complex fields can also cause problems when processing the data and, in order to avoid ambiguity when processing such a field, it can be split up into subfields. In the MARC machine-readable cataloguing system, for example, a personal author's name is recorded (in simplified form) in a single field as follows:

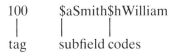

The $a subfield code marks the surname and $h the first name. The number 100 signifies that the data element is a personal author and is called a tag.

A set of records stored on a magnetic disk will normally have a prescribed order. Often this is by the key field which is usually part of a record that identifies it uniquely. A record number is a commonly used key field. Using the mechanism of the disk and the disk operating system, an individual record can be retrieved from the disk. The place where the record is stored on the disk is calculated from the key field. Hence although the records may be stored in sequential order, they are accessible and can be retrieved individually. A technique called the index sequential access method (ISAM) was devised which provides a programmer with the ability to build a sequential file on disk but which can be easily updated. The individual records are put together on disk sectors and tracks, each cylinder containing an index to all the records stored in the cylinder. If a particular cylinder becomes full, there are one or more tracks or cylinders that have been set aside for overflow records

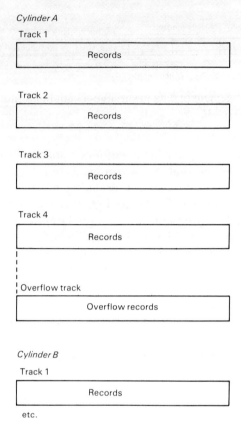

Figure 3.10 Arrangement of data records with tracks to accommodate overflow records.

(Figure 3.10). Thus new records can be added in their correct place without having to rearrange the whole file. The logical arrangement is maintained although records may not be physically next to each other. In practice, for a large file, a hierarchical system of indexes may be necessary. There might be a track index for the records on each track, a cylinder index for the records on each cylinder and a master index on top (Figure 3.11). The ISAM technique provides reasonably fast access to individual records at the same time as keeping the records in sequence, which will be important for processing records in batches, e.g. for printing lists. In Figure 3.11, if it is required to locate record number 15, the program would search for the nearest number lower than 15 in the master index.

This index would show the location (address) on the disk of the relevant cylinder index. A search would then be made of the cylinder

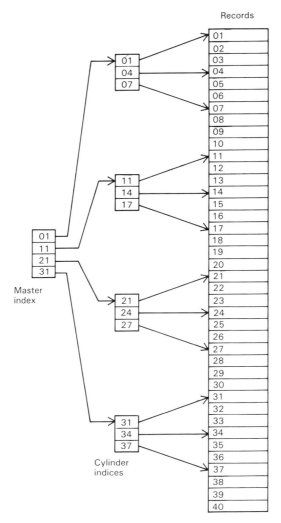

Figure 3.11 Example of master and cylinder indices for index sequential organization.

index to find the entry with the nearest lower number, in this case 14. This entry would lead to the point on the disk which contained records starting with 14, in this case 14 to 16. A sequential search of the remaining records would soon locate record number 15. In practice, the number of records would be much larger than is shown in the example.

If it is not important to process records sequentially, they can be organized randomly on the disk. The space on the disk is split up into a number of cells (say 1 to n). The key field is subjected to a formula that

Table 3.1 Example of disk file with access by hash coding technique

Record for	Characters for hash	Numerical equivalent	Position on disk (hash code)	Overflow* position
Able, J	AB	65×66	41	
Brown, T	BR	66×82	163	251
Brown, W	BR	66×82	251	
Jones, L	JO	74×79	97	
Smith, T	SM	83×77	142	252
Smith, W	SM	83×77	252	
Wills, A	WI	87×73	102	

* Overflow starts at location 251.

Example: (ABLE, J) AB = 65 × 66
65 × 66/250 = 17 rem. 40
hash code = 40 + 1 = 41

translates it into a cell number. The idea is to invent a formula that translates each key field into a unique cell number so that every record can have its own place on the disk. In practice, there is often a large number of empty cells or, if space is at a premium, it is necessary to have overflow areas when several records generate the same cell number. The process is normally known as hashing, and the devising of suitable formulae has been the subject of much research.

A simple example of a hashing algorithm is given in Table 3.1. It is required to store customer records on disk and to use the customer surname to obtain access to a particular record. The hashing algorithm uses the numerical equivalent of the first two letters of the surname. The range of possible combinations is 256 × 256 (each ASCII character occupies eight bits, giving a range of numbers between 0 and 255). Hence SMITH would generate the ASCII code 83×77 (the numbers equivalent to SM).

It is important to know the approximate number of records in the file as the amount of space which should be allocated in an ideal situation would be exactly the amount required to store those records. Assuming there are about 250 records in the example in Table 3.1, and multiplying together the two characters from the surname, dividing by 250, then taking the remainder plus 1 as the location for the record, would produce numbers ranging from 1 to 250. This is equal to the number of records and ideally the arrangement would ensure that each record generated a unique hashing code so that it had its own location.

There are two occurrences of the names Smith and Brown. An overflow record will need to be created for the second occurrence of each name and its position will be stored next to the first record with the same name. The overflow records themselves will be stored in locations 251 and 252. It can be seen that a more complicated algorithm which included the customer's initial would have reduced the need for overflow records. The hashing technique, if well designed, provides fast access to data, as normally only one disk read is necessary to locate the data. However, the technique can be difficult to manage with large files which are also getting bigger. In addition, if files need to be arranged in different orders, they will need to be sorted. This will be time-consuming, as each record will have to be located individually at different places on the disk.

Another method of organizing data is using tree structures. Such techniques are useful for looking up entries in dictionaries, for instance. Once an entry is found, it can be associated with a pointer to where related data are stored. The simplest example of a tree structure is the 'binary tree'. An example is shown in Figure 3.12. A binary tree consists of a series of 'nodes' linked together in a tree. The entry (or key as it is often known), a pointer to where linked data can be found and pointers to the two branch nodes are stored at each node. Each node branches into two other nodes and is connected to them by means of the pointers. Each pointer is an address where the connected node can be located. One of the keys stored at the branch nodes is a lower number or comes earlier in the alphabet and the other a higher number, or comes later in the alphabet than the key at the node pointing to it.

In the example, it is assumed that it is required to look in the dictionary to find whether the word 'computer' is present, and then to retrieve the data linked to it. The word being searched for is first compared with the key stored in the root node, i.e. 'information'. As 'computer' comes

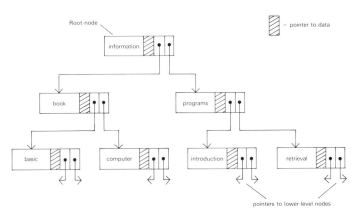

Figure 3.12 Example of a binary tree.

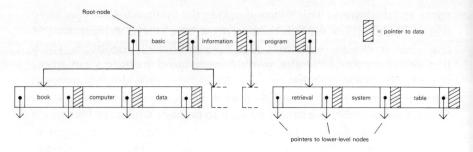

Figure 3.13   Example of a B-tree.

before 'information' in the alphabet, the next step is to use the 'earlier' pointer to find the next node, in this case containing the word 'book'. A comparison with the key at this node is again carried out; this time 'computer' is later in the alphabet than the word 'book'. Selecting the later pointer leads to the node containing the key 'computer'. The associated data can then be retrieved using the pointer to where they can be found. This pointer is shown at each node in Figure 3.12 as a shaded area.

There are ways of improving the speed of the search in a tree, one of these arrangements being called a 'B-tree'. Instead of having only one key at each node, this number is increased. An important reason for doing this is because of the physical design of the disk. Data are normally written to, or read from, the disk a sector at a time. In this case, it is advantageous to make the size of a node coincide with the size of a sector and store a number of keys in each node. An example of a B-tree arrangement is shown in Figure 3.13. There are three keys per node in this particular case. Compared with the binary tree, the B-tree reduces the number of disk accesses required to find a particular key. With tree structures, it is important to get a balanced effect. An unbalanced computer tree would resemble a tree which had grown with many missing branches. When a tree is filled with data, techniques are used to readjust the pointers and to move the keys around to achieve this balanced effect. A method of managing the available disk storage must also be available. In some cases, data keys must be removed from a node or an entire node may need to be removed altogether. Once a particular sector is empty, it can then be reused for another node.

There are other arrangements of data which provide advantages in certain circumstances. The representation of data on disks is a complicated subject and the foregoing discussion gives but a flavour of the various available techniques. Indeed, with some database management systems (Chapter 4), extremely complicated logical structures can be devised without worrying about the physical arrangements which are taken care of by the database software. Often, these logical structures (hierarchies of data, etc.) are physically stored by chaining records together. A chain is formed by placing the position or address of the next or previous record, or both, in the record itself. A record can be part of a number of chains and the process of adding or deleting records can become quite complex.

Systems for information retrieval and data management

This chapter deals with systems for information retrieval on microcomputers. In addition, the features of database management systems and the use of microcomputers as intelligent terminals for accessing remote databases are described. Chapter 5 deals mainly with systems for library housekeeping but the line between the two areas is difficult to draw and hence some overlap is inevitable.

4.1 INFORMATION RETRIEVAL SYSTEMS

4.1.1 Essentials of information retrieval systems

Online computer-based information retrieval systems were developed in the 1960s, for example by Lockheed Dialog and Systems Development Corporation (SDC). They were introduced in order to provide fast access to bibliographic records and, at the same time, to improve on the performance of manual search tools such as printed indexes. As such, they usually provide only a reference to a document, and possibly an abstract, rather than the full text of the document itself. Bibliographic databases are, in such systems, stored on disk and searches are made at a terminal connected directly to the computer (Figure 4.6 shows an outline of the equipment), and answers can be displayed directly on the terminal.

Today, it is possible to connect a computer terminal to a wide range of online computer-stored data around the world. These host computers can store many databases and have enormous power which is used to service many hundreds of users simultaneously. A few search terms entered at a keyboard can quickly retrieve details of documents or data to satisfy a request.

Information retrieval systems are also available for microcomputers. Their mode of operation is basically similar to those designed for larger computers but they are limited in certain ways in what they can provide. Indeed, some of the systems are scaled-down versions of operational systems for larger machines. As retrieval systems have become more widespread, they have been used for an ever-increasing range of data. In addition to bibliographic records, they are used for such applications as real estate for sale, research projects, online yellow pages, etc.

The optimum organization of a database for retrieval will depend on the particular needs. Of importance will be:

1. the structural characteristics of the data and their use;
2. the overall size of the database;
3. the speed of retrieval required;
4. the frequency of updating required.

In a classical information retrieval system, data tend to be arranged in a single record as shown in Figure 3.7. A number of inverted indexes, which can be likened to those in the back of a book, provide the fast retrieval speeds required. A bibliographic database can become quite large as documents are often entered into it with only a vague idea of whether they are going to be relevant. A fast retrieval speed is usually of more importance than a fast updating speed. Although the online database vendors, such as Dialog, provide a fast response to queries, updating the databases themselves is not usually such a time-critical process. Normally a typical database is updated at weekly or even longer intervals, although there are exceptions. Often, once a record is established, it is not changed or deleted until it is removed with a number of others.

At the other extreme to the large online systems is the single-user microcomputer information retrieval system, the use pattern of which may not have the same constraints. It may, for instance, be possible to make do with a slower retrieval speed in exchange for faster updating. The design of the retrieval system will be very dependent on this decision. However, if a software package is chosen which provides certain features such as fast retrieval speed, it may not be possible to change the system significantly if priorities change. If flexibility is required, it may be better to go for a general-purpose database management system (section 4.2) which may offer inferior retrieval functions but more flexible data management features.

4.1.1.1 Inverted lists or indexes

The creation of inverted lists is one mechanism for increasing retrieval speed. Search terms are taken out of each record, or perhaps assigned from a controlled vocabulary, and are entered into lists which are ordered in some way to allow a search request to be matched quickly against the entries in the lists. There might be different lists for the various types of data, author, title words, terms from a controlled vocabulary, etc., or they may all be grouped together. The entries in the inverted lists are often linked to their respective records in the main file through a postings file which stores the record numbers corresponding to the entries in the inverted lists. Figure 4.1 shows the creation of inverted list entries for three records from a sample bibliographic database. The files might be arranged and searched as in Figure 4.2.

With this arrangement, searching is usually a two-stage process, the first being to search the inverted lists and the postings file to find the number of records that satisfy the search request. The original records which are retrieved by the search are displayed at a second step and their locations are obtained from the postings file. This two-stage process is sometimes carried out in one step. Tree structures might also be used,

Records in main file (file will contain many more)

| 014263 | SMITH, W | AN INTRODUCTION TO COMPUTING | PRIME PUBL., 1983 |

| 015463 | SMITH, W | INFORMATION RETRIEVAL AND COMPUTING | JAMES, 1982 |

| 018214 | JONES, N | AN INTRODUCTION TO BASIC PROGRAMS | PRIME PUBL., 1984 |

Inverted list entries from above records

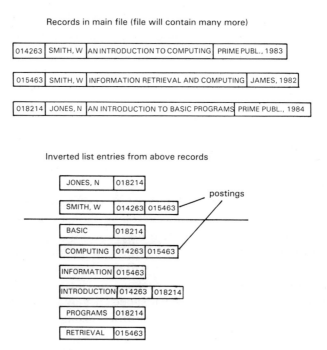

Figure 4.1   Inverted list entries generated from records in main file (entries for publisher, record number and date not created).

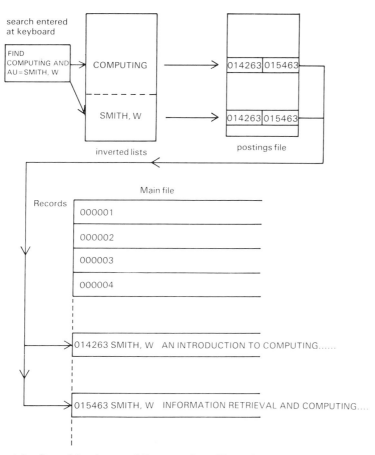

Figure 4.2 Searching inverted lists, postings file and main file.

for instance to search the inverted lists. Both binary- and B-trees are described in Chapter 3.

The difficulty in updating the database can be seen from Figure 4.2. When a record is added or deleted, not only is the main file one of variable-length records but also the entries in the inverted lists and in the postings file have to be altered. The size of these indexes can grow rapidly, especially for bibliographic records, and even more rapidly if an abstract describing the content of a document is also searchable by the inverted list technique.

4.1.1.2 String searching

The size of the lists can be reduced and the maintenance problem eased by minimizing the number of types of data elements which are inverted for searching. On some systems, it will still be possible to search on these data elements using a technique known as string searching. The records in the main file are scanned sequentially from the beginning of the file until a match is found. Needless to say, this technique is relatively slow but can be valuable if the data are not searchable through indexes or if retrieval speed is not critical. In some cases, string searching can be carried out on subsets of the file. This will consequently be faster than searching the whole file. At the extreme, inverted indexes can be dispensed with altogether which, especially with large files, would remove much of the updating headache. Of course, the main file must be updated but the whole process then becomes more manageable. It is likely, as well, that updating of records will be an important factor in in-house systems.

4.1.1.3 Search strategies

Once a database and its inverted indexes have been set up, a search can be carried out using one or more search terms. In the records shown in Figure 4.1 a search for all documents containing the word 'COM-PUTING' might be as follows:

FIND COMPUTING   (entered at the keyboard)

The answer from the computer would be:

SET 1 : 2 hits

(Figure 4.1 shows there are two records containing the word 'COM-PUTING'.)

The search is given a set number so that if the search results need to be displayed, or the search refined, it can be referred to directly. Hence to display records for set 1:

SHOW S = 1; F = ALL

would be entered. It is sometimes possible to show all or part of the retrieved records. In this case 'F = ALL' means show full records and S = 1 is the set number. The above commands are those adopted for the European Common Command Language (CCL) but they are only a convention and there is a variety of different commands in use. The variety can be quite confusing and its elimination was the main aim behind the development of the CCL.

A more detailed search could be carried out by combining two, or more, terms using Boolean logic, in this case the word 'COMPUTING' and an author 'W SMITH' (see also Figure 4.2):

FIND COMPUTING AND AU = SMITH, W

This would retrieve records containing both these terms. The following example:

FIND INTRODUCTION AND (BASIC OR COMPUTING)

would retrieve records containing the word 'INTRODUCTION' together with either the word 'BASIC' or the word 'COMPUTING'.

It is also possible to search for part of a search term. Thus the truncated term 'COMPUT$', with the dollar being the truncation symbol, would retrieve records containing words such as 'COM-PUTER', 'COMPUTING', etc. The same symbol can also be put in the middle or to the left of the term in some systems. Records containing a particular term can be eliminated using 'NOT' logic.

All the above searches can be carried out without accessing the main file. Only when the retrieved records are to be seen is it necessary to enter the main file. Other search techniques are possible, such as the string searching mentioned above, and some of them require the main file to be accessed. String searching allows the searcher to specify the relative positions of search terms or that terms should only be searched in a particular type of data element. This can also be done in the inverted data structure if the relevant data are carried in an inverted list or attached to it. Of course, a more complex inverted data structure will add to the maintenance problem, but will speed up searching when more sophisticated search techniques, such as word adjacency, are used.

4.1.1.4 Controlled vocabularies, thesauri and indexing

The examples of searches just described show the application of what is sometimes called **free-text** searching. Words or groups of words freely thought up to describe a sought-after subject are matched by the computer against the data in each record. This type of subject search may be sufficient for some questions but not for others. For instance, in a database of real estate, it may not be possible to retrieve details of all houses which are, say, 'detached' using the data describing the houses if that word is omitted from some of the records. In addition, records describing 'semi-detached' houses may also be retrieved if the retrieval system treats a hyphen as a space. In a similar way, some types of search query, such as those for the subject of a document, are often difficult to match exactly with records for relevant documents; hence the aids to retrieval such as the truncation device described above.

Even with these devices, the retrieval efficiency may not be sufficient. The recall (the percentage of relevant records in the collection that are retrieved) and the precision (the percentage of retrieved records that are relevant) may not be large enough. Both these measures can be improved in some circumstances by employing a controlled vocabulary. In the real estate example, a list of 'types of house' would include the words 'DETACHED' and 'SEMIDETACHED' (with no space or hyphen), etc., one of which would be assigned to each house record when it was entered. Thesauri have been produced for a wide range of subject fields. Controlled vocabularies for subject indexing can become quite extensive for large document collections, and techniques are used to ensure that searcher and indexer (the person assigning the terms) use the correct terms. At its simplest the vocabulary can be a list of preferred terms, but structural aids, such as showing the relationships between broader, narrower and related terms, can be used. Some vocabularies are based on classifications using a code or notation to describe each subject.

If desired, the controlled terms can be entered into the inverted lists instead of the free-text terms. This may cut down the number of terms in the lists and simplify maintenance. There are disadvantages, however. The vocabulary itself must be maintained and terms assigned to each record. It is also preferable, although not essential, that the retrieval system maintains the vocabulary. If it does not, it can be maintained manually outside the system but this usually means extra work.

A controlled vocabulary can be applied at search time instead of when a record is created. In this case it can be used to help generate the search terms. Most retrieval systems will allow the inverted lists, and, if available, the controlled vocabulary to be displayed online. This can be used for both indexing and searching. There has been considerable debate on whether to use free-text searching or a controlled vocabulary. If it can be afforded, having both free-text and controlled vocabularies may be useful as they can come into their own in different circumstances. For small collections of records, as may be the case with many microcomputer systems, the user may be able to make do with something quite simple. The final decision will need to be taken on the basis of perceived costs and benefits.

4.1.2 Information retrieval systems for microcomputers

There is a range of available information retrieval systems for microcomputers on the market with a variety of prices. A list of available software is given in Appendix A. Some of the systems will naturally provide more features than others but it is important to analyse carefully the particular needs and choose the software appropriate for the job. Software features can be divided into those that are necessary, those desirable and those unnecessary.

Any retrieval system will provide three essential ingredients:

1. Database creation and management (input of new records, amendments and deletions, creation of searching structures, e.g. inverted indexes);
2. Search commands, normally in online mode with fast response time (usually a few seconds) and Boolean logic;
3. Display of search results.

4.1.2.1 Database creation

One of the first tasks will be to decide on the data elements for the database and their characteristics. This demands careful consideration because the database structure may be difficult to change after it has been set up and records have been entered into it. Most software will have a module to set up the skeleton of the database. An example of building a database using the University of London FIRS retrieval system is shown in Appendix C. This is a simple system, but shows the basic principles. Software may also provide a format checker to check such fields as data and record number. The package will have a limit to the size of fields and records and to the total number of records in a database.

Before input of data, the indexing system will need to be set up. If free-text indexing is used, a decision will need to be taken on which data elements are to be made searchable (Appendix C) and how. Elements such as the title of a document will probably require each word to be individually searchable. Authors' names will also be searchable individually but the forenames and surnames will need to be kept together. Some data elements will be searched as a single element (e.g. record number).

The use of a controlled vocabulary will present another level of difficulty as the indexing mechanism will need to be set up. The example in Appendix C does not support a computer-stored controlled vocabulary but a manually maintained one could be used in conjunction with it. Input of data into a record may be onto a preformatted screen, and it may be possible to design the layout of the screen and possibly alter the screen colours to suit the individual needs. If variable-length fields are used, particularly if they are long, it may be necessary to present them on screen one at a time. The first data element is sometimes a record number which is presented by the program. It may be necessary to have a second record number under the user's control. If a computer-stored controlled vocabulary is used, the assigned terms might be checked automatically and new or mistyped terms would be flagged (marked).

In order to amend a record it can be located using the input/ maintenance module by means of its computer-assigned number, and in this case the number must be known. It may be possible to retrieve the record using the retrieval module and then go straight into update mode. Such a feature might be useful if it were convenient to use the retrieval and updating modules together. This approach might also be useful for the deletion of data; for instance it might be desirable to delete a set of records that satisfy a certain criterion, e.g. older than a certain date. They could be retrieved by the retrieval module and then deleted in one step.

4.1.2.2 Creation of inverted indexes

When a new record is added to the database or an existing record amended, the inverted indexes will need to be updated. Some systems may require the whole of the inverted index to be recreated after every change to the master records, but they should be avoided, if possible, as it can be a time-consuming process for large databases.

4.1.2.3 Searching and retrieval

Following a search it will usually be possible, as a second step, to display results on the screen or to print the records on a printer attached to a microcomputer. Some systems print or display the entire record only but it might be useful to have a range of user-definable subsets of the database to be extracted and used for other purposes. It may be required to create a report from the results and this could be done using a word processor. The machine-readable records retrieved from the search could be submitted directly to the word processor and edited.

4.1.2.4 Production of printed catalogues and indexes

Production of printed catalogues and indexes may be important, particularly in a library with a larger number of users than (say) a single-user microcomputer could cope with in online mode. It may also be necessary to have access to the database in different places: the production of multiple copies of catalogues and the indexes is one answer to this problem. If multiple terminal online access is required a multiple user computer system will be needed. There are several answers to this hardware problem, one of which is to use a minicomputer! If printing is required, the software should be examined to see how this can be done. Some systems will allow several different printing formats and sequences. It may be necessary to consider alphabetical filing rules, e.g. to interfile names such as those beginning with Mc and Mac.

Other features of the software which should be taken into consideration include:

1. system reminders to create back-up copies of databases (tidy housekeeping procedures are essential to maintain the integrity of the database);
2. access security (different passwords for various categories of user);
3. user-friendly search facilities (for users unfamiliar with the retrieval system);
4. software capable of supporting simultaneous use by a number of users, e.g. use of LANs;
5. permanent storage of search strategies;
6. system recovery procedures to minimize data loss;
7. ability to output in standard word processing form, or in a database format.

Section 4.4 deals with the 'down-loading' of machine-readable data from online database vendors into a microcomputer. Software is available to carry this out but, once the data are in the microcomputer, a retrieval system should be able to take a batch of records directly without the need to re-input it manually. Such a transfer would normally require a format change program to make the records compatible with the local system.

Some information retrieval systems for microcomputers have been derived from mainframe systems developed by online database vendors, others from minicomputer systems for in-house library and information service operation; still others have been devised as original microcomputer systems, and there are undoubtedly other categories. It would be wise when considering selection to examine the history of the development of each system and its current range of applications. If it is expected that the system may have to cope with the range of library housekeeping applications as well (Chapter 5), some compromises may have to be accepted. As already noted, another approach may be to adopt a database management system which will probably provide maximum flexibility but will usually require greater knowledge of software. These systems are discussed in section 4.2. The use of optical disks in conjunction with microcomputer information retrieval systems will grow in importance and should be taken into account when deciding on a system. Optical disk developments will be considered next.

4.1.3 Information retrieval with optical disks

Write once and erasable optical disks, as well as magnetic disks, can now be used with microcomputers. In addition, a growing number of bibliographic databases are becoming available on CD-ROM and some software producers have adapated their information retrieval systems to allow searching of these databases to take place using a microcomputer. It would have seemed amazing just a few years ago to be able to search a database of hundreds of thousands of records using a microcomputer costing only a few thousand dollars. Bibliographic databases provided on CD-ROM normally contain both the basic records and the inverted indexes. With a capacity approaching 600 Mb, it is easy to see how these huge databases can be accommodated.

The CD-ROM drive can be attached to an existing microcomputer, providing the correct interface is available. Portable microcomputers are also available with CD-ROM drives. Searching is almost identical in most cases to searching a smaller database stored on magnetic disk on the microcomputer, and probably no slower than an online search of a database stored on a large host information retrieval service, if the logging-on time is taken into account. With such large databases stored on a microcomputer with CD-ROM, the response time can be slow, but the CD-ROM version has other advantages over both the searching of databases on remote hosts and the use of printed sources. The advantages over online access to remotely stored databases include:

1. predictable costs compared with paying online connect time charges;
2. no pressure to search in as short a time as possible;
3. increasing the number of searches reduces the cost per search;
4. inexperienced users of online services are more likely to use them.

and over printed publications include:

1. CD-ROM takes up much less space;
2. is faster to use;
3. provides similar sophisticated access paths to those obtained presently with online searching using remote hosts;
4. multiple copies can be distributed to users at a particular location as they are not expensive to make.

One of the problems faced by the bibliographic database producers is the loss of revenue from other forms of publication of the database. The database producer has had to adjust to the changes in technology. A further complicating factor is that the CD-ROM can in theory be used to transfer machine-readable records to a local retrieval system on a much larger computer. Thus a user could capture a whole database for a possibly low price. Such eventualities have to be guarded against contractually. On the other hand, another type of user might want only to search the CD-ROM file on a single-user microcomputer. In this case it is difficult to justify charging a price much in excess of the cost of the subscription to a printed index, or what the user currently might have spent on online charges.

The shelf life of CDs is still not proven as it is still a relatively new technology. However, most CD-ROMs are reproduced from time to time anyway. Another factor is that, although prices have come down, they have yet to reach the low prices of audio CD players. Nevertheless, a growing number of large electronics companies now produce CD-ROM and microcomputer companies, such as Apple and Microsoft, are taking an extremely active interest in them. The challenge is still to the information community to generate the information products to profit from the evident advantages of the CD-ROM on a mass-market basis. Some novel products have already been produced, such as multilingual dictionaries, encyclopaedias, computer manuals, books and aircraft service manuals.

The combination of the storage of text, sound and images will provide opportunities for a new approach to information dissemination. It is the authors' view that the compact disk format will become widely accepted: which version this takes remains to be seen. The multi-media possibilities are potentially far-reaching and there will no doubt be a battle between the major players in this area. It will take some years for the clear winners to be seen.

The retrieval of information from videodisks using microcomputers is also possible, as described in Chapter 2. Data in machine-readable form can be stored on a videodisk and retrieved in a similar way to that of a CD-ROM. Moving or still images and sound can also form part of the retrieval process. An application which was given wide coverage was the Domesday project which put a large database of multi-media material onto a variation of the LaserVision system (LV-ROM). Major problems with videodisks are the cost of the equipment and the small number of products on the market. It is very likely that the introduction of the multi-media CD, which also offers text, images and sound on the same disk, will enable a much less costly product to be manufactured, even if the capacity is much smaller. Despite the cost of production, videodisks have been successful in interactive training situations and in stores at points of sale.

4.2 DATABASE MANAGEMENT SYSTEMS

4.2.1 Database management system features

Database management systems (DBMSs) do just what the name suggests: manage a computer-stored database or collection of data.

DBMSs were originally developed for large computers to assist with the development, implementation and maintenance of related computer systems.

At first, computer systems were designed around particular applications or departments in organizations. Separate systems were developed for, say, the personnel and payroll departments. It was realized that the data were duplicated in a number of systems, e.g. details of employees' names and addresses. When someone left a company or was promoted, several files had to be altered. In addition, changes in company policy could mean a larger number of changes to all these independent systems. More seriously, the fact that programs reflected the existing organization made it more difficult to change management structures.

File management systems were introduced to give programmers a consistent set of routines for managing files of computer-stored records. They did not, however, solve many of the fundamental problems of the management of data for the organization. Database management systems were evolved to provide the sort of assistance required by programmers to enable them to provide more efficient computer systems.

DMBSs for large computers are usually expensive: several tens of thousands of dollars is not an unusual price to pay for the software alone. The fact that they work indicates the sort of savings and benefits they can bring. To illustrate the basic principle of how a DBMS centralizes the data for an organization and provides a subset of the data to a relevant department, take as an example the technical service operation of a library. Such a service will be responsible for ordering, receiving, cataloguing, classifying, etc., books. Other library departments will require information on different aspects, e.g. the book circulation department will need data on users' names and addresses and which books are on loan to whom. A traditional approach to the automation of the various departmental systems might be as shown in Figure 4.3. The section responsible for ordering books has a file of books on order and received and a file of suppliers. The cataloguing section maintains a file or catalogue of books in the library. The book circulation department has a file of books for the purpose of controlling circulation, a file of loans and a file of library users.

The DBMS approach might look like that shown in Figure 4.4. All data are centralized into a database and the various departments in the library enter data and retrieve them according to their interests. The programmer developing a particular application can specify the data needed just for that application. If the design of the whole database is sensitive to all the library's needs, it can lead to a high level of

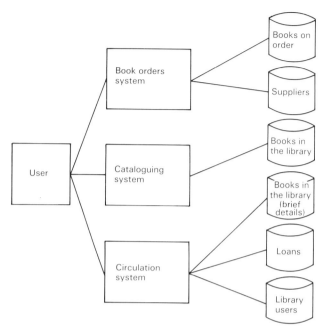

Figure 4.3 A library automation system with separate files for different departmental systems (simplified).

independence between applications, i.e. changes in one having little or no effect on another. In addition, departments can have access to all the data in the library of interest to them, even that from other departments. Duplication of data is reduced and the result can be a more effective organization for less effort. Just as important, both management and the library user may want an overall picture and can more easily obtain it. For instance, a user interested in a particular book may be happy to wait, if it can be easily determined that it is on order. If the book files are integrated from the user's point of view, this information can be found out with a single online query to the database. The user can then follow the status of the book as it progresses through the system, i.e. received but not in process, being catalogued, available, on loan, etc.

A DBMS will comprise a number of modules to operate on the central database, i.e.:

1. A data definition language (DDL), a mechanism for organizing and structuring the database and defining the data elements;
2. A data manipulation language (DML), used by programmers to manipulate data, often used in conjunction with a high-level language such as Cobol;

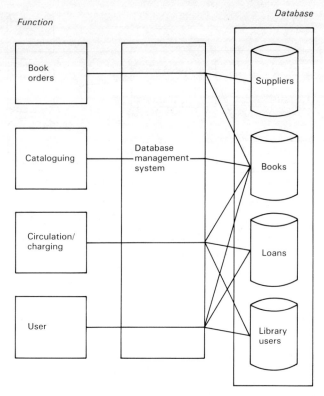

Figure 4.4 The database approach to a library automation system (simplified).

3. A query language, for users of the database who need answers to *ad hoc* questions – it should be easy to use and supply answers rapidly;
4. A report writer, for producing printed, customized reports;
5. A data input subsystem;
6. A communications subsystem to support a number of online users.

Of course database management systems will vary in what they offer but, for large computers, there are generally accepted features which must be available. The term 'database' is often used for a collection of data managed by a DBMS.

4.2.2 DBMS data structures

Database management systems can be characterized by the way they hold or structure their data. Information retrieval systems, such as those described in section 4.1, generally have a simple structure in the master record where there is often no relationship between data elements other

Table 4.1 Books on order in a relational database

Order no.	Author	Title	Supplier no.	Date
01625	Brown, T	Computer systems	124	831211
01626	Able, M	Introduction to PL/1	024	831212
01627	Smith, W	Basic for students	124	831213
01628	Nichols, M	Introduction to Pascal	025	831213
01629	Black, T	Logo for children	024	831214

than that they are side-by-side in the record. It can be very like the sort of data structures found in relational databases in which data are arranged in simple tables called relations. The other main category of DBMS uses complex data structures in which elements of data are organized hierarchically (one-to-many) or in networks (many-to-many).

Relational database management systems (RDBMS) operate on data tables or relations, an example of which is shown in Tables 4.1 and 4.2. A relation can be regarded as a matrix, with a number of rows and columns, a row corresponding to a single record in an information retrieval database (see Figure 4.1) and a column to all instances of a particular data element. A relational database can comprise a number of these tables and the RDBMS is able to manipulate them to produce the desired results. Tables 4.1 and 4.2 show a simple database for ordering books which contains a 'book' relation and a 'supplier' relation. The two relations can be manipulated to produce, for instance, a list of books on order to each of the suppliers. This is shown in Table 4.3. The arrangement of data in the two relations avoids the duplication of data. Supplier details are stored once only in a separate relation rather than with each book on order. Thus, if a supplier's address changed, it would only be necessary to change the appropriate entry in the supplier relation. Again, if orders to a particular supplier were changed to another, only the relevant supplier numbers in the 'books-on-order' relation would need to be changed. These changes could be made by the data manipulation tools supplied with the DBMS.

Table 4.2 Supplier relations in a relational database

Supplier no.	Supplier name	Address
024	Mount & Son	26 South Street, Anytown
025	Jones and Co.	PO Box 1, Westchester
124	Surton Books	246 Time Street, Dounton-on-Sea

Table 4.3   Production of a report of books on order organized alphabetically by supplier from the relations in Tables 4.1 and 4.2

Jones and Co.		
Nichols, M	Introduction to Pascal	831213
Mount & Son		
Able, M	Introduction to PL/1	831212
Black, T.	Logo for children	831214
Surton Books		
Brown, T	Computer systems	831211
Smith, W	Basic for students	831213

This is only a very simple example of the operation of a relational database management system. In practice it is necessary to have expertise in this area to take full advantage of a DBMS. However, some RDBMSs for microcomputers are fairly easy to use (see below). The analysis of each application requires the construction of relations which are normalized. There are different levels of normal form of a relation, most of which aim to simplify the relation by, for instance, eliminating repeated data elements and complex links between the keyfield and others.

Network and hierarchical database management systems allow data to be stored in ways which exactly reflect their structures and links. Rather than eliminating the complex links, as relational systems do, the exact desired structures can be supported by hierarchical and network structures. Theoretically, it can be shown that a hierarchy with one-to-many links is a trivial example of a network structure with many-to-many links. These DBMSs allow links to be created and destroyed subject to an overall database organizational plan called a schema. In the example shown in Figure 4.5, if a teacher takes over an existing course from another, the links between teachers and courses can be broken and re-formed as required. Systems provide rapid access to, and maintenance of, a database. It is vital, however, to design the database correctly, as it can be difficult to change the schema significantly if it is not satisfactory once the database is in operation and of some size. Contrast this with the relational approach in which links are usually implied by common data in different relations (see, for instance, the supplier number in Tables 4.1 and 4.2).

4.2.3 Database management systems for microcomputers

DBMSs for microcomputers are, in general, much more modest than those for larger computers and a good deal less expensive. Some of

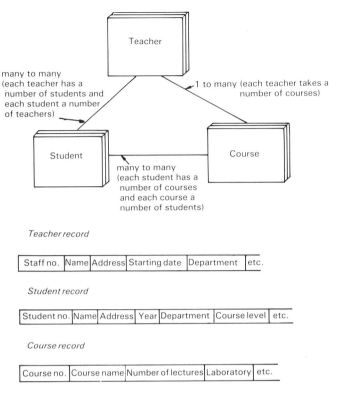

Figure 4.5 Schema for a network database management system for a teacher–student course database.

them, in fact, do not deserve the label in the strict sense of the definition. This lack of sophistication can be a positive advantage in some circumstances, however, because:

1. many applications on microcomputers are themselves fairly modest;
2. lack of sophistication can also mean simplicity of use.

In practice there is a wide range of DBMSs masquerading under that description. The simplest will do little more than manage a single file to produce printed reports. The most complicated has many of the features of systems for large computers.

Bearing in mind the warning about definition of the term DBMS and taking a wide and pragmatic view of the available software, the packages can be looked at in three groups:

1. file management systems;
2. systems which provide a simple data manipulation language;

3. fully fledged DBMSs which have a data manipulation language which can be used in conjunction with a programming language such as Cobol.

File management systems provide the ability to create records in a file, according to a particular specification, to add, modify and delete records and sort them into specific orders before printing them in a variety of formats. The procedures to carry out these operations are usually simple to learn.

An information retrieval system, such as described in section 4.1, will have a file management system built into it. Bibliographic retrieval systems often hold data for a document in a single record and, generally speaking, the database approach involving, for example, the manipulation of relations as shown in Tables 4.1, 4.2 and 4.3 is not a common feature.

There are a number of simple database management systems which are rather more powerful than file management systems. Some are classed as relational and the authors of some of this last group would claim that the very simplicity lies in the use of relations, but that the approach allows the construction of as complicated a database as the network approach. dBase IV is a popular example of the relational approach and, in addition to its data management features, it has a retrieval language which can employ inverted indexes for fast retrieval.

The choice of a DBMS for microcomputers is now extremely large and there is fierce competition between the major suppliers. As well as being able to manage and retrieve data, print reports, etc., the database systems must work with other software packages. Indeed some packages have database systems fully integrated with spreadsheets, word processors, etc., and the various modules are sold as a single package. Microsoft's 'Works' is an example. Sometimes, a single programming language can be used to write applications which use the various modules together. For instance, a database containing details of office letters, memos, etc., could be built up and linked directly to the documents themselves, which were prepared on the word processor. Such an application would be easily managed with an integrated package. Customized data entry screens could be developed to help the user enter the details of each letter, e.g. name of receiver, date sent, subject, file number and name. These might then be automatically transferred to a memo blank before being typed. The memo might then be sent by electronic mail. This database could then be searched at a later date to retrieve a particular letter.

The facilities to be considered when choosing a database management system in this simple category include the following:

1. Data element definition: the types of element which can be defined, e.g. alphanumeric, numeric, monetary amount;
2. Record characteristics: maximum field length, number of fields, fixed- or variable-length fields/records, maximum record length and records per file;
3. File handling: multiple file/relation support and manipulation, acceptance of data in external database structures and production of sub-files to take to other systems, ease of redefinition of database;
4. Searching capabilities: availability of a query langauge to allow online searching of the database and its ease of use, including Boolean logic, truncation, support for inverted indexes, range searching, e.g. greater than, less than;
5. Data manipulation language: necessity to use this language in order to make the system work, simplicity of use (some systems can learn by showing them an example), power of the language and its function, e.g. is it used for producing reports or is a separate report generator available;
6. Integrity and security of data: back-up facilities, restart from error condition with minimum loss of database, if system is multi-user, procedures to ensure same elements of data are not operated on simultaneously;
7. Reports: creation of customized reports, sorting of output on any field, degree of expertise required;
8. Easy of use: e.g. easy-to-understand documentation.

Some of the trends in DBMS design, such as the GUIs and hypertext, will be dealt with in the next section. However, another important development is the use of DBMSs in conjunction with a local-area network. One way of using DBMS on a LAN is in conjunction with a file server. This can mean, in effect, that the database program is stored in the user's machine but the files, which might normally also have been stored on the user's machine, are stored on the server. They can then be used by other users. This technique has the advantage that large databases can be stored on the server and this machine might have a large disk with a magnetic tape back-up unit attached. One of the problems with this approach is that the data traffic over the LAN can be quite high.

A more recent trend is the use of 'client/server' systems. With this approach, a more logical split of the processing between the user's machine and the server is achieved. The database is stored on the server in a form which allows standardized requests for data to be put to it. In effect the requests for data themselves are separated from the other activities, the latter being carried out in the user's machine. This cuts down the amount of traffic on the LAN, but still allows the database to be stored once only and be available to other users. An interface language called SQL (structured query language) has emerged as a *de facto* standard for manipulating such databases. SQL is a language designed to be used in conjunction with other programming languages, it being used when database manipulation needs to be carried out. It originated on large computers but is also available for microcomputers. Although there are different dialects of SQL, its availability on different machines brings closer the goal of compatibility of mainframe and microcomputer databases. An example of an SQL statement operating on a relational data base is (see Table 4.1):

> SELECT AUTHOR, TITLE
> FROM BOOK, WHERE ORDER NO: > 01627

This command would select all records in which the order number was greater than 01627 and would pick out the 'Author' and 'Title' fields from these records. Another, but more complicated statement, could be used to generate the report shown in Table 4.3. It would involve the **union** of the two relational tables, 4.1 and 4.2. The above statements are not unlike the command language used to put queries to information retrieval systems.

An SQL statement can be included in a program in the user's microcomputer and used to, for instance, extract data from the database on the server. The future of microcomputer DBMSs seems to be in this area, with a small number of SQL-type servers surviving in the long term and with the development of a larger number of 'front-ends', i.e. programs to provide particular solutions for the user in his own machine.

4.3 GRAPHICAL USER INTERFACES AND HYPERTEXT FOR INFORMATION RETRIEVAL AND DATABASE MANAGEMENT

The introduction of GUIs has affected database software as well as other microcomputer programs. DBMSs can be operated by the user using windows, mice, etc., rather than by entering commands directly. Items can be selected from pull-down, or drop-down, menus as with many other programs. A further development is that software is available to allow items of data to be associated with each other by means of explicitly constructed links. They are not the orderly links created according to a set schema as in the classical hierarchical DBMS. Rather, the links can be freely created according to the decision of the database creator. The systems which allow databases to be constructed in this way are known as 'hypertext' systems. A further development which is influencing this area is the ability to store graphics, video and sound on the microcomputer. A completely new approach to information provision is possible with such systems. Hypertext systems have their roots in the 1940s when Vannevar Bush, one of President Roosevelt's advisers, outlined an information retrieval scheme which associated information together in this way. However, the term 'hypertext' was coined by Ted Nelson some 20 years later. Some hypertext schemes have been designed to try to mimic the way human beings are thought to organize information in the brain.

Practical hypertext systems, which could be used widely, had to wait for the introduction of the microcomputer and the GUI to provide a user interface that allowed the user to interact with the machine in an optimum way. The 'pieces' of information in a hypertext system are stored at nodes; links can be made between any of the nodes by the database producer and by the user. It is possible for the user to navigate through the database by selecting a particular route. Text, graphics, still photographs, video and sound can be stored at individual nodes. One could imagine a music database which stored short pieces of music, the relevant score, pictures of the composer, scenes from an opera performance, pictures of soloists, etc., at the nodes. Links would be made between some or all of these items. Other links might be built between different pieces of music by the same composer and music by different composers of the same period, etc.

The GUI provides the tools to wander through the database. These include graphical **buttons** (like a push-button radio, selection being by clicking with the mouse) to select a particular way to go, and graphical **browsers** which basically show the structure of the database in a graphical form. The structure of hypertext systems is not unlike that of a thesaurus. Some hypertext systems also have attributes of more normal retrieval systems and DBMSs, such as inverted indexes.

Hypertext structures are also evident in other programs. It is likely that some of the structures will be incorporated into GUIs themselves and be generally available to program developers. They are also used in a range of software sometimes known as personal information managers. Such systems are probably better classed with office software but they provide the ability to enter and retrieve a wide range of information of interest to the individual, such as telephone notes, plans and documents. Some systems allow the user to retrieve files stored on the microcomputer using search terms which are then used to search the entire contents of some or all the files on the microcomputer.

The hypertext area has been particularly supported by Apple Computers and perhaps the best-known microcomputer hypertext system is

Apple's 'HyperCard'. Another well-known system is Owl International's 'Guide' which is also available for IBM machines. The Hypercard system is not a piece of hardware, but a software package. Although hypertext seems to be an exciting development with great potential for use in many information storage and retrieval and database applications, there are some who say that it is easy to get lost in a maze of associations and that the links are usually only one person's view. Human thought is so varied and the brain can form links in ways which we cannot mimic in today's computers. Nevertheless we are seeing important changes which will inevitably lead to systems which are more in line with user's needs. It may well be a combination of the new ideas and technologies in ways that are not presently obvious which provide the greatest progress. These are interesting times!

4.4 MICROCOMPUTER-ASSISTED INFORMATION RETRIEVAL AND DATA COMMUNICATION

4.4.1 The online search process

The process of online searching of remote databases in most cases involves a dialogue between a searcher and a host computer. A computer terminal, operated by the searcher, is connected to the host computer by means of a telecommunication link. An outline of the equipment is shown in Figure 4.6. The link between terminal and host is often via a packet-switched network (section 2.7).

The flow of data is, in one direction, from keyboard to host (requests) and, in the other direction, from host to visual display screen (information) as shown in Figure 4.7. In this dialogue, the host computer imposes constraints on what the searcher can do and when. For instance, commands must usually be constructed in exactly the required format (see section 4.1 for examples of the search process) and often it is necessary to wait for a reply from the host before entering the next command, even though the content of that command may not be dependent on the answer to the previous one.

4.4.2 Microcomputer assistance

Inserting a microcomputer between the terminal and the searcher's modem provides computing power to interfere with the streams of data going to, and from, the host computer (see Figure 4.8). The microcomputer can be made to manipulate the data which flow in either direction to the benefit of, and under the control of, the searcher. In addition, it

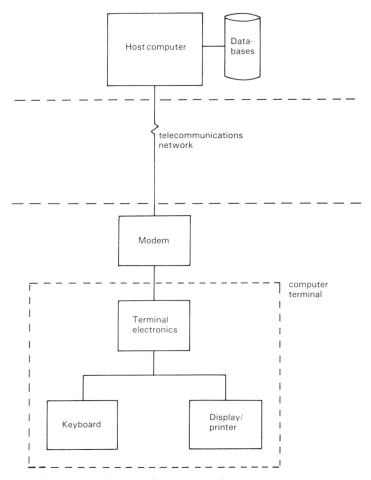

Figure 4.6   Equipment for accessing a remote host computer.

can reroute data to, and from, different devices in the microcomputer, such as magnetic disks, again under the control of the searcher. 'Down-loading' or the capturing of data sent from a host computer can be carried out. This can be achieved by diverting the stream of incoming data onto a storage device, such as a disk (see Figure 4.9). The transmission of data from the microcomputer to a host computer is sometimes referred to as 'up-loading'. If the storage of data coming from the host, and the transmission of data already in the microcomputer to the host, can be done conveniently and rapidly, it can provide some advantages over searching techniques with a normal terminal. These include the following:

1. Simplified procedures for logging-on to the host computer;

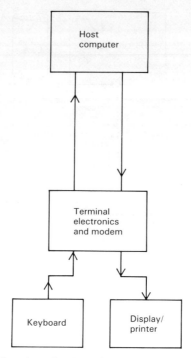

Figure 4.7   Flow of data from keyboard to host and from host to display.

2. 'Store and forward' techniques for search data;
3. Storage of search results for later use (in several ways);
4. Automatic transfer and reception of data (unattended);
5. Aids to searching such as the provision of advice on using the host computer systems, translation of commands from one host language to another, help to inexperienced users and enhancement of the search strategy and, in restricted circumstances, searching using natural language input.

Perhaps the simplest, and most obvious, use of the microcomputer is for storing data locally in the microcomputer before going online to the host computer and then forwarding the data, as and when required, directly from microcomputer to host computer using simple procedures.

Logging-on through a public data network can be a time-consuming and frustrating task, particularly at busy periods. By permanently storing the network and host user-identifiers and passwords in the microcomputer, logging-on can be made a very straightforward process, normally reducing it to a very small number of key-strokes on the keyboard. In addition, auto-dialling can be carried out. 'Smart' modems

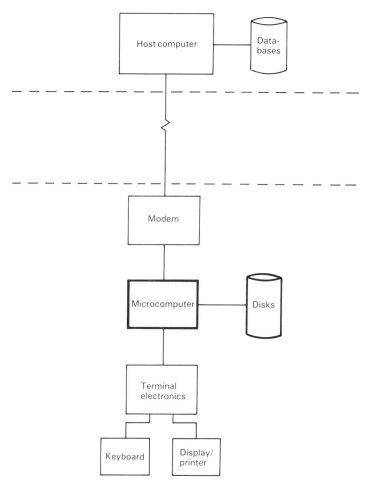

Figure 4.8   Equipment for accessing a remote host computer with microcomputer assistance.

are available which can store frequently used telephone numbers and even the communications software (Chapter 2).

The same principle of storing data in the microcomputer before connection to the host can also be applied to search strategies and other commands which are to be sent to the host and which can be worked out in advance (see Figure 4.10). The advantages of being able to carry out the forwarding of pre-stored data to the host are evident on analysing the charging policies of many host database providers. The practice of levying a relatively high charge for online connect-time (the time the user is connected to the host), irrespective of whether any searching is actually being done, penalizes the person with poor keyboard skills. A proficient typist cannot match the usual transmission speeds of the line at which pre-stored data can be transmitted. Proceeding at a higher speed, the search can be carried out more quickly, thus saving connect-time or giving extra time for more interactive search operations to be carried out.

A further degree of sophistication is the ability to store data that are being entered at the keyboard during an online session. It then becomes an easy matter to instruct the microcomputer to re-send the data if, say, the message was not correctly received by the host. Similarly, the sending of data can be delayed until a whole line is ready to go, and thus the correction of typing errors by simple backspacing (locally) will again aid input. It must be emphasized, of course, that the microcomputer is usually programmed so as not to interfere with the use of the equipment as a normal terminal.

4.4.2.1 Down-loading

Some advantages of down-loading are:

1. Data can usually be stored at the speed they are received and thus the speed of the search is not limited by the speed of the printer; the results can be printed at leisure once the search is finished;
2. The search results can be edited, possibly to eliminate unwanted references, to make multiple copies or perhaps to make a more impressive-looking report (a word processor can be used for this);
3. The search results can be transferred into a local information system, either on the same microcomputer or on some other local computer (see bulk transmission below) – normally a reformatting program that translates the format of the down-loaded data into the format of the retrieved data will be needed;
4. Search results can be transferred from one database on the host to another, or from one host to another, e.g. a search for chemical compounds in a sub-structure search system which can then be input to (say) a *Chemical Abstracts* bibliographic search;
5. Retrieved data could be communicated to another computer at another location (a form of electronic mail).

4.4.2.2 Unattended transmission and reception

It is possible to arrange for data to be transmitted to a host computer at a prearranged time and/or have the microcomputer available to receive data at any time. With this ability, advantage can be taken of less expensive, off-peak telecommunication rates or host charges or to improve the efficiency of the search operation itself. The whole process

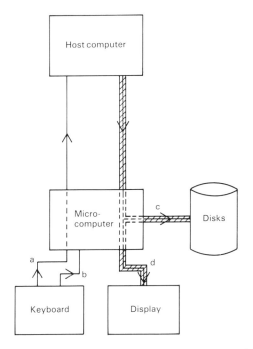

Figure 4.9 Flow of data during down-loading operation. (a) Searcher gives instructions to host computer to start to down-load. (b) Searcher gives instructions to microcomputer to collect and store data. (c) Down-loaded data going onto disk. (d) Simultaneous display of down-loaded data on screen.

saves operator time and takes pressure off the central computer since response time for a particular terminal (microcomputer) is no longer as critical as it was with the previous completely online operation.

Some online retrieval services provide data manipulation programs that allow local microcomputers to process down-loaded data. They can be manipulated on a microcomputer using a program, such as a spreadsheet or a database. Spreadsheet programs are described in Chapter 6.

The microcomputer can be used to provide a number of search aids to the online database user. Some of them are available on the host computers themselves, but can be more convenient to use if they are available locally. Other help features are not available on the hosts and a number of them can be placed in a local microcomputer.

4.4.2.3 'Help data'

Essential information on command languages, frequently used data-bases and other useful facts can be stored in the microcomputer. Once

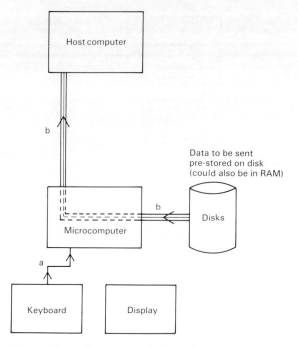

Figure 4.10 Forwarding of pre-stored data from microcomputer to host computer. (a) Searcher gives instructions to microcomputer to send data. (b) Microcomputer collects data from disk (if necessary) and sends to host.

stored, they can be quickly called-up on the screen during a search. An example might be if, having logged-on to a host computer, the searcher needs to know the format of an infrequently used command. Reference to printed manuals would waste time.

4.4.2.4 Command language translation

Some online information services use the same command language (see section 4.1) and the Commission of the European Communities has sponsored the development of the Common Command Language (CCL). Despite this, there is a plethora of different command languages which present difficulties to the online searcher. In principle it is possible to translate the commands from one service to those of another. In practice not all the commands are likely to match but, nevertheless, software exists which will allow a searcher to use a single language with a number of different hosts using a microcomputer. For each command entered in one language, the microcomputer can be programmed to analyse and translate it into that of the host to which a connection has been made. Some systems use a guided approach to development of the query through the use of menus with search terms being entered one at a time. Only when the search is ready for transmission is it translated into the language of the chosen database and host, which may be selected by the system, rather than the user. GUIs can be helpful in simplifying the interface for the user. Differences in databases, retrieval systems and database management system design, together with varying ideas on the setting up of the same or similar databases on different systems, put a large number of problems in the way of the microcomputer systems designer in this area, but some software has been successful albeit with some limitations.

4.4.2.5 Help for inexperienced users

A further level of assistance after command language translation is the provision of searching facilities for a user who is unfamiliar with information retrieval systems. Such systems:

1. elicit the question from the user;
2. decide which database(s) to search;
3. decide which host computer to search;
4. formulate and carry out the search automatically;
5. display the results to the user.

Some systems are available to carry out these functions but they are restricted in the number of databases and hosts they can search.

4.4.2.6 Search enhancement

At its simplest the microcomputer can scan the words or indexing terms which are present in a list of retrieved references and present them to the searcher with the most frequent words appearing first. Those that are relevant and not already in the search can be added to it by the searcher.

4.4.2.7 Expert systems

Such systems are designed to solve practical but complex problems, which normally require an expert to interpret and solve. This is done using a computer system to store and apply the reasoning process used by an expert, with the intention of arriving at the same conclusions that a human expert would reach if faced with the same problem. Existing expert systems do not completely replace the human in decision making although they do well in some applications.

If the knowledge of the search intermediary could be stored in the microcomputer, it would be possible for an unskilled user to carry out a complex search without the aid of such an intermediary. For instance, it is possible to search an author's name automatically in a particular database if the rules for constructing that item of data are available to the program. However, it is difficult to cope automatically with errors in the format, which might be spotted by the searcher by browsing.

4.4.2.8 Bulk transmission of data

The amount of data usually transferred to the host computer during an online search is relatively small. The microcomputer is capable of transferring much larger amounts of data and this facility can be used as a general-purpose file transfer procedure such as for:

1. the transmission of inter-library loan requests;
2. general message transfer or electronic mail.

Electronic mail systems are discussed in Chapter 6.

4.4.3 Software packages for assisting information retrieval

Packages for microcomputers exist at various levels of sophistication, the IBM PC being clearly the machine for which the most packages are available. There is a group which allows a microcomputer to operate as a computer terminal. It may be just as a single asynchronous terminal, which is sufficient for obtaining access to online hosts. Other packages and/or hardware circuit boards are available to emulate terminals that are used with specific larger computers, e.g. to emulate the IBM 3270 terminal.

A second group of software products has been designed for general-purpose communications and these packages have not, in the main, been programmed with the information retrieval process in mind. For example, some of them can only transmit a whole file of data and not a line at a time, the latter being a useful feature for transmitting search data to an online host. A third set of packages comprises those especially written to assist the information retrieval process. They may be general purpose in nature, i.e. designed to access all host services, or they may be specifically oriented towards a restricted number of hosts and/or databases. Generally speaking, the more features offered, the less generally applicable they are. Some packages are aimed at the experienced searcher and others at the inexperienced user. A list of software packages is given in Appendix A.

Applications in information retrieval and management | 5

In this and the next chapter, we will examine the ways in which the microcomputer can contribute to the remaining tasks of the library and information services (LIS). For the sake of convenience, these have been divided into discrete topics, but the LIS manager must always look for ways in which to integrate these functions in order to reduce duplication of effort, eliminate transcription errors, etc. Much off-the-shelf software now on the market provides just this integration, in that the software is provided as a series of modules covering specific functions, which together form a complete system, from acquisitions to online catalogue. Modules can be bought as required and/or as funding permits: each module will work with all others, allowing records to be transferred from one to the other.

The main objective is to indicate the factors which must be taken into account when studying automation of these routines, and to examine how some of the software deals with this work.

5.1 SERIALS CONTROL

Serials control, often in the past the Cinderella of automated systems, consists of a number of individual elements, though all revolve around the same basic set of data relating to a journal subscription. The LIS manager must consider not only the recording of serial **subscriptions** but also requires a system whereby individual **issues** can be recorded as they are received, a policy for dealing with long-term retention and disposal (including binding), a means of controlling and recording subscription rates and renewals and a means of referring from previous titles to ensure that holdings records are complete. In addition, exploitation of serials holdings may require formal systems to ensure proper circulation of new issues to interested users.

Whilst these may appear as a disparate list of elements, they need to be treated as parts of a single serial recording system, since to do otherwise would result in various files operating with little or no connection between them. This 'one-stop' approach can be achieved using DBMS software and constructing a suitable record, or by implementing one of a number of dedicated serials management programs.

DBMS software, with a suitable record structure, will permit searches on all fields within a record, either individually or in combination. Thus, details of outstanding subscriptions, holdings lists, etc., can be produced with relative ease, while implementing the program's report generator will permit the selection of specific fields for a catalogue of holdings, a circulation list or a subscription list. If the record structure incorporates a field for subject heading or classification number, subject listings can be produced and/or included in select bibliographies, etc.

DBMS software, however, would not be suitable for use simply as a serials receipt system: simply recording issues as they arrive is a waste of the software's capabilities. However, incorporated with the other facilities mentioned above, it would be a worthwhile operation.

DBMS programs could also be used for individual routines within the heading of serials control, if, for some reason, it was considered unnecessary to implement a full-scale serials control system.

Circulation lists could be maintained as a file of journal titles and the names and addresses of recipients. Keying in the title on receipt would generate a printed record consisting of the date of receipt, the names of those to whom the journal was to circulate, and some suitable text message, if required. An additional benefit of such a system would be the ability to generate a list of the journals which each user receives, to act as a check on accuracy and currency of the records. Periodically, users could be asked to confirm that they still wished to receive these titles, and to amend the list as required.

Malmberg has provided a brief description [1] of PERCICO (periodicals circulation and control system), developed specifically for medium-sized services, which will handle up to 1000 titles and 1000 users on circulation lists. Its cost-effectiveness is indicated by his claims that the procedure for recording receipt and starting 'hundreds of journals on their circulation route has been reduced from 1–2 hours to 15 minutes'.

Subscription records: DBMSs offer online searching of records relating to a subscription, plus the ability to sort the entire file on various fields and so to produce output arranged by title, renewal data and price, etc. Overdue subscriptions can be found as easily as listing all titles or finding one supplier. Total values of subscriptions payable in a year can be calculated automatically with those DBMSs which have mathematical facilities, while regular 'searches' can be made to determine subscription costs due in any month or week.

Holdings lists/catalogues could be produced from DBMS files using report generator facilities at more or less regular intervals, depending on how frequently the subscriptions list changed. The result would be a catalogue or holdings list for distribution to departments, branches, etc., which could have additional sequences (e.g. by subject heading or keyword, or by location).

A major problem with **union catalogues** of serials holdings is the sheer size of the final catalogue, and the need to make amendments at more or less regular intervals, usually to produce a revised (printed) version, though there is, of course, no reason now why the file should not be maintained on disk and searched for locations, etc. In these days of reduced resources for LISs and in the knowledge that few services can be self-sufficient, resource-sharing is an important consideration, and the union catalogue has a major role to play in this context, not least by eliminating unnecessary duplication of subscriptions [2].

The initial data entry task is a major one (as it would be with a manual system), but its maintenance and updating is simplified and made faster by the use of an automated system. Amendments can be made as they are notified either to the central point responsible for the catalogue or to individual members. Updated versions can be distributed on disk or via a telecommunications link (e.g. BT Gold) to those with appropriate software – and distributed more frequently than would be possible with a printed version – or printed for distribution to those lacking the software. Even if different software is used by members (who may have requirements which cannot be met by that used for the union catalogue), the ability of contemporary software to store data as ASCII files means that, generally speaking, the catalogue can be read into a wide range of software: the principal requirement is a common operating system.

Since there appears to be no commercial software on the market specifically for union catalogues, either DBMS [3] or word processing programs can be used. The former, of course, will offer more powerful online search facilities, though practical use of union catalogues will normally be limited to ascertaining the location of a specific journal title and issue, in which case search facilities do not need to be very sophisticated. In addition to these programs, however, standard information retrieval packages such as MicroCAIRS and InMagic have been used with success by special and industrial libraries and information services to record serials information. As these are also used by these services for their information retrieval (IR) applications (indexing and abstracting services, for example), there is a standardization of software which can be of considerable benefit to the service.

Considering that union catalogues tend, almost by definition, to be large, it is unlikely that they can be effectively held on floppy disks (though they can be distributed that way): a hard disk system will be required.

Record size will vary with the number of subscribing services and thus with the number of potential locations, though these can be coded in some way, as is usually the case with manual systems.

Word processing offers a more straightforward way to create a union catalogue, but printing the catalogue in various sequences (by location or subject, for example) will require the additional facilities of a DBMS.

For serials control in general, the alternative to using a DBMS program, of course, is to use one of the dedicated packages now on the market. These have been designed specifically with the needs of the routine in mind, but some have, in addition, a telecommunications link with a major serials supplier. With this facility, the user has online access to accounts information and claims, as well as the ability to record receipts, holdings, etc., and to analyse subscriptions in various ways [4].

Thus, Blackwells and the Dawson Group both supply serials control software (Pearl and SMS, respectively) with optional links to their respective databases of serial titles, in which the user can browse, order titles and down-load record data for the control routines, thus eliminating a considerable amount of rekeying of data. Dawson's program also provides analyses of circulation lists by borrower and department, list of subscriptions due to expire and details of titles by relevant funding code or section.

OCLC's Serials Control System allows the user to transfer records from their online union catalogue for incorporation into the holdings file: alternatively, records can be created in-house, and there is a variety of report features available.

Systems developed without this telecommunications link, but with all the other facilities required, include Swets and Zeitlinger's SAILS program, and the serials control modules for Bookshelf and CALM (computer aided library management). These last two form part of a complete suite of programs for LIS applications.

5.2 CIRCULATION CONTROL

The circulation control system is probably one of the most popular candidates for automation, consisting as it does of so much routine. The basic requirements of a circulation control system are to record items on loan and to whom, to find and trap items requested by other users, and to indicate overdue items. An additional facility of considerable potential value is the production and compilation of statistics at predetermined intervals, though, as we shall see later, there is evidence to suggest that the commercial software currently available for circulation control (and other applications) fails to provide adequate management information in this respect.

Circulation control systems must also provide messages appropriate to the operation, which will indicate errors, warn of overdue or reserved items, etc.

Most microcomputer packages for circulation control use bar-code readers as the simplest and most effective way of matching reader and item. Alternatives such as keying-in names and titles at each transaction, or even numbers for user and item are time-consuming and prone to operator error, unless the software includes an error-trapping routine for the number input. Thus, Plymouth College of Further Education uses the CARS/CLASS software for circulation control and an online catalogue without bar codes: users are allocated individual numbers which contain a security digit to prevent inaccurate keyboarding [5]. On the other hand, the same system in operation at Harper Adams Agricultural College has taken up the option to use bar codes [6].

A small LIS may be able to set up perfectly adequate circulation control using DBMS, provided that the number of transactions is small (see below).

Systems do not differ from existing bar-code readers operating on larger computers: the 'pen' is passed over the labels on the user's card and the borrowed item to record a loan. Requested items are searched for by number and are flagged so that, on return, a message is displayed preventing re-loan or return to the shelves. Overdue items can be sought by due date and notices printed automatically. To aid the standard operations such as flagging reserved items, some systems provide a set of command bar-code labels which are a coded preset operation for the number which then follows.

For microcomputer systems, the bar codes can be generated by an ordinary dot matrix printer (rather than the previously required expensive printers).

The normal approach to a microcomputer-based circulation control system is to create files which link the item number with its bibliographic record and the user number with user details such as address, duration of course, loan entitlement, etc. Precisely what is included, particularly in the user file, will obviously depend on the specific requirements of the LIS. Systems have been tried which use only numbers for item and user, the full details of each being obtained from a printed list, but this also is only feasible with small systems which have a low transaction rate. This approach does have the advantage that it can be set up quickly, since there is no need to key in full records. A decision on whether this approach is feasible must be based on a careful analysis of the circulation control sytem and the requirements of the service, and merely emphasizes that microcomputer systems do need as detailed a systems analysis as larger operations.

In the specification of a circulation control system there are a number of points to bear in mind, other than the obvious one of whether the package has the capacity to handle all of the loan records. Messages relating to various functions will be required and will include the fact that an item is overdue or that a user has other overdue items; that the item is required for, say, the short loan collection; or that a user has exceeded his loan entitlement. The system may have to cope with varying loan facilities for different categories of user, as well as different loan periods for the various types of material.

A microcomputer system can be used as a terminal to a larger system, with loan records being up-loaded daily or weekly, as required. This will increase the power of the system, though some online access to records will still be required. An alternative is to use the microcomputer system as a back-up to the computer which normally handles loans.

Bookshelf includes a module for circulation control in its suite of programs. It is integrated with the online catalogue, so that loans are effectively recorded against the catalogue entry and consulting the catalogue will indicate whether or not a book is on loan. There is also an automatic display for each user of that user's entitlement, any reserved items and any fines due. Bookshelf also allows various user categories and loan periods to accommodate most requirements.

As we suggested above, it is possible to use DBMS software in a small unit as a circulation control system. Theoretically, software such as dBase, for example, would allow the creation of three files, one for bibliographic details, one for user information and a third for transaction records. This last file would use the numbers which also appeared in the other two files and thus permit the joining of the files when required (e.g. for overdue notices). Online searching (for overdue and reserved items) is possible, and report generator facilities will allow the production of any relevant notices and letters.

A feasible alternative for a LIS with a low daily transaction rate is to batch the transaction records and key them in at the end of the day (this has been tried in small school libraries, for example). This will free the system for other uses during the day, but it does require some temporary means of recording loans, and the duplication of work may reduce savings in other areas. On the other hand, having a loans file could make certain types of analysis easier, thus providing useful information on loan rates, subjects in demand, etc.

5.3 ACQUISITIONS

An acquisitions file is intended to indicate the status of each title on order, together with information on its ordering (supplier, date, order code), for whom it was ordered and other relevant facts. It will also indicate titles overdue, with reasons for the delay, and it can answer enquiries from users about the progresss of titles they have ordered. It is often an automated routine because it is not unusual to find the same information being repeated at various stages during the ordering process. The same detail of author(s), title, publisher, etc., can appear on record cards, official order forms, list of overdue titles and so on (which, of course, is why many LISs use multipart order slips which can be filed where appropriate). The microcomputer simply extends this principle and offers many more access points to the file.

Word processing software does offer a simple way to produce copies of printed orders and reference lists of titles on order, but generally it will not be flexible enough for acquisitions.

For small libraries, DBMS programs (particularly if they are used for a catalogue) can provide the required degree of flexibility in acquisitions, and, as books are delivered and catalogued, etc., the basic record is amended ('date received', 'at cataloguing', etc.) until it eventually becomes the catalogue record. In addition, lists of overdue titles can be simply produced by a search for a relevant date, and a mathematics facility will allow calculations of the value of orders, costs of multiple copies and other calculations required.

This progress through a series of amendments as the book is ordered, received, catalogued, classified and added to the online catalogue is, of course, the principle behind the integrated software now available. Bookshelf, for example, contains an acquisitions module which accepts details of each title order. Individual records can be displayed in response to catalogue enquiries (section 5.4.2) to show titles on order, but it serves primarily as an order record containing all the relevant information. Claims for outstanding items can be created, and the system will cope with full or part supply of titles in an order – a useful point, since partial supply is the norm. The module will also handle donations and exchange items (for which, of course, an order is not created), and when a title is received, there is an automatic procedure to provide accession numbers, labels and bar codes. From the records of titles received, it is possible to create accessions lists of recent additions.

So far, we have only considered systems which will generate orders which then have to be printed in hard copy and posted to the supplier. A number of the larger booksellers and library agents now provide a package which will derive orders from their own databases of holdings.

Thus, users of Blackwell's system can browse through their database of titles and order direct: the subsequent progress of orders can be similarly checked online, and there are facilities for claiming overdues and maintaining accounts.

5.4 CATALOGUING AND ONLINE CATALOGUES

In earlier editions of this book, we suggested that the microcomputer could be used to produce catalogue cards, while indicating that this posed a number of problems. It was also not seen as the best use of the microcomputer's facilities, since it effectively meant using the system as a glorified (though relatively flexible) typewriter. Since it appears that few, if any, LISs have gone along this route, we do not consider it in this edition, other than to say that it is possible, with some effort. We shall instead concentrate on online catalogues, since it is here that most advance has been made.

5.4.1 Online catalogues

Online public access catalogues (OPACs) have been the subject of considerable research in recent years, including a British Library R and D-funded project [7, 8]. Technology and software have now developed to the state that comprehensive online facilities can be provided with microcomputer-based systems as well as with larger systems. OPACs can take the entry created during the acquisitions stage and, once it is amended to comply with the cataloguing rules in use, store that entry as part of the LIS database of holdings.

In the process of this research, however, interest has been re-awakened in the problem of user-friendly systems which will provide enhanced access to the collection. User-friendly access means the provision of clear, simple instructions and the use of pre-programmed keys for commands, together with fast response times for basic enquiries at least (authors, titles). Slower response times will be acceptable for more complex searches.

Enhanced access methods include not only the ability to combine terms in Boolean searches (which we would now accept as a standard requirement), but also the provision of an online thesaurus to aid in term selection, the ability to browse through the index and perhaps the ranking of items to reflect matches with the user's chosen terms. Much of this effort (to improve access to the collection) stems, implicitly or explicitly, from the realization that, to date, online catalogues have been little more than electronic card catalogues, in that they have effectively only converted the old card catalogue (with all its problems) into a computer file which can be searched in broadly similar ways. Such an attitude obviously fails to make full use of the facilities available from computer-based systems. It also fails to take into account the psychology of the user, since it tends to force him or her to think as the catalogue (or cataloguer) wants, and not as he or she normally does about the subject.

The realization that more could be done is not, however, entirely new: Cochrane, for example, has written extensively on the subject of improved subject access since the 1960s [9]. However, it was lost in the first fine flush of enthusiasm for automated systems which would provide online access and in the technical problems which it initially presented. Many online catalogue suppliers, however, are now looking at the problem anew (as we suggested, it is not just a question of technology) and developments and improvements will start to appear on the market in the foreseeable future. Certainly, this was a major focus of the Okapi work referred to earlier (reference [8]).

The whole question of improved access is beyond the scope of the current work, but the reader is advised that it is a 'burning issue' which will be discussed (and gradually implemented) for some time to come.

It goes without saying that online catalogues require hard disk storage facilities – a 1 Mb floppy disk can hold much less than 4000 250-character records, because space is needed not only for the records themselves, but also for any indexes required. A safe estimate of the ratio of space required by indexes is $2 : 1$, that is twice as much space as the records themselves.

The specific requirements of online catalogue software to be established in the initial investigations relate to two general features: the record structure provided and the search facilities available. Record structure can be further divided into the structure proper and the number of records which can be handled. This last is now, more often than not, limited less by the software and more by the hardware, though suppliers will indicate some upper limit on records: the CARS/CLASS system already mentioned as in use at Plymouth College of Further Education, for example, will hold some records for some 60 000 items.

Limits may be placed on the size of fields permitted within a record, though this is not always the case: using Bookshelf, for example, a bibliographic record can be of any required length. Whether this is significant or not will again depend on the analysis of requirements, which should establish the range of record sizes required by the service. It may be that relatively few bibliographic records in the system exceed a certain figure and, provided that this figure can be accommodated by the software, restrictions on record or field length will not cause a problem. If, on the other hand, there is great variety in record lengths owing to the nature of the material, a more 'elastic' limit will be needed, or at least a maximum equal to or in excess of the maximum bibliographic record. Choice could be based on a simple utilitarian rule which says that the system should be selected which can accommodate most (around 90–95%) of records, since the remaining 5–10% occur so infrequently that they will not constitute a significant problem. The point is an important one, since software capable of accepting any length of record may be more expensive than a program with fixed lengths. The suppliers of the CARS/CLASS system suggest that the 110-character limit for author, title and publisher, for example, can be shown to be adequate for 98% of all entries, and it is certainly worth considering whether extremely detailed records are required by users of the service. Against this must be balanced the need to improve access, as suggested above, though improved access is provided less through very detailed catalo-guing and more through the provision of suitable access points such as subject descriptors of some type, as well as authors, titles, etc. (This point about improved access, incidentally, contradicts what we said in the second edition of this book, where we suggested that Boolean searches are not a feature of a monograph catalogue. With this growing awareness of the need to provide more detailed access to records (and thus to the collection), our earlier statement must be corrected: Boolean searches of some complexity will rightly be a facility of future catalogue searching.)

As an example of the type of software now available for an OPAC, we shall look in some detail at Bookshelf, since it has been referred to on a number of occasions so far. This is, of course, not to suggest that it is the only program available for this function, but it does indicate the facilities one can expect.

The Catalogue and Enquiry Module of Bookshelf, like all its modules, is menu-driven, though there is also a command-based operation for the experienced user. In addition, the LIS can have specially designed help screens at appropriate points throughout. A full bibliographic record (which can be of any length) consists of 24 fields, of which only the standard number (usually an ISBN) and title are mandatory: all other fields are optional, but can be set by the LIS as mandatory, depending on the cataloguing practice of the service. Fields provided include General Media Description (as prescribed in AACR2), author (individual or corporate), edition, place and year of publication, publisher – in fact all the fields normally required for a fairly full bibliographic record. Some fields relate to housekeeping functions, such as name of person recommending the title, source and price, while a further field contains any number of keywords. There is also a field for free-text notes.

Before setting up the system, fields to be indexed (which will be used for searching) must be defined. Seven of the eight menus available relate primarily to cataloguing and related processes (one controls the printing of spine labels and bar codes), while the eighth provides access to the Enquiry routine, i.e. online searching. Searching can be on individual words or phrases in the fields of a record, and the standard Boolean operators of AND, OR and AND NOT can be used to refine searches precisely. Additional facilities are right-hand truncation and the ability to store search results for further study or to be combined in further searches. Searching is command-driven and operates on the indexed fields of a record: the results of a search can be displayed on screen in one of six formats (as with commercial online databases) ranging from ISBN, author and short title to full record. Viewing a reduced format is useful if a large number of records are retrieved since the user can browse through them first before selecting a fuller format. Finally, indexed words can be browsed in order to establish the system's preferred terms.

Because it is an integrated system, the Catalogue Module will operate with other modules (if they are installed), so searching will also indicate titles on loan (from the circulation module) and those on order (from the acquisitions module).

We can see then, that Bookshelf, as an example of an online catalogue system for microcomputers (it is also available for larger systems) displays a full range of facilities for the user, including powerful Boolean searching. Figure 5.1 shows displays from the Catalogue Maintenance function, used when creating a record.

The need for user-friendly displays is demonstrated in Figure 5.2, which shows screen displays from the CARS system. Note also that, in this system, Boolean operation is not provided by ANDed statements, but simply by the entry of a second word. There is an argument to suggest that this is easier for users to understand than the complexities of Boolean operators: on the other hand, the limitation to the equivalent of AND statements means searches cannot be refined as effectively as those in Bookshelf.

The use of Bookshelf to automate a multi-site service has been detailed by Powne [10].

As we have suggested, Bookshelf is not the only package available for this application, though it is representative of the possibilities. Other similar programs include Ocelot, Micro Library, CALM and Librarian.

However, many smaller LISs will feel that the cost of these modules is beyond their scope and they may prefer to use a DBMS program instead. Certainly, such programs are capable of acting as an online catalogue, though it must be said that their generally business-oriented nature means that creating an OPAC could be difficult, mainly because the interface between the system and the user is not sufficiently

```
BookshelF                                                    05 NOV 90
                        CATALOGUE MAINTENANCE

1) Standard No. A21_ _ _ _        2) GMD T         3) Class WA 108_ _ _

4) Title  1 Lecture notes on epidemiology and community medicine_ _ _ _ _ _
          2 _ _ _ _ _ _ _ _ _ _ _ _ _ _ _ _ _ _ _ _ _ _ _ _ _ _ _ _ _ _

5) Init.  6) Surname
1     RDT   Farmer_ _ _ _ _ _ _ _ _
2     DL    Miller_ _ _ _ _ _ _ _ _

7) Edition 2nd ed._ _ _ _ _ _       8) Editor _ _ _ _ _ _ _ _ _ _ _ _ _

9) Place                 10) Publisher                        11) Year
   Oxford_ _ _ _ _ _ _       Blackwell_ _ _ _ _ _ _ _ _ _ _      1983

12) Accession      Location        Status    Due date      No. of
    1 C13572....   JR:SL....        A        ........      copies
    2 C13649....   JR:SL....        A        ........       7
    3 C13650....   JR:SL....        A        ........

Please enter a standard number (as ISBN or other, if prefixed by a letter)
```

```
BookshelF                                                    05 NOV 90
                   CATALOGUE MAINTENANCE (cont'd)

13) Collation _ _ _ _ _ _ _ _     14) ISSN _ _ _ _      Entry date 28 Aug 86

15) Series title _ _ _ _ _ _ _ _ _ _ _ _ _ _ _ _ _ _ _ _ _ _ _ _ _ _ _
16) Series no.   _ _ _ _ _ _ _ _ _ _

17) Notes  1 _ _ _ _ _ _ _ _ _ _ _ _ _ _ _ _ _ _ _ _ _ _ _ _ _ _ _ _ _
           2 _ _ _ _ _ _ _ _ _ _ _ _ _ _ _ _ _ _ _ _ _ _ _ _ _ _ _ _ _

18) Keywords                          19) Subjects
    1 Community medicine_ _ _ _ _ _       1 _ _ _ _ _ _ _ _ _ _ _
    2 Epidemiology_ _ _ _ _ _ _ _ _       2 _ _ _ _ _ _ _ _ _ _ _
    3 _ _ _ _ _ _ _ _ _ _ _ _ _ _ _       3 _ _ _ _ _ _ _ _ _ _ _

20) Recommenders        21) Reservers                    22) Groups
    1 ..................    1 ..................            1 _ _ _
    2 ..................    2 ..................            2 _ _ _

23) Source _ _ _ _ _ _ _ _ _ _ _ _ _ _ _ _ _ _ _ _ _
Enter any free text relating to the physical description
```

Figure 5.1 Demonstration of catalogue maintenance from Bookshelf.

'friendly' [11]. Many DBMSs assume a knowledge and experience of their use at a level which many LIS users will not reach, simply because they do not use the system frequently enough. Cardbox Plus, for example, though used by a number of LISs for journal and other indexes, requires the user to be familiar with its search operators of SELECT, EXCLUDE and INCLUDE. These act just as Boolean operators, but this and Cardbox's 'levels of operation' are not conducive to successful operation by the naive end-user. One way to overcome this problem is to use a DBMS such as dBase III Plus which has the facility to create interfaces (menus, etc.) similar to those used by Bookshelf and

```
                          Book search

You may search for books either by :-

1    Dewey Class Number

2    Author

3    Words in the Title

4    I.S.B.N.

5    Accession number


Enter your choice (1-5) [_]



                       Author Search

This search finds the nearest author to the one entered
and may be continued forwards or backwards.


Author    [HARPER,F.           ]

Class no. 631.5
Author 1. HARPER,F.
Author 2.
Title     PRINCIPLES OF ARABLE CROP PRODUCTION.
Publisher GRANADA,1983. (+13305)
I.S.B.N.  0246117419              Accession no.  13304

F(forward) B(backwards) Q(quit) _



                Search for words in the title

After entering a word the system will search for that word and display
the nearest. You may then either accept that word or move backwards
or forwards until an acceptable word is found. On entering a second
word the search will be restricted to books containing both words.
To finish entering words just press the return key. The book details
will then be displayed.

Word to find  [EARTHWORM         ] EARTHWORM        Occurs   1   Matches
   1

Found   1



Class no. 636.087
Author 1. NIAE
Author 2. FOOTE,N.
Title     EARTHWORM CULTURE FOR FEED PRODUCTION & ANIMAL WASTE CONVERSION.
Publisher NIAE,1982.    [PAMPHLET]
I.S.B.N.                          Accession no.  17100


F(forward) B(backwards) Q(quit) _
```

Figure 5.2 'Search' demonstration from CARS.

the others, and many LISs have reported on the successful use of dBase in this way.

As a further example of the use of DBMS for cataloguing, Findlay and Motherwell have described [12] an ingenious method to help inexperienced cataloguers daunted by the complexities of MARC records required by a large online catalogue. They have developed a dBase III program for cataloguing which asks a series of questions or presents menu options, the answers to which are used to create a dBase III record containing codes which match the MARC field codes. (Incidentally, the basic record is taken from an existing file of records for books awaiting cataloguing or ordered but awaiting delivery, a further example of the potential to integrate files and eliminate duplication of effort.)

Once the dBase III records have been created in this way, they are converted into text files in which the fields are marked by special delimiters and then processed on a host computer which creates MARC fields, indicators and sub-fields, and thus a MARC record which can then be loaded onto the online cataloguing system.

A further option is the use of information retrieval software for online catalogues, all of which offer searching facilities of sufficient complexity and will accommodate the required size of record. A number of special libraries have reported use of such software [13] with successful results. BRS/Search, for example, is used at the Turing Institute in Glasgow for a combined catalogue and database of holdings. Although it has a relatively small bookstock, the Library subscribes to a number of journals and reports in the area of artificial intelligence. Each report and journal is indexed analytically, and the database contains entries for all journal articles, conference papers and reports, as well as the monograph stock. The software provides searching by author, title keywords, journal title and abstract terms.

There are many such programs available, often with very sophisticated facilities for storage and retrieval: not surprisingly, these programs tend to be more expensive, though prices are comparable with the integrated modules. Some, such as MicroCAIRS, are derived from mainframe or minicomputer software, and their ancestry shows in their power. These programs provide for maximum records of considerable size, usually more than would be needed for a monograph catalogue, but as we suggested above, their sophisticated retrieval mechanisms will accommodate the enhanced searching which OPACs should now provide. Micro-CAIRS, for example, will accept records up to 16 000 characters in length and with a maximum of 80 fields per record. Possibly its most powerful feature is the ability to create an online thesaurus as an aid to searching the database. This thesaurus provides all the usual facilities of broader, narrower and related terms, and it can be browsed by the searcher, in order to select search terms [14]. It should be noted, however, that even a relatively unsophisticated program such as Cardbox-Plus allows the user to browse through the terms indexed for each field, though this is only an alphabetical listing and not a thesaurus of terms.

A number of packages fall between the typical DBMS program and the integrated software such as Bookshelf or the mainframe derivatives such as MicroCAIRS. These programs are typically intended for information retrieval rather than an OPAC, and though they have been well-used in the former role, there appear to be few reports of their use in the latter.

A glance back over the previous pages will indicate that today we have essentially two types of program capable of providing an online catalogue, which we have chosen to call 'library-specific' and 'information retrieval'. The former acknowledges the usually monograph nature of the materials included in its database, and provides an appropriate record structure. The latter, intended originally for more textually based items such as journal indexes with free text abstracts (and occasionally full text items), is perhaps more flexible, but could be said to be too sophisticated for monograph records. This situation is, we suggest, evidence of a dichotomy in thinking which may well be obsolescent. We are at the stage of at least contemplating, in larger LISs, the approach exemplified above by the Turing Institute Library of a **single database** of records relating to all forms of material, and thus a single enquiry point – surely more beneficial to users than multiple points which depend simply on form of publication? This will be particularly attractive if the move towards enhanced access suggested earlier continues, and access to monograph literature becomes as sophisticated as that which has operated for journal indexes for some time. (As we have already indicated, our suggestion in earlier editions that OPAC users did not want such sophisticated access is withdrawn: it is possible to provide some aspects of enhanced access, and once it is available, it is certain that users will use it and expect it in other systems to which they have access.) The LIS manager contemplating an OPAC will do well, therefore, to consider this question from the start, and to move towards a single integrated database of holdings. Manson has reviewed some of the software for online catalogues (together with programs for other applications), and has listed packages available at the beginning of 1989, though, as she rightly says, 'the market is very volatile' [15].

5.4.2 Retrospective catalogue conversion

Once an OPAC has been implemented, the LIS manager is faced with the problem of what to do about existing records in the manual system (assuming that an online system is not being implemented for a new service). There are two possible solutions. The first and probably most common is to close the existing card catalogue, to make no further entries to it after a chosen date (when the online system is fully operational) and to record all new stock in the online system. This has the advantage of simplicity from the LIS's point of view and, although as the card catalogue gets older, less and less use will be made of it, it does mean that the user has two places in which to look for some time.

The alternative is to convert all or some of the existing records to the OPAC [16]. As with circulation control, selection of which records to convert can be based on some identifiable criterion such as level of use or age (certain monographs are unlikely to be sought frequently since they are obsolescent). Comprehensive retrospective conversion has the advantage of eliminating the problem of two files to search, and gives the opportunity to amend records as required. It is not, however, a task to be contemplated lightly by any but the smallest LIS, since it involves a considerable amount of work in creating the entries, error checking, and so on. It may not be possible to spare the time required, or the resources may not be available to employ additional temporary staff for the task. Edinburgh University Library, for example, is using the REMARC system to complete its retrospective conversion of the Geac online catalogue and has estimated that the task will take at least five to seven years to create the fully networked library database. Whilst this is a particularly large system, it does indicate the potential scale of the problem: Kosa has suggested that the cost of retrospective conversion using an online shared cataloguing system is in the order of $1–2 per record [17] – for manual rekeying it will obviously be much higher.

If it is decided to convert all or some of the existing records, that can be done most easily by using a centralized or shared cataloguing service, such as OCLC, to obtain records for the existing stock and to down-load these, amending and reformatting them if required to suit local practice. On the assumption that the records are available from the shared service, this is a very fast method of conversion, with the minimum of rekeying of data. It does, however, normally require software to reformat down-loaded records.

This method, though it has been implemented using microcomputers as part of the process, is probably only feasible for the larger LISs which, in turn, tend to use systems larger than microcomputers. The smaller LIS using a microcomputer-based OPAC is unlikely to have the numbers of stock items to justify the expense of down-loading records from a shared cataloguing system, and will almost certainly be faced with the task of rekeying records or simply starting the OPAC from a suitable date and allowing the card catalogue to atrophy [18]. However, as Hays has pointed out [19], an alternative solution for the smaller library is at hand in the shape of optical disk technologies. Hays describes the systems supplied by a number of American companies, in which bibliographic records (usually MARC records) have been stored on either videodisks or CD-ROMs which can then be bought by an LIS. With the appropriate software, these databases (consisting of millions of records) can be searched for relevant records, which are in turn down-loaded onto hard disks for incorporation in the OPAC. Records can be edited before down-loading to conform to local practice. Although the method requires either a subscription to the service (for updated disks) or the outright purchase of a set, it does eliminate the need for much rekeying or the need to use a shared cataloguing system, which, as Hayes points out, can result in many false drops, i.e. records which are not part of the LIS stock.

5.5 SUBJECT INDEXING

Since we described, in the previous edition, various uses of microcomputers to create subject indexes (i.e. to manipulate the index terms assigned to a document in order to create a set of index entries), little or no further work has been reported in the literature. This is possibly because most LISs are now content to allow the software in use (e.g. for information retrieval) to employ subject index terms when producing printed versions of databases, or to include terms which can be searched using Boolean operators. Indeed, it may be the case that as the use of DBMS, information retrieval, full text retrieval and online catalogue software proliferate, the need for pre-coordinate indexing will decline. Certainly, there has been a rush of full text retrieval software in the recent past, which suggests a growing commercial interest.

Pre-coordinate indexing places limits on retrieval in that it requires the user to select the system's terms, which may not be the terms he or she normally uses (a common problem with the technique, though it can be alleviated by the use of a thesaurus): contemporary software (and recent and promised developments) suggest that the ability to retrieve based on *any* term in a record or document will reduce or possibly eliminate the need to do more than include index terms (e.g. keywords) in a record – though this, of course, still raises the problem of keywords which do not match the user's vocabulary.

A subject index can be produced using information retrieval software or a DBMS, by reformatting the record layout and sorting on index terms in separate fields.

Browsable thesauri are available in packages such as Micro-CAIRS [20] and, as we indicated earlier, indexed terms can be scanned in DBMS software such as Cardbox Plus. Batty [21] has shown how dBase II can be used to create a vocabulary and thesaurus of some 200 terms for a specific subject area.

Full text retrieval has made significant progress in the last few years [22]. Many online hosts provide full text files either online or on CD-ROM, and microcomputer software can be used to search these CD-ROM versions: in one such system, the full text of some 220 biomedical journals published between 1987 and 1988 has been placed on 80 CD-ROM disks [23]. In addition, there are now various packages for indexing and retrieval of documents produced using word processors or text editors. Programs such as Recall, Zyindex and Concord can accept word processed material, index every significant word (using a stop list which can be amended by the user), and then use this index to retrieve documents as required. Boolean logic is supported, and Recall, for example, can display the sought term in its sentence, paragraph or full document. Given the growing quantity of electronically prepared material, programs like this have a clear role in certain LISs which would, in the past, have stored the printed version of these documents.

It should also be noted that some indexing facilities are provided by word processors. Wordperfect, for example, which has been used to write this book, allows the user to select terms from the text which are to be included in the index. These terms are then arranged alphabetically in the index, with page numbers. The index thus created then becomes a Wordperfect file itself and can be printed or browsed. In addition, Wordperfect can search files for a particular term and then display it in context.

5.6 SMALL-SCALE INFORMATION RETRIEVAL

In this section, we shall look at some of the ways in which microcomputer software can be used for smaller-scale information applications; smaller, that is, than is the case with online catalogues or indexing collections. Many such applications have been reported, since they offer several advantages: since the files are, generally speaking, small, they can be set up quickly, they offer some immediate and tangible benefits and, since they are aimed very directly at users, can promote the image of the LIS. Within this category, therefore, we include small bibliographic and non-bibliographic files, current awareness and selective dissemination of information (SDI) services.

Current awareness and selective dissemination of information are methods by which information on new material of potential interest to users can be conveyed to those users: this material can range from the bibliographic (new titles added, recent articles) to the factual (news items noted, forthcoming conferences, new product literature). The essence of the service is to keep users up to date: SDI may be differentiated, however, in that it is usually supplied to an individual, whereas current awareness services are aimed at the wider group of LIS users. The distinction is not a hard and fast one, however.

For SDI to be selective, it has to be matched against the known subject interests of the individual, i.e. a subject profile, so that the user receives only that information which is relevant: the main aim of SDI is to save the user's time by not providing material which is of no interest. In order to do so, a search strategy consisting of the user's interests (expressed in relevant terms) must be created and stored permanently, though with the ability to amend it as interests change in time. Subject terms used in the search profile should be drawn from the same authority list of thesaurus as that used to index the database: similarly, a uniform set of journal titles may be needed, and some form of date or acquisitions indicator will be required in order to ensure that only new records are retrieved at each run.

The search profile expressed as a search strategy is run at regular intervals against any relevant databases maintained by the LIS: this could include a periodicals index, or non-bibliographic database of, for example, forthcoming conferences or trade and product literature. Added to the search profile at each run will be some form of data indicator. Output can be arranged in any suitable way: the possibilities include by subject, date or journal title (i.e. a form of current contents list).

The search facilities required for SDI are clearly a feature of DBMS and information retrieval software, as is the ability to save these strategies for regular recall at appropriate intervals. It is unlikely that stored searches will be available in OPACs, except on a temporary basis (as with Bookshelf), though such programs do have facilities to create recent acquisitions lists for a current awareness service.

Current awareness services can generalize on this procedure by simply retrieving all recent additions to the database and re-sorting them in some useful order, so that the output can be distributed to users in the form of a recent additions list or included in some form of newsletter. Subject bibliographies can be produced by searching for appropriate subject headings or classification numbers: this is a common practice in public and school libraries, where such lists are produced on specific themes, often relevant to some topic of the day.

In effect, these products (current awareness bulletins and SDI) are produced as a by-product of the main database, but the simplicity with which they can be produced means that they need no longer be the major chore they once were. It may also mean that such services are produced more frequently than is possible with a manual system which involves retyping card entries, thereby improving the currency of the service and, no doubt, enhancing the image of the service [24].

Small-scale bibliographic or information files are a common application in LIS, and usually utilize a DBMS or information retrieval program. The material recorded can vary considerably, as with the SDI and current awareness services indicated earlier, and such files usually form an adjunct to the main database or catalogue (which serves to emphasize again the potential value of having a single database for the LIS, instead of one large and (possibly) several smaller files). Johnson, for example, has developed a Cardbox Plus database with bibliographic and other data relating to the computer and communications industries, because 'there is no published or online guide to this type of data for the computer industry that is sufficiently up-to-date, comprehensive and with good UK and European coverage' [25]. The original bibliographic basis of the file has been augmented by such material as press releases and news items from journals, showing the flexibility of the system.

A very different application (though again using Cardbox Plus) has been implemented at the former College of Librarianship, Wales (now the Department of Information and Library Studies of the University of Wales), in order to create author bibliographies from a database of modern Anglo-Welsh authors [26]. Some 5000 records formed the basis of 24 author-bibliographies which included works by and about the author, authors' contributions to journals and reviews of the authors' works. The various arrangements are eventually written to a word processor file for final editing and publication as a bibliography.

Many LISs create other forms of non-bibliographic files, often of factual information provided as part of the reference service. Some of these are used directly, others require an intermediary. Typical files contain such diverse data as the opening hours of public buildings and offices, names and telephone numbers of local officials, brief local histories (with references to more detailed sources), and so on. One public library reference service maintains a list of accommodation for students in the area using IBM's Filing Assistant software. Students can request details of the accommodation by specific area, price or facilities provided. Microcomputer-based versions of these records (usually using DBMS software) provide much improved currency, since it is easier to keep the files up to date, a variety of access points and a range of printed versions which can be taken away by the user if necessary.

A somewhat different problem faced Manchester Commercial Library in its efforts to provide information on local companies, information which was not readily available from the usual published sources. In the end they were able to buy over 7000 company records from Dun and Bradstreet on floppy disks (at a cost of £350 per 1000 records) and to use this database with dBase III Plus to provide an online system which is approached through a set of menus [27]. This application is another illustration of the advantages conferred by current technological developments in microcomputers, namely, the portability of records and files between different systems. Standardization of operating systems together with a standard format for data enable users to transfer data between systems in a way which was largely impossible a few years ago. It should also be noted that this has gone (or can go) a long way to prevent the usual re-invention of the wheel at regular intervals.

5.7 INTER-LIBRARY LOANS

Developments in telecommunications have facilitated the use of microcomputers as terminals capable of transmitting inter-library loan (ILL) requests either to a central agency such as the British Library Document Supply Centre or between libraries (we should also note the growing use of fax and electronic mail in this respect).

The requirements of the application are the ability to create requests in the required format (e.g. BLDSC loan forms) and to transmit these to the appropriate destination. In addition, various statistics and financial data are required by management. Many LISs, for example, analyse their ILLs to identify monograph and journal titles which are frequently requested and which they should, therefore, purchase for stock, rather than relying on the ILL system. The restrictions on resources of the last few years have increased the volume of inter-library lending, as more and more LISs realize that they cannot be self-sufficient and so need to cooperate more in order to avoid wasteful duplication of resources.

A typical commercial program for inter-library lending (a number of LISs have developed their own in-house software for this purpose) is AIM (administration of interlending by microcomputer), originally developed at Leicester Polytechnic and now marketed by the Dawson Group. Loans to other LISs, as well as requests to BLDSC and to other sources of supply, can be handled (AIM uses a format essentially the same as that of the printed BLDSC form), overdue items are monitored, and a variety of printed options is available for standard letters of notification, etc. [28].

Noel-Lambot and Somville have described [29] an in-house program to handle inter-library loan requests which also produces statistical analyses of requests and a variety of print-outs: the analyses include details of the most requested periodicals, alphabetical lists of all periodicals requested, with frequency count and details of the eventual supplier.

An alternative approach to the question of inter-library lending by microcomputer is exemplified by OCLC's Interlibrary Loan Micro Enhancer. Inter-library lending is possible through a subsystem of the OCLC online system, but as with all interlending schemes involves a great deal of routine work monitoring loans and requests for loans. OCLC have, therefore, developed a package for inter-library lending which runs on their M300 range of workstations (which are variants of the IBM PC range). The system operates with a variety of menus and user-entered options, and has the useful facility of specifying when the system will go online to begin searching for records: this means that it can be set to operate at quiet or less busy times (when the terminal is not otherwise needed) or at off-peak times for reduced telecommunications costs [30].

5.8 USER EDUCATION

It seems a natural development to use the microcomputer for user education, since computer-aided learning (CAL) is a major application of microcomputers in schools and colleges. The methods used for user education within LISs vary: in some cases a preliminary course of instruction can be given and then reinforced by suitable software which assesses how much the student has learned and retained. In other cases, instruction is provided by the program, with or without relevant questions. Thus, a guide to the layout of the LIS can be in the form of a simple instructional package which responds to questions on location of materials, whilst a learning program for, say, the use of reference works would include questions to assess the user's progress.

Such programs can be used as a refresher course or for a specific course of instruction. Because of their specific contexts (other than for very general introductions to, for example, the classification scheme), programs tend to be written in-house to suit particular applications. dBase II was use in this way in the Department of Information Science, University of Strathclyde to provide a computer-aided learning program for the use of dBase II, and the principles could be applied to any learning situation. A suite of such programs could be developed, leading on from the general to the specific.

Such a suite of software would begin with an introduction to the LIS and its layout, move on to the use of the catalogue, and from there to the use of typical reference tools such as bibliographies, abstracts and indexes[31]. Expert system shells are a potentially useful tool in this area, since they can be built with advice and help screens with relatively little difficulty, and can also monitor the user's progress through the various parts.

The Library of the University of Waterloo in Ontario has developed a system to simulate the services of a reference librarian, primarily using expert system techniques. The various modules provide advice and instruction on query negotiation (clarifying what the user wants), use of specific reference tools (e.g. the interpretation of entries), referral to appropriate reference works for specific enquiries, basic information on services and locations, and classroom instruction on library techniques[32]. The developers of this program see one of its major advantages to be a reduction in the basic demands made on reference staff, since, although many such demands are simple, they can be numerous and time-consuming.

A further advantage of such programs, particularly those which deal with reference works, etc., lies in their use to overcome the problems of the infrequent user who does not develop a familiarity with the relevant work. Using a CAL package can allow the user to refresh his or her memory (without having to admit the fact that he or she has forgotten!).

6 Management and administration of information services

Certain aspects of work within library and information services arise simply from the fact that they are, in their own way, business operations with typical management and administrative functions. Budgets must be prepared and accounts kept, correspondence and reports must be prepared, statistical information has to be collected and presented, and so on. How much of this there is will depend on the size of the service, but some elements will always be present.

Given that software has been developed to handle almost every aspect of business from budgeting to Statutory Sick Pay records, this is one area which can be automated with little difficulty using standard software.

6.1 WORD AND TEXT PROCESSING

For this, the obvious answer is the ubiquitous word processor, for which there are programs of varying sophistication for every make of micro-computer. At the bottom of the range, word processors may offer basic facilities (see below), while top of the range products such as Wordperfect come close to desktop publishing in the functions which they provide. The choice is such that the requirements of most LISs can be met by one or more of the packages on the market: choice, as indicated in Chapter 8, must be based on an analysis of requirements.

The advantages of word processing, well known though they now are, can be summarized as follows:

1. Storage and production of standard documents to which minor changes are made in order to 'personalize' them;

2. Storage and production of draft documents which can quickly and easily be amended to produce perfect copy;
3. Storage and production of lists, catalogues, etc., which are amended at intervals, so that up-to-date versions can be produced with the minimum of retyping.

Use can thus be summarized as any textual information which has to be replicated at regular intervals or in quantity, with or without amendment. In view of their use for many in-house publications, the ability of a word processor to handle journal or magazine-type layouts may also be an item for consideration. The standard features of a word processor appear to have changed as packages have become more sophisticated (what was considered a 'luxury' feature five years ago is now standard), but the very basic features can be listed as follows:

1. **Text formatting:** setting left and right margins, line spacing, justification, page size, page numbering, centred text (for headings);
2. **Text editing:** deletion of single words or blocks of text, transfer of words or blocks of text to other points within the document, appending text from a disk file, insertion of new text, global search and replace (i.e. replace all occurrences of one word with another), easy movement backwards and forwards in the text.

These are, as indicated, the basic functions required: a word processor which lacks some of these could hardly be considered a word processor at all. An overall format of margins, line spacing and so on can be set at the start of the document, but changed to suit specific parts of the text (single line spacing and wider margins for a quotation, for example). New text can be inserted at any point in the document, and this new text can be typed in at the keyboard, moved from somewhere else in the document, or added from another document altogether. Moving text usually involves defining it in some way as a block and then indicating the point to which it has to be moved. Describing the operation takes longer than doing it: the whole process can be carried out with a few keystrokes.

Presentation of text on the screen is important, because that is normally how initial corrections and checks are made. Some programs will display on screen the codes and characters needed to create certain effects, such as bold text or underlining, but this can make scanning the text confusing. Others will conceal these codes, so that the general effect on screen is of the completed (usually printed) document, and this feature, known as WYSIWYG ('what you see is what you get' – pronounced wizziwig!) is to be preferred. (Some programs use colour in various ways to indicate such features as bold or underlined text. This may depend on the screen used.)

More advanced features of the software are as follows:

1. *Record merging:* this usually involves calling up a name and address from a file and merging it with a document (often a standard letter). Some programs have the added facility of selecting names from the file on the basis of some criterion (e.g. postcode);
2. *Arithmetic:* it may be possible to carry out calculations on figures included in the text. This ability can range from simple adding of columns to automatic recalculation of all related figures when one is changed;
3. *Graphic images:* the better word processors can also handle graphic images, a feature which is becoming more and more desirable in contemporary text handling. The images are usually produced using painting or drawing programs, but they can also be input via a scanner. Although the detailed handling of such images is best left to the specialized packages, some word processors can carry out basic operations such as scaling the image, moving it around on the page, or providing captions. WYSIWYG word processors have the advantage here, since the image can be seen on the screen as these operations are carried out, but some character-based word processors have a page review facility which provides a WYSIWYG 'version' of all or part of a page;
4. *Spell checks:* a dictionary is included which can automatically check spellings and highlight words not in the dictionary. Note, however, that not all highlighted words are necessarily misspelled, since the dictionaries are normally limited in scope. American word processors will have American spellings, of course, but it is often possible to add words not included in the dictionary, so that they are not queried on subsequent use, and UK dictionaries are also available. Wordperfect also has a thesaurus function which can be used to select alternatives: whether this improves style is another question! Furthermore, spell checks will not indicate when a word has been misspelled in such a way that another feasible word has been created: for example, if 'from' is mistyped 'form', there will be no warning given;
5. *Background printing:* also known as concurrent printing, this facility allows the user to work with one piece of text while another document is being printed;
6. *Review:* a review facility allows the user to scan a document quickly in order to check its contents without being able to edit in any way. The most popular use of this function is to remind the operator what is in a file, since it eliminates the need to load the file first.

There are one or two other features which should be considered. Word processors provide facilities, as suggested above, for enhancing in various ways the printed version of a document, provided that the printer is capable of accepting such commands. The range of such options varies with the program, but the usual features now found include underlining, super- and sub-scripts, bold, italics and a growing variety of typefaces, styles and founts. It is therefore possible, for example, to choose the most appropriate founts, etc., for headings and sub-headings in a document. Of course, the founts must be provided, and some companies have benefited from sale of fount libraries for microcomputers. Figure 6.1 illustrates the possibilities in a short piece of text (admittedly created specially for the occasion!).

Programs also vary in the way in which they set such print features as margins, typeface, line spacing, etc. In some cases, all the necessary commands must be inserted at the start of each document: if changes are required in the body of a document (as in Figure 6.1), the appropriate commands must be inserted where required. To switch these commands off, the original commands must be re-inserted, though it is possible to do this using the text move facility. In other cases (the more usual) a default set of options applies, and these can be changed as required within the text. The new commands can be switched on and off with one or two keystrokes. The problem is that the default options may not be the standard required, and so they will have to be changed for every document typed, although certain packages will allow a new default set to be created. This is often the case with American software which will have default settings suitable for quarto paper: alternative settings for A4 will have to be created in the UK.

More advanced word processors allow pages to be layed out using measures more akin to those used by the typesetter. Thus, inches, picas and points are used, instead of, or as an alternative to, characters per line and lines per inch.

Given the comprehensive set of commands now available, it was inevitable that various combinations of keys now have to be used with word processors, leading to an apparent complexity in use. Thus, Wordperfect on an IBM PC (used to create the text of this book), uses all ten function keys alone or in combination with the Control, Alt or Shift keys, giving 40 initial functions in all. Each function then has between two and six further options, and some of these have further 'sub-options'. It sounds hideously complicated, but in practice (and with practice) it works satisfactorily: the most-used functions are quickly memorized and Wordperfect's online help facility means that every other function can be found very quickly. Students have been taught to use Wordperfect effectively for written work within two or three hours, depending on their previous experience. It should be noted that its operation on an Apple Macintosh is considered to be much easier.

CHAPTER 6

"Knowledge is of two kinds. We know a subject

ourselves, or we know where we can find

information upon it" - Samuel Johnson.

When Johnson wrote these words, it is unlikely
that he had the information worker in mind,
but it may serve as a working hypothesis of
the work required in that profession[4].

Note 4: it should be stressed that this is only a working
definition.

Figure 6.1   Print options in a word processor.

As with all software, features over and above what are assessed as
standard requirements will have to be selected on the basis of what will
be needed or useful in the specific context, but it should be borne in mind
that the availability of 'additional' features may stimulate better
products and printed output.

6.1.1 Desktop publishing

Desktop publishing (DTP) is a comparatively recent concept which has
captured the imagination of a large number of microcomputer users.
With the appropriate hardware and software, it enables documents to be
produced with a quality approaching that of documents produced
professionally. For a time, the enthusiasm for DTP could be described as
being over-optimistic, or worse. DTP is only coincidentally connected
with publishing: its main application is for internal documents, but if it is
possible to produce a document in a form which is suitable for external
publication, then it may be advantageous to do so.

An important feature of DTP is that it is necessary to consider the
computer software packages which will be used to manage or create the
data to be printed, as well as that used to make up the page of the final

document. Word processors, spreadsheets and database packages are, therefore, an essential part of DTP, depending precisely on what has to be printed.

The production of high quality documents can be achieved with large and small computers. However, the field of DTP is normally associated with microcomputers. Indeed, DTP was born on the Apple Macintosh. DTP can be carried out on the full range of machinery, ranging from the inexpensive home computer to the 32-bit microcomputer and powerful engineering workstations. For professional results, DTP requires a microcomputer with considerable power, partly because of the need to process, print and display graphical data.

For serious DTP, a 32-bit processor is recommended, and several megabytes of RAM will be needed for the more advanced packages, especially if multi-tasking is required. A hard disk drive capacity of 40 Mb is advisable, and more should be obtained if possible, especially if images are to be stored. It is essential to have a screen which can display data graphically, and, in order to design a page on the screen, it is desirable (and in some cases essential) to have a screen which can display an entire A4 page, and possibly two side-by-side. It will also be helpful to have a screen with a higher resolution than normally found on a microcomputer, as this will enable extremely small fount sizes to be seen clearly. A colour screen might also be required, in order to handle colour images. If particular screen founts are to be used, it will be necessary to install them.

The choice of printer depends, in part, on the quality of output required. Laser printers are the obvious choice, but there are other possibilities (see the discussion on printers in Chapters 2 and 9). Storage of a range of founts will also take up memory space in the printer, though founts can be down-loaded from the computer or stored in plug-in fount cartridges. If the laser printer is to be used heavily, it is worthwhile investing in a more expensive model. The Postscript page description language needs to be considered, since, even though Postscript printers tend to be more expensive, there are advantages such as the fact that founts of different sizes do not need to be stored: they are generated mathematically from so-called outline founts. In addition, a Postscript page can be printed on compatible printers with differing resolutions. It is even possible to use a phototypesetting device to produce the page at a much higher resolution than a laser printer.

A scanner can be used to capture data from the printed page, and images can be incorporated from video sources. Characters can be analysed and recognized by optical character recognition (OCR) equipment, while captured images can be processed in a variety of ways (see below). Phototypesetters, also know as image setters, give output with a resolution above 1000 dots per inch, and hence are used to produce quality output.

Broadly speaking, applications software for DTP can be divided into three areas:

1. The capture of data from outside and its preliminary processing: this includes OCR and image processing software. OCR software falls into two groups depending on the method of analysis used. One uses a matrix-matching technique to match stored characters with those input. The other analyses the features, such as ascenders, descenders and circles in characters. The first is useful with fixed-width founts, such as those produced by a typewriter. The second type is more successful with a wider range of typefaces, styles and founts. Some systems also match the captured data with machine-stored dictionaries. Image processing software can crop, rotate, stretch and reduce the size of an image, and perform extremely sophisticated operations on individual parts of the image. Some of the software mentioned below can process images, such as paintings, and include page make-up packages;

2. Software which manages data in the computer. This covers the wide range of packages available for the microcomputer. Examples of packages include:
   (a) word processing
   (b) spreadsheets
   (c) database management
   (d) painting
   (e) drawing (including computer-aided design)
   (f) business graphics;

3. Page make-up and typesetting software: computers were used to assist with typesetting long before DTP became available. Typesetting data are added to the material to be printed using codes. A related approach is the use of SGML (standard generalized markup language). This language is handled by a range of typesetting systems. One advantage of these coding approaches is that they have been developed for the printing trade and therefore offer good control over layout, founts, etc.

DTP is more normally associated with the WYSIWYG approach. The page itself can be seen more or less as it will appear in print, but on the screen. For the design of magazines, individual pages can be built up by gradually bringing in data, e.g. from the packages mentioned above. Thus, text would be acquired from the word processor, spreadsheets would provide spreadsheet data (figures), images from painting and drawing packages, etc. Some packages also allow typesetting codes to be used.

When DTP packages first appeared, they provided few of the tools used by professional typesetters. However, they have improved rapidly with time, and prices of professional programs have come down. DTP packages now have a wide range of typefaces, styles and founts, can undertake kerning, hyphenation with the aid of dictionaries in more than one language, and allow images to be manipulated in various ways. They can also handle spot colour and four-colour separation tasks. DTP packages are available for LANs, enabling more than one user to work on document make-up. Specialist DTP packages, such as those specifically for designing forms, are on the market and, as mentioned above, word processors continue to improve the quality of their output.

Professional typesetters normally require substantial training to achieve the skills necessary to produce a professional product. Although DTP programs have made it much easier to produce higher quality documents, design skills are just as important in DTP. It is all too easy to produce a result which actually detracts from the document's readability, rather than enhances it. However, some extremely good results can be obtained with a relatively low level of skill, as long as some basic rules are followed.

6.2 MANAGEMENT INFORMATION

Libraries and information services have to operate within a budget (be it large or small) and all keep some statistical information on their loans, numbers of users, etc. How much effort is put into the recording of this will depend on the time available, the expertise available and the amount of information needed. Even if there is a limited amount of such work, it will be useful to use microcomputer-based systems to reduce the work involved and, perhaps more importantly, to do work of this kind which was previously impossible. The provision of useful management information is now an important requirement in the efficient and effective running of information services, which can no longer afford simply to react to user demand. The emphasis today is on **proactive** services, services which seek out information demands and needs and seek to meet them. Proactivity requires, *inter alia*, information on the use of the service which can be used not only for problem solving, but also for **problem finding**. Unfortunately, while most of the larger automated systems do provide what passes for management information, it is rarely used by LIS managers, since it does not meet contemporary needs. This fact has been realized by the suppliers of large automated systems and it is likely that, in the next few years, we shall see major improvements in this respect. For the time being, however, much can be achieved with a

microcomputer system. Rush has provided [1] a comprehensive statement of the needs for a microcomputer-based system to support
management functions in LISs, emphasizing the need for more *effective*
management and decision making.

6.2.1 Administration

The administration of information services covers a number of topics,
ranging from those with direct parallels in the business world such as
personnel records and salaries to routines more specific to the information service. Of course, a number of these routines may be handled by
other departments within the parent organization – the personnel office
or salaries section, for example – and the LIS manager need be
concerned only with records of staff illness, annual leave, etc. There are
business programs to cover all of these possibilities, but here we shall
concentrate on the routines of more direct concern.

At a basic level, we can begin by examining a common routine,
namely, the service of sending out or provision of regular lists of some
description to an identified group of users. Typical examples are listings
of recent additions, select bibliographies on topics of current interest,
in-house journal indexes, and so on. Such lists would now be prepared
with a word processor, as suggested in the previous section, and, as we
also indicate there, such lists can be combined using a mail merge facility
with the names and addresses of recipients. The whole process becomes
automatic. Since it is feasible to select names from the mailing list on the
basis of some criterion, this will ensure that the most appropriate
audience is 'targeted'. This is a similar technique to that used in
commercial mail shots, in which individuals can now be identified on the
basis of forename (certain forenames are a good indicator of age) or post
code (an indicator of the area in which one lives and thus of such factors
as home ownership), and targeted with information (actually, often junk
mail!). The commercial system may be open to some criticism, at least in
its application: the application of the principle to information dissemination is more laudable.

Sections within large units must often maintain an **inventory** of
equipment and furniture, usually to allow for checks on the location of
valuable items. A typical inventory will contain details of make and
model, serial numbers, location and date of purchase and/or installation.
There may also be details of maintenance and maintenance agreements,
to ensure that these are renewed when necessary. Inventory lists can be
maintained easily with a word processor, and this is particularly useful if
the details included are subject to alteration and amendment at more or
less regular intervals. Listing inventory items with a DBMS may not be

necessary (i.e. the additional facilities of a DBMS would not normally be needed), although this would be a sensible approach for a multi-site system: equipment within each site could be traced easily. Similarly, listing by date of purchase would give an indication of equipment that is due for replacement or that is out of warranty and in need of a maintenance agreement.

By using a DBMS package and including fields for a record of breakdowns, repairs, etc., it would be a simple task to identify troublesome machines, as well as to analyse the overall pattern of maintenance and repair. Such an analysis could be used as a **predictive** tool, enabling the LIS manager to take preventative action in good time.

In general terms, there is much that the small LIS can do in the realms of administration with a standard DBMS. A relational package like dBase will remove much duplication of effort, since files can be linked in various ways. Saye and Wilt provide an overall view of the potential of DBMS in decision making [2], while descriptions of specific applications appear regularly in the appropriate journals (see section 8.1). Devadason has described a system for manpower planning which can provide models of present and future requirements [3], while Jackson and Aluri have shown how dBase III can be used to handle the problem of continuations and standing orders, often a complex problem which causes difficulties in budgeting [4].

The potential of the microcomputer to alleviate the administrative problems of the small LIS, in particular, is great: a glance at the professional journals will indicate how much can be done. As we have said, the only limitation is the imagination!

6.2.2 Statistics

The amount of statistical information maintained by an LIS will vary, often depending on size, on how much statistical data are needed, and not least on how well the LIS manager can handle the data! Expertise (and need) may range from adding weekly loans figures and producing the occasional graph to complex operations on patterns of use, distribution of users, and so on. Generally speaking, there are three types of statistical software available: true statistics programs, business statistics software and spreadsheets. Their use can improve the quality of presentations at budget time (and on other occasions, of course) and they can also be used to reveal new aspects of the service in a problem-finding capacity.

The true statistics packages now available for microcomputer systems, such as SPSS, will carry out all of the standard statistical operations, including means, medians, chi-squared test, regression analysis, etc.

They may be too sophisticated for many areas of LIS work (and for many librarians), since they assume a knowledge of statistics such that the user not only can enter the appropriate data, but also understand the significance of these operations and the results. However, those that have knowledge can use these programs in analyses of user populations, book usage patterns and similar large-scale projects. The business statistics packages tend to be less demanding, since they are aimed at a population which is not necessarily expected to have that expertise readily available, or which demands a more user-friendly approach.

Features to look for when selecting a program are self-evident. It must cope with the range of data to be analysed and carry out all the required operations. In general, the LIS manager should have one of the three types in his or her armoury, since not only will it prove useful in the ways suggested above, but it will also indicate other possibilities, as expertise develops. In selecting a program, it will also be necessary to assess the level of knowledge required to operate it successfully and to be clear whether any special peripherals are needed. A graph plotter may be required, for example, as may colour for easier interpretation of the results, and even if analyses are not to be printed, the screen must be capable of presenting the results clearly, which will normally require the installation of a graphics card.

The form in which figures will be presented must also be considered. On many occasions, a simple tabular format may be sufficient, but more interesting and effective results are produced by being able to present data as graphs, bar charts, pie charts, etc., and to include these in published or circulated reports.

As was suggested above, very sophisticated analyses of data can be produced with this software, and the interested LIS manager is advised to consider these packages carefully, since their use may enable him or her to improve significantly the quality and range of information available for decision making and the development of services. The more advanced statistical techniques are presented in Simpson's standard work on statistics [5], while Hernon has a very useful description of the available software, output variations and a case study [6].

6.2.3 Finance

The spreadsheet, which, it was suggested, is an alternative method of carrying out statistical analyses, has a further and equally important role when it comes to handling and administering the LIS budget. Prices of the range available run from around £50 to several hundreds of pounds. As with word processing software, certain features which a few years ago were seen as luxuries, are now available as standard on available packages.

Spreadsheet programs consist of a matrix of boxes or 'cells', into which the user enters data or formulae. The maximum number of cells is determined by the program, but may also be restricted by the available RAM – how much RAM is needed will be stipulated. A cell is defined by the vertical and horizontal coordinates (usually represented by a letter and a number) which are based on the columns and rows set up by the user. The number of cells is finite, but typical packages now handle several thousand cells.

Column width determines how big a number can be entered, and a maximum will usually be stated. The cells can contain words, data or formulae which act on data elsewhere on the spreadsheet: how extensive these formulae are is another determining factor in selection, and most packages provide a wide range. If a formula or equation is not provided, it may be possible for the user to add it by manipulating the data in cells, though this can be a complex task. It should be possible for a formula to use data that are themselves derived from a formula. The formulae are normally 'invisible' until the cursor is placed over the relevant cell. Once the calculations have been carried out, the cell contains the derived answer, although the formula remains for future use.

All spreadsheets will print data exactly as they are recorded, and most also allow the presentation of graphs, bar charts, etc., which may be more effective. As we indicate later (section 8.3.5), integrated software such as Microsoft Works provides a spreadsheet with word processor and database package, which means that data in the spreadsheet can be incorporated into word processor files.

Spreadsheet software can be used within an LIS in various ways. Recording expenditure in the budget is one obvious application, but use can extend to circulation control statistics – indeed any type of data recording and analysis. Smith has described, for example, the use of Multiplan to model and cost online searches, in order to balance the need for further refining a search with the cost to that point. It is also suggested that the model would be useful in an investigation of the microeconomics of online searching [7]. The particular power of spreadsheets, however, lies in their ability to model operations, often known as 'what-if' calculations. For this, a spreadsheet is created with every element in, for example, the annual estimate – salaries, repairs, heating, etc. Formulae express all the relevant relationships between these data. It is then possible to see automatically and instantly the effect of a salary increase, an increase in costs, or both, on the estimate and to make suitable adjustments. Similarly, a spreadsheet built up of the standard ratios of books to students and of loans to stock in an academic institution could immediately indicate the impact of an increase in student numbers on required stock. Used in this way, spreadsheets are an aid to planning and to problem finding, as well as problem solving. While they are only as good as the estimates which they contain, it is always possible to add real data as they become available, thus refining the 'predictions'.

Spreadsheet programs usually offer a report generator which will allow the insertion of additional text, will rearrange the sheet, add page numbers and so on. In addition, it is possible to view different parts of the sheet side by side, thus making it possible to see related data which are, however, physically separated on the sheet.

The microcomputer as a resource | 7

We have concentrated throughout this book on the application of the microcomputer to information management routines within library and information services. However, some indication must be given of the demands created when the LIS manager includes microcomputers and software as a resource, alongside the more 'traditional' non-book materials. Provision of software and some (more limited) provision of hardware is now commonplace in the public sector library services (schools, public and academic), though it may be less evident in information services within commercial organizations, since users in these organizations will normally be provided with software in much the same way as they are provided with pens and paper.

7.1 HARDWARE

The factors to consider when selecting hardware are described in Chapter 9, and these factors apply with equal force when selecting hardware for LIS users. In many academic libraries, where the parent institution has standardized, for teaching purposes, on one make of microcomputer, choice is not necessary, but few academic institutions have, in fact standardized: Burton's survey indicated that ten different makes were provided for users, and several provided more than one make [1].

Without such a policy of standardization, the library manager is free to choose any suitable hardware system which falls within the budget allocation. Naturally, the opinions of others should be sought as well, and these should not be limited to the staff of the computing or mathematics sections, valuable though their comments will be. Within schools and colleges, for example, the business studies department may well be using Apple Macintoshes or Amstrad word processing systems, and there will be certainly be a number of BBC microcomputers in various forms (Model B, Master and Archimedes). It may be necessary, therefore, at least to consider whether one of each should be provided.

As with any computer application, the available software will be the principal determining factor: there will be little point in providing an otherwise excellent microcomputer if the relevant software available for it is not suitable for potential users (e.g. at an inappropriate educational level), or if the range of programs is very limited. Of course, the fact that this hardware has been chosen by the various departments should suggest that suitable software is available.

The storage of hardware should pose few problems beyond those associated with any item of valuable and (relatively) delicate equipment. Security will be important, and there are various ways in which microcomputers can be permanently or semi-permanently secured to furnishings, including adhesive pads and/or anchoring bolts with special keys. Chapter 9 also considers the question of the ergonomics of hardware design and the environment in which the system will operate. Generally speaking, microcomputers will require some sort of physically separate location, either to provide an appropriate environment or to avoid the irritation to other users of the noise from keyboards, cooling fans, etc. Since several microcomputers together can generate, over time, a significant amount of heat, this too suggests a separate location in a well-ventilated area. Shoolbred has described the factors which influenced Birmingham Polytechnic Library in setting up its microcomputer facility [2].

Maintenance can be as problematic as it is for systems used by the service, and whether or not a maintenance contract is taken out for the post-guarantee period is a matter for in-house policy. The cost of maintenance contracts must, however, be included in estimates, and it should be noted that this can be up to 10% of the total purchase price of the system. Maintenance contracts can be recommended, however, in view of the regular and varied use which will be made of the hardware by users of varying degrees of experience!

7.2 SOFTWARE

When only one make of microcomputer is provided, this will obviously simplify the choice of software, by limiting it to that which will run on the systems provided. However, as has already been suggested, many libraries provide a number of different makes, and they will have to consider how far to provide the same (or very similar) programs in versions for each make. This has proved to be a particular problem, for example, in the libraries of colleges of education, which provide software for student teachers during teaching practice sessions. Since the hardware used in schools can vary, the college libraries have to consider how far they duplicate provision of the same program in order to cater for some or all of the makes and models that a student teacher may encounter. This will be a matter for individual library policy: standardization within education authorities will obviously help, but, as has been suggested above, such standardization may not be widespread.

Software made available for loan has to match the hardware of users, which means that libraries offering this service have to consider the range of microcomputers which their borrowers may be using. Whilst this range is obviously large, it is possible to justify limiting it to the most popular makes of home or personal computers, the names of which can be gained from 'league tables' which appear frequently in the microcomputing press: local variations could be obtained from a survey of users and an examination of enquiries for software or from local retail stores, who may be willing to provide information on the systems they have found most popular. (Of course, they may not be so willing if they realize that the library is proposing to lend programs, since this could affect their sales.) At the time of writing, it is probably true to say that the overall variety in hardware used (and thus the range of software which has to be provided) is, in fact, somewhat less than it was five years ago, as certain makes have become front runners and others have dropped out. A glance at shelves of software suggests that Atari, Amstrad, Amiga, Commodore 64 and BBC are the most widely supplied.

What kind of software is provided will also be the subject of in-house policy. Within educational institutions, this will largely be determined by the subjects taught, but both educational and public libraries will have to consider the provision of other types of software. Selection can be based on well-established principles comparable to those for book selection, and can include assistance from journal software reviews (see also Chapter 9).

From time to time, the question of whether libraries should provide games software may be raised. However, if libraries can provide recreational reading and video recordings of popular films, there seems little justification for not supplying some at least of the endless variations of arcade-type games so popular with home computer users. More expensive software in the shape of adventure games should also be considered.

This software may be supplied on cassette tape or magnetic disks, and must therefore be handled and stored in the same way as audio cassette tapes and other magnetic media (see section 9.2.3).

Provision of microcomputer centres (with software), in the face of a continuous high demand from users, will have to be regulated by a scheduling policy for the daily use of machines. 'Rationing' access time on the basis of courses or classes will help to limit game playing within the centre, and will ensure that resources are used to the full. However, this policy can cause problems at certain times in the year, particularly for students in academic institutions. The knowledge that they must soon give up their place to another class or student causes panic when assignment deadlines are creeping ever nearer!

Library managers will also have to consider whether to make back-up or working copies of software, storing the master copy safely, so that, should anything happen to the cassette or disk, the programs are not lost. This is standard for business applications software, suppliers of which provide instructions (and exhortations) to make working copies of software. It would seem advisable for libraries to copy this practice, and simply to make another working copy should anything go wrong. However, how often do libraries keep back-up copies of the *books* they stock? If a book is damaged, it is either repaired or replaced, the borrower being asked to contribute to the cost of a replacement copy. It must be pointed out, however, that, since software cassettes or disks are so much easier to damage than a book, libraries could be faced with frequent replacement of software. Even if users are required to make good the cost of damaged software, the library is still faced with the extra cost of reordering and reprocessing the replacement copy.

In earlier editions of this book, we observed that a few software suppliers stated that their software could not be loaned by libraries: the suppliers feared, with some justification, that their software would be copied and they would lose revenue. As we said then, this is precisely the same argument that had been applied to the copying of music recordings borrowed from a library. Recent software purchases suggest that this proviso is no longer as widespread. An amendment to the Copyright Act of 1956 has placed computer software within the Act, thus removing at least one area of doubt.

Since the last edition of this book, the question of software piracy has been raised on several occasions in various ways and by various interested bodies. The concern has led to the formation of the Federation Against Software Theft (FAST) which is encouraging strong action against software pirates as well as endeavouring to persuade individuals that it is wrong. Many educational establishments now require student users of software provided under educational licences to sign a declaration which, among other things, points out the illegality of software copying. What we said in the previous edition remains true: it is in everyone's interest to ensure that abuses are kept under control, since, if suppliers are forced out of business, there will be less competition and less software (at higher prices).

The problem still remains for libraries lending software that, with programming experience (and some young people now have amazing ability in this area), it is possible to change a program and to record those changes on the disk or cassette. While both of these can be 'write-protected', the write-protect mechanism is easy to bypass: on a $5\frac{1}{4}$ inch disk it is simply an adhesive label which covers a notch on the envelope. The next person to borrow the disk may then find that the program does not match the documentation or does not work properly. Preventing such changes is not always easy, since it would be impossible to check every disk or cassette on return, and the only simple way may be to use some form of adhesive label which will indicate immediately if it has been removed or tampered with, thus suggesting that the disk or cassette should be checked.

In previous editions, we indicated that cataloguing computer software was a problem, since Chapter 9 of *Anglo-American Cataloguing Rules*, 2nd edition (AACR2), was not satisfactory in terms of the elements required for the description of a program. Considerable debate ensued over this problem, with various authors suggesting alternative rules or guides to the available rules [3], but eventually Chapter 9 was completely revised to provide the rules necessary for the cataloguing of microcomputer software [4].

7.3 VIRUSES

Since the earlier editions of this book, computers of all sizes have faced a growing menace in the shape of computer viruses, programs which can be inserted into some part of a computer system and which then replicate on other users' programs, disks or terminals, either through a network or by direct transfer to a disk. Viruses, as a phenomenon, appear to have originated in a relatively benign form (the use of medical terminology is difficult to avoid!): one of the first displayed a Christmas tree and seasonal greetings, but more serious and dangerous forms were soon developed by those who felt it was amusing and/or challenging to break into a system and to create a virus.

Viruses vary in their symptoms and effects, from the benign to the deadly. Some simply produce a so-called amusing display on screen, though they may cause systems to freeze, so that they have to be re-booted, with potential loss of data entered to that point. The 'Ping-pong' virus will cause a bouncing ball to appear on the screen, but can corrupt files if it becomes attached to them. More serious viruses will destroy entire files, often when a specific date is entered or a particular

operation is carried out. Towards the end of 1989, there was considerable concern in many organizations about the possibility of a 'Friday
13th' virus, which was supposed to have been inserted in a wide-area
network and which would wipe all records and data when triggered with
the date of 13 October. It turned out to be a false alarm, but more
well-founded concern was expressed over a virus which was distributed
in large numbers to potential users in the form of a disk purportedly
containing information on AIDS. Anyone running the 'program' would
have immediately infected their operating system with catastrophic
effects on files and records.

The problem with viruses is that, like their medical equivalents, they
are difficult to detect (very few are like the 'Ping-pong' virus, which can
be detected simply by running the DOS checkdisk command
(CHKDSK): if it is present, a 1024 byte bad sector is reported) and they
can spread from disk to disk and system to system, either when the
infected disk is used or when some specific event occurs (such as a
predetermined date). In terms of the loan of software, it would be
relatively easy for an infected disk to be returned to the library, issued to
others and so passed on to all of their disks in turn.

Fortunately, the medical analogy can be continued to the extent that
various companies have produced anti-virus programs which can be used
to detect a virus and 'disinfect' a disk: one such program can check for 42
viruses and their variants. However, new computer viruses are appearing all the time, and will remain a problem for some time to come.
Libraries lending software will have to include a routine to check for such
'infections', just as many organizations now do as a matter of course.

Selecting the software | 8

Selecting the software for a particular application can be a lengthy task, and it will not always be easy. However, together with staff involvement in the development of an application, it is probably the most important aspect of the whole process – to select the wrong program from the wide range now available for all aspects of information management will only cause frustration and disappointment on the part of both staff and users.

Since the second edition of this book, many more packages have come on to the market which are aimed at the library and information handling market. These programs take account of the specific requirements of that market (they may, for example, provide 'ready made' fields for ISBNs, with validation) and many have proved very successful in terms of the numbers of users. Many such programs (Bookshelf, for example) are provided in modules for specific applications which can be bought as required, but which allow data to be transferred from one module to another as required.

In addition, the standard business software of DBMS, spreadsheets and word processors have a place. Because of the high cost of many of the modular library-specific packages, these business programs have more appeal for the smaller library. Certainly, the various surveys of the use of microcomputers have shown that this business software remains very popular [1, 2, 3].

In sum, therefore, the LIS manager can find software for every conceivable routine and application, some of which takes account of the specific requirements of the LIS environment.

It should, however, be noted that software may be incompatible with the routine, usually in the sense that the program is too elaborate for the particular application. Trevelyan and Rowat investigated the use of seven kinds of systems software for six library routines, including circulation control, acquisitions and cataloguing [4]. By defining the requirements of each activity and utilizing data from five different types and sizes of library, they attempted to indicate the feasibility of using the programs under study for a given task in a library of given size. Some useful conclusions were reached on the use of these programs for the routines studied.

For example, DBMSs were not considered appropriate for circulation control because the record structure required is too simple. Similarly, notification (i.e. accessions lists, current awareness and bibliographies) is not a complicated enough application for a DBMS, though a file-handling package would be a feasible solution provided that no abstracts were included, since such programs have restrictions on field lengths. (It should be noted that Trevelyan and Rowat define DBMS as the 'true' DBMS of the minicomputer and mainframe, rather than the DBMS which one normally speaks of in reference to microcomputers.)

The point is that a detailed analysis of a particular application or task may indicate that some applications software would be a case of using a sledgehammer to crack a nut. The library-specific software discussed in Chapter 5 would not fall under this restraint, since it is designed for the range of library applications.

A further important point concerns the method by which records are accessed in a database. If fast access is required (for circulation control, for example), sequential or indexed sequential access methods will be too slow: an inverted file structure will be required. Areas such as cataloguing (but not the online catalogue), where instant file access is less important, may be sufficiently well served by sequential or indexed sequential methods. (These terms are explained in Chapter 3.) Modern dababase software is now more likely to use inverted files for access, so the problem of choice is less acute.

In the last analysis, a microcomputer is a small computer and may be unsuitable for no other reason than the sheer size of the files involved. Even with contemporary storage capacities and processors, the micro-computer may prove to be too slow in handling very large files, and it may be more cost-effective to implement a minicomputer or even a mainframe: the microcomputer could serve as an intelligent terminal to the larger system and could be used, for example, for the local processing of smaller files to subsets of the main files after they have been down-loaded.

8.1 SOURCES OF INFORMATION

The first problem faced by anyone wishing to select software for an application is the lack of a single, formal and comprehensive catalogue of available software which will constitute a one-stop place to look. There is no true bibliographic control over software comparable to *British National Bibliography*, but there are a number of places in which details of software can be found. The problem is compounded by the very rapid growth of applications software.

Advertisements and reviews are, over a period of time, probably the most comprehensive (though confusing) source of information at present. Advertisements can be followed up by a request for literature, which will not, of course, be totally objective, but will at least provide some information on which to base the selection decision. Advertising claims can be balanced by journal reviews. These are carried by most of the microcomputing journals and some others within the library and information field: the *International Journal of Information Management* carries regular reviews of relevant programs. General journals will carry reviews of software intended for the general business market, and some effort may be needed to relate these to an information context.

A number of journals dedicated to the subject of the microcomputer in information work are now available, however. *Library Micromation News* is a useful source of comment on specific applications programs and provides descriptions of individual implementations, written by librarians. It has additional value in that, being published from the Library and Information Technology Centre, it is more relevant in many ways for the British scene. In addition, *Vine* carries regular reports on new software and applications, usually of greater length than those in *Library Micromation News*.

Microcomputers for Information Management is a major vehicle for lengthy articles on all aspects of micrcomputers for information work, and it includes advance notice of new software, as well as descriptions of their use. *Computers in Libraries* and *The Electronic Library* both contain valuable descriptions of programs and reports by librarians, and, while it is not restricted to microcomputer systems and applications, *Program* is an equally useful source of in-depth articles describing working applications. It should be noted that the domination of the (business) software market by American products often means that journals may not give details of British agents (if, indeed, there are any): obtaining such software may be difficult, as will assessing the reputation of the supplier and obtaining support for the program.

Online sources of information, though lacking in detail, are more up to date, and information on packages can be found through a variety of access points, including supplier, application and hardware type or operating system: reviews and evaluations are not provided, however. Dialog, for example, has *Business Software Database* (file 256), *Menu: the International Software Dababase* (file 232) and *Microcomputer Software Guide* (file 278), while its *Microcomputer Index* (file 233), though an index to 50 microcomputing journals, includes the software reviews from those journals. Dialog's *Computer Database* (file 275) also includes software evaluations, and the full text of these is available on *Computer ASAP* (file 675).

In the UK, the library of Aslib and the two computing organizations, the National Computing Centre (NCC) and the British Computer Society, have details of available software. In the case of Aslib, this consists of suppliers' literature, backed up by an index to journal articles. NCC also carries out evaluations of applications software, though this is done by their own staff and is primarily concerned with establishing that the program does what it claims – in itself a valuable piece of information!

The Library and Information Technology Centre provides advice on a number of programs and can also offer demonstrations of packages to those interested. Some of these demonstrations are arranged specially, in that the software is provided specifically for the demonstration, but the Centre also has several programs permanently available. Demonstrations can be booked and expert advice and comment are also provided.

8.2 WRITING IT OR BUYING IT?

Applications software can be obtained from three principal sources:

1. bought off-the-shelf (and used with or without modification);
2. commissioned from a software house;
3. written in-house, either by a member of staff or by available computer staff.

Program writing is a lengthy and complicated task which can take many man-years: a programmer can expect to produce less than 100 lines of tested, error-free instructions in a high-level language in one working week: this includes all the necessary documentation. The complex search routines, etc., required for information retrieval on large files can contain several thousand instructions and represent many man-hours of work. Whilst efforts are being made to automate this aspect, it remains a fact that commissioned or in-house software will almost certainly be expensive. It will also take some time to produce an error-free program, as it will have to be tested and corrected at regular intervals. The process can take several months – more if the application is particularly complicated. The time needed to prepare full documentation must also be considered.

The advantages of such software are, of course, that it is tailor-made for the particular application and, in the case of commissioned software, there will be a high degree of support from the supplier. This last cannot always be said of in-house software. This may be produced by computer department staff at little or no apparent cost, but it may not be possible to get the necessary support and documentation. Too often reliance is placed on being able to contact the programmer if a problem arises – but what happens if the programmer resigned two weeks ago and took all his notes with him?

Generally speaking, the last two options are not recommended for the librarian seeking to implement routines on a microcomputer, though they have been used by some librarians. The librarian interested in writing programs can consult Hunter's book on Basic programming [5] or Davis on Pascal programming [6].

Off-the-shelf software, on the other hand, is readily available for all library routines, and it can be up and running very quickly. The business software will not, of course, be tailor-made (unlike the library-specific software), but the range of software now available is such that it should be possible to find a very close match to requirements. Where the software does not match, the library manager should be flexible enough to consider whether the existing routines could be adapted to the program.

In examining the various claims of advertisements, reviews, etc., the library manager should approach the software with an open mind, and be prepared to translate examples given in these sources into information retrieval and library management terms. For example, if the programs can search for 'all employees in Manchester who speak French and are less than 40 years old', then it is likely that it will also handle typical Boolean searches for bibliographic records.

8.3 SOFTWARE ASSESSMENT

Having pursued some or all of these avenues of information, the librarian will eventually be in a position to examine a number of programs that appear to be likely candidates for purchase.

A regular feature of the microcomputing journals is the summary or state of the art report, which considers the general requirements of a particular type of program and then lists a selection of those available, indicating how each matches up to these requirements. These articles are extremely useful, in that they can indicate to the inexperienced user exactly what to look for in a program, especially if a number of such reports are studied [7].

Their form of presentation can be adopted, and at an early stage it should be possible to draw up a chart or check-list of the necessary features of the required program, indicating in some way those that are essential and those that it would simply be useful to have. The chart will, of course, differ for each type of program, but this approach will ensure that a uniform assessment of each program is arrived at, as well as making it easier to compare programs and trade-off features where necessary. As an indication of the kind of chart which can be drawn up, Appendix 8.1 gives a summary of the points made in earlier chapters regarding software for information retrieval and library and housekeeping applications, though these summaries should be regarded as suggestions only: individual situations may necessitate amendments.

It will also be useful to include in these check-lists some information about the hardware on which each program will run. Although hardware is the last link in the process, it must be considered in principle at least: the necessary hardware may prove to be too expensive, not easily available, etc., and this information will add to the total picture. Selecting hardware is no longer the constraining factor it once was, with the development of a *de facto* standard in MS-DOS and the wide range of systems which can run MS-DOS programs: nevertheless, software will have requirements of memory, disk storage, etc., which will have to be taken into account.

When using check-lists, a separate form for each program is to be recommended, though this can make comparison of a number of programs difficult, unless a summary chart is also produced. Appendix 8.1 lists software-specific criteria, but there are a number of general points which should also be considered.

8.3.1 The supplier

What reputation does the supplier have locally (or nationally) in the provision of software? This is important not so much for the quality of the software itself as for the support and training which is available. A reputable supplier could provide names of former customers who may be contacted for their opinions on service, support and maintenance: alternatively, he should at least be willing to arrange with other customers for contact to be established (some customers, though perfectly satisfied, may not want to be inundated with requests to see their system in operation).

It will obviously be necessary to establish with the supplier precisely what level of support will be offered and at what cost. Do not expect too much in this respect: very inexpensive programs may well have little or no after-sales service beyond a back-up copy of the disk, but it should still be possible to telephone for initial advice, particularly if things go wrong in the early days. In most other cases, support will include advice (possibly via a help line), free or reduced-cost updates to the program as they are issued, and some degree of operator training. Suppliers may also include installation of the software and a preliminary check that it is working properly, since this eliminates the first problem faced by most users, namely, that they themselves make mistakes when setting up the system. However, a comprehensive service will be an additional and ongoing cost: it is not unkown to pay up to one-third of the purchase price per year for software support.

As with hardware, a software supplier should be reasonably local, since this will make it more convenient to visit his premises or for him to come to your premises: it also minimizes the cost of telephone calls. It is preferable for the supplier to come to the site where the software will be used, as he can then see more readily the precise context in which the program will operate, including any unusual or unique requirements.

If the supplier provides training in the use of the program, it will obviously be more useful for this to be carried out on-site (though this may involve an extra charge). In this way, the training can be applied to relevant tasks and be more relevant. Training, however, will only be available for the more expensive software – it would hardly be economical for a supplier to spend a day on-site for a £30 program!

Single sourcing (the buying of hardware and software from one supplier) has many obvious advantages, not the least of which is that there is only one person to argue with when something goes wrong!

8.3.2 Software demonstrations

Demonstrations are a very useful way of assessing the potential of a program, and suppliers should be willing to give such demonstrations, but they do have their limitations.

Normally, they will not be using very large data files, and so it will only be possible to estimate how well the program will handle typical library files for searching, indexing, etc. However, it should be possible to assess how 'user-friendly' the program is (see below) and the overall ease with which the program can be used.

It will be more useful to visit users of the software to see it in operation in a 'real' situation, even if this is not an exact parallel: it will still be using real data in a live situation, and will provide a more accurate picture than is possible with a showroom demonstration, though the latter will be the first step in eliminating anything obviously unsuitable. As we have already suggested, the Library and Information Technology Centre can arrange demonstrations of a range of programs in a relevant context and application.

Demonstration disks of the software may be available, and these can be considered a worthwhile investment. Whilst they will also be limited in the amount of data they can handle, they provide yet another opportunity to study the program at leisure and in a relevant context.

The price of demonstration disks is relatively modest and is normally deducted from the full purchase price. Prospective users should, however, distinguish between demonstration disks that simply show the program running with data already provided on the disk, and those that allow the user to set up a small file in order to show the program's facilities.

8.3.3 Documentation

The documentation which comes with the program should be examined carefully. This is the operations manual for the software and it should be clear and concise: if it is not, there could be many problems and much frustration, since it constitutes the only immediate source of information on running the program. Ideally, it should provide step-by-step guidance for the non-technical, first-time user, as well as serving as a reference manual for the experienced operator. This will normally require two separate sections, since to combine the two approaches will only baffle one and frustrate the other. The best documentation includes a 'tutorial section' which takes the user through the main features and operations one by one, so that a basic competence can be built up gradually. More complex commands and facilities can be obtained from the reference section.

8.3.4 User-friendliness

This much over-used phrase (which grates on many ears!) has been interpreted in different ways by software houses. It refers not only to the way in which instructions on the screen are presented, but also to the total interaction of the operator and the program. In summary, user-friendliness relates to:

1. screen presentation of operating instructions;
2. error prevention and data recovery;
3. information on what is happening;
4. confirmation of action to be taken.

Instructions should be clear and unambiguous, and should proceed in a logical manner. Consistency is also important: the same symbol, mnemonic or instruction should always be used for one operation, and the language employed should be as natural as possible. Software has progressed a great deal in this respect and there is no longer any justification for incomprehensible instructions and comments which have to be looked up in the back of a manual.

Mnemonics used for the sake of speed and simplicity (i.e. single key operations) should be obvious ones and truly mnemonic, i.e. capable of being remembered. They should also be unique: one (now thankfully obsolete) program known to the authors used the letter 'n' as both 'no' and 'next' in successive instructions.

The WIMP (windows, icons, mice and pointers) environment has greatly improved interaction with computer systems, since keyboarding is reduced to the minimum required. Icons and mice allow the user to point to and select an image which represents the required instruction, which is then carried out: the user no longer needs to type in the instruction. The WIMP environment generally provides an object-oriented approach which appeals to both novice and experienced user, as well as making record entry easier to those lacking typing skills.

An earlier but still popular approach is that of the menu, a list of alternatives which are selected simply by pressing the appropriate key, which may be a number or a mnemonic letter. This approach presents on screen all the options allowed at any stage and shows how to implement them, but even menus can vary in friendliness. In some cases, all that is displayed is a list of options with numbers: others may expand this with a command such as 'Press A to view the author index', or 'Move cursor bar to desired option and press the enter key'.

While a well-constructed menu will leave little or no room for error, menus can be a source of frustration for the experienced user who knows what to do. He or she has to plod through the menu each time, and so it is useful if two levels of operation can be provided which cater for both the novice and the expert, enabling the latter to 'jump' straight to the required option. An experienced-user level may make greater use of abbreviations and mnemonics.

If a program receives an instruction for which it is not programmed, or if the wrong kind of data is entered, it will normally do one of two things: either it will display an error message to alert the operator to the mistake and offer the opportunity to re-enter the correct data or to correct the mistake, or it will 'crash'. The former is the better and, with contemporary software, the usual response, but programmers cannot always anticipate all the errors which an operator can make, and so crashes may occur, though under more limited circumstances. Nowadays, the most likely source of a crash is a hardware problem.

If a crash does occur, it should be possible to retrieve the files as they were at the start of the session **and** most of the data which were entered prior to the crash. Otherwise, it will be necessary to establish just where data recording stopped and re-enter everything from that point. As we have said, in an ideal situation there will be no crashes, but an alternative will be to indicate which errors will cause a crash, so that operators can be suitably careful.

A program should always tell the operator what it is doing once an instruction has been given: there is nothing more nerve-wracking than to enter a command, only to see the screen go blank! Questions which go through the operator's mind at times like these are 'Did I press the correct key?' and 'Have I lost an entire morning's work?' At the very least, there should be a screen message of the 'Please wait' variety: better still is a (brief) statement of what the program is doing (e.g. 'Saving file NNNN'), which also confirms that the correct instruction has been given. Software should also ensure that the default option for certain instructions is appropriate. For example, when deleting files, the default option (which would be invoked if the enter key is pressed without thinking) should be 'No': the operator has consciously to press the 'Yes' key to delete the file or record.

Related to this is an opportunity to confirm that what has been entered (the text or data) is correct. This can relate to the data just entered (are there any typing errors or missing fields in a bibliographic record, for example?), and it should be possible to make corrections with an edit facility before saving the record.

8.3.5 Software integration

The ability to use data files of whatever sort with more than one program offers considerable flexibility, as well as saving time in re-keying the same or similar data. Library and information services often work with files which have different functions but use the same or similar data. If integration of this kind is available, it means that only one data file need be set up: the data can be used in various ways by different programs or modules or programs. The alternative is to enter the data for each application: a time-consuming task which does much to negate the savings gained by the use of the computer in the first place. It is also prone to transcription errors. Integrated business packages are now available which combine DBMS, word processing and spreadsheets: records set up under the DBMS can be extracted and used with the word processing module, for example, and in this way can have more text added. The appearance of the finished product can also be changed. Thus, a seletion of records could be extracted from a database, inserted into the word processor, and printed as a bibliography or subject list aimed at sections of the user population, or in response to a specific enquiry. The more powerful DBMSs are multifile systems, capable of accessing various files in response to an enquiry (see Chapter 4). Similar links can be found between word processors and spreadsheet programs, so that statistical or financial data can be inserted into reports with ease.

Transferring files between programs is also facilitated by the ability of programs to store data as ASCII files which can then be read by a range of other programs.

From the LIS point of view, the development of integrated library-specific software provided in modules is much more significant, since, as we saw in Chapter 5, this allows records to be created and transferred from one module to another as required, thus fulfilling a major aim of library automation, to reduce the duplication of keyboarding, and thus eliminate errors and save time.

APPENDIX 8.1 CHECK-LISTS FOR SOFTWARE SELECTION

Information retrieval software

Maximum record size
Maximum file size per disk
Maximum number of fields
Variable length fields provided
Search facilities:
    maximum number of terms per search
    logical operators
    qualifiers (e.g. $<$, $>$, $=$, Range)
    'wild card' searching
Sort facilities:
    multiple sorting
    merging subsets
    depth
Print formats:
    full record
    label
    report generator
Amend record format
Stored searches
Program utilities incorporated:
    back-up
    directory
    file copy
Block transfer of records
Block delete of records
Support contract
Hardware:
    operating system
    cost
    local availability

Spreadsheet software

Maximum number of cells
Maximum column width
Formulae
Speed
RAM required
Graphics output
Report generator
Split screen
Support contract

Word processing software

Right and left margins
Line spacing
Justification
Page size
Page numbering
Headers and footers
Single word deletion
Block deletion
Text transfer
Search and replace
Paging
Mathematics
Record merging
Spell check
Concurrent printing
Underlining
Enhanced printing and additional founts
Support contract

Selecting the hardware | 9

In an ideal situation, microcomputer hardware will be the last element in the selection process. Generally accepted practice is that the requirements of a particular application will determine the software needed and the software will, in turn, determine the hardware on which it will operate. To choose the hardware first may place an unnecessary restriction on the programs which can be used and thus on the ways in which the application can be automated.

However, in these days of IBM compatibility and the current *de facto* standard operating system of MS-DOS, this question of hardware selection is less problematic. If the hardware is acquired first for whatever reason (it may be provided by the parent authority, or the authority may have standardized on a particular make), provided that it is an IBM-compatible system, most of the standard software will run on it, simply because it is written for MS-DOS. The advent of the IBM PS/2, which was intended to establish a new industry standard and which has replaced the IBM PC range, has had considerably less impact on the market than the original IBM PC, with the result that MS-DOS systems appear to have a relatively assured future. Currently, there is much speculation about the potential role of the Unix operating system, as it acquires a more user-friendly interface, but at the time of writing there is little library-oriented hardware using this operating system. Once again, though, we can say that this trend will have to be watched.

The only major contender which is not IBM-compatible is the Apple Macintosh range, not least because of its excellent print facilities and its use of a WIMP environment. Most of the standard software is available in a Macintosh version, and probably the only major criticism which can be levelled against the Macintosh (at least in the low to middle end of the range) is the small size of the screen, though its clarity and resolution may exceed that of some larger screens.

The LIS manager may therefore be faced with a choice of hardware, all of which is capable of running the selected program(s): each system will accept the programs, but will also offer other features of varying usefulness. The situation is directly analogous to selecting a car even when the required engine size, fuel consumption, etc., have been established. The final choice (of microcomputer and of car) will then be determined by these other features in conjunction with those which, it has been determined, the system **must** offer. It would, of course, be naive to assume that cost will not be the major factor in selecting hardware: many will be working within a budget. However, the trend of falling hardware prices, commented on in the last edition, has indeed continued, so much so that it is now possible to spend as much on software as on hardware: stand-alone Amstrad 1512 systems, for example are currently advertised at under £500, while the software which they can run may cost £400 and more per program.

9.1 SOURCES OF INFORMATION

The most immediate and obvious source of information about available systems is the advertisements in the microcomputing journals and the manufacturers' literature, augmented by the various reviews (bench-tests) which are reported in the journals. As with software, advertisements must be treated with caution, but product literature will supply the necessary technical information about the system, including memory (RAM) and disk capacities, input/output ports for peripherals, available software, etc.

The bench-tests in the journals are, generally speaking, more objective, though they can rarely assess long-term reliability and in most cases assume a degree of technical knowledge. Many journals use a system of bench-marks to provide a concise evaluation of hardware. Bench-marks are the time taken to carry out a set of standard operations, comparable in many ways to government fuel consumption figures for cars, in that they allow a comparison of the various systems' capabilities to carry out identical operations.

What Micro? carries a monthly list which provides basic information about almost every microcomputer on the market. The information is brief, but does indicate cost, manufacturer, processor, operating system and available options, as well as RAM size and disk capacity. This can be a useful way to draw up an initial selection list for further investigation.

It will also be worth while to discuss requirements with a reputable supplier, who can offer advice on a suitable choice of hardware. However, suppliers are often agents for a particular make, and they will naturally prefer that make to others. Their advice should be complemented by the comments of system users, and again a supplier should be willing to supply names and addresses of current users. Comments from users on hardware can also be obtained when investigating software, as suggested in the previous chapter. As with software, user experience is particularly valuable, since it is based on experience in a working environment.

9.2 CRITERIA FOR SELECTION

There are a number of points about hardware systems which will influence the final selection. Broadly speaking, these relate to the CPU itself, to data storage and to other peripherals, including the printer. (It is assumed here that the reader has already studied the earlier chapters on the operation of a microcomputer system.) Rapid developments in technology mean that the available choices change frequently: the size of the problem is admirably summarized by Eyre [1].

9.2.1 The CPU

As we saw in Chapter 2, microcomputers can use a range of processors, and while these may be broadly similar, some offer advantages over others.

The speed with which a processor operates is also related to the clock speed of the processor, which is essentially the factor that controls how fast the necessary signals are transmitted within the microcomputer. Clock speeds are measured in hertz (Hz), but the situation is confused in that manufacturers may use the same processor but configure it to run at different speeds. The higher speeds (e.g. 15 MHz or 25 MHz for the 386 processor) are obviously to be recommended. The 32-bit processors now available provide even more processing power and speed.

However, some common sense should be applied here: there is little point in having an extremely fast system if much of the time is spent staring at the screen and just thinking, or if disk access times for the next record are extremely slow.

The system will obviously have to have the required operating system for the program(s) selected. As was suggested above, while Unix may become the operating system of the future, the user is currently best advised to consider MS-DOS.

The RAM capacity is an important consideration because, as we saw in Chapter 2, this is where the program (or program modules) and data will be stored temporarily during operation. This means, of course, that it must be large enough to hold the program and the data to be manipulated: it should be remembered that bibliographic and textual material will take up a considerable amount of RAM. Generally speaking, 'big is beautiful', and will also allow for future developments.

Typical current requirements are for 1 Mb RAM, and many systems can be upgraded with add-on cards to 1 Mb beyond this. (The minimum requirement for RAM will be stated by the software.) Indeed, memory is now so cheap that 2 Mb or more will soon be the standard, allowing the system to run more than one program at a time, or to carry out background printing.

On a more practical level, it should be remembered that an operator may have to sit in front of a microcomputer for quite lengthy periods, carrying out a variety of tasks. It is therefore most important to consider the overall **ergonomics** of the system to ensure that fatigue and general discomfort are minimized. Many trade unions have established policies on the use of VDUs, in particular to minimize health risks, and it will be necessary to ascertain whether such a policy is in operation.

The ergonomics of a microcomputer system are complex, consisting of the overall layout of the hardware itself and the environment in which it operates [2]. Users should be able to sit comfortably, and screen displays should be clearly visible without glare or poor focus and contrast. Screen legibility will be affected by ambient lighting, and the screen should be positioned to avoid reflections. There is an optimum distance between the eyes and the screen, and it should be possible for the operator to rest the eyes by looking past the screen at more distant objects (which should not, however, be a distraction).

Greatest flexibility is provided by screens which can be tilted and moved from side to side, together with detached keyboards placed in the most comfortable position. Purpose-built furniture ensures that keyboard and screen are in the optimum positions with respect to the operator, and is a worthwhile alternative to placing the hardware on a standard desk.

Screen displays can be improved by attaching a polarizing filter to eliminate glare and reflections, and to improve contrast. Though they can be expensive, such filters are useful when it is difficult or expensive to provide a better lighting environment. The screens are easy to attach and remove.

The keyboard should be clearly laid out and easy to read, with a matt surface which does not reflect overhead light. Any special keys should be clearly marked, so that they are not touched accidentally. A point worth noting is that keyboards will differ in some respects from those of a standard typewriter: this will affect touch typists in particular. Some systems have special function keys which can be programmed by the operator in order to simplify operations (some software will also allow keys to be 'programmed' as **macros**, which can be used, for example, to type frequently used words at a single keystroke).

The use of a mouse to select from a menu or to point to and implement an instruction has greatly simplified the operation of systems, as we have already said. Most people who regularly use a mouse prefer it to the keyboard (though the keyboard must still be used at times), and mice are certainly one way of overcoming unfamiliarity with a keyboard – still a feature encountered in staff, despite the supposed widespread use of microcomputers in schools.

A number of other facilities are now standard features of hardware, although it must be stressed that their overall value will depend largely on individual needs and applications in both the short and long term. It is possible, for example, to purchase optional extras such as bar-code readers, joysticks and paddles (normally only necessary for games), sound and speech synthesizers, and graph plotters, these having obvious use in statistical presentations. Bar-code readers have a similarly obvious use in circulation control (see section 5.1), and Buschman *et al.* have described a bar-coding project using microcomputers [3]. Such options are available from both the original manufacturer and from the numerous suppliers of additional products for microcomputer systems.

For telecommunications links, an RS232 port will be required, and this is now a common feature on contemporary hardware.

Multi-user systems, a feature of more expensive equipment, allow a number of microcomputers to share common (and often expensive) peripherals such as disk drives and printers. In theory, each station behaves as if it alone were connected to the peripheral, calling data from disks, etc. Problems can occur when a number of users are connected at the same time (as with online systems), and the specification of a multi-user system will indicate the maximum number of users possible. There must be provision to prevent an operator changing a record or file when someone else is working with it (known as record and file locking). Since floppy disks do not have the access speeds and storage required, multi-user systems must have hard disk storage.

Multi-user systems have probably been overtaken as a means of sharing peripherals and providing interconnection of microcomputers by local-area networks. These are a necessity for larger libraries requiring more than the number of terminals available under multi-user systems.

9.2.2 Data storage

The normal requirements of the LIS mean that hard disk systems are a prerequisite, since they offer the necessary storage capacity, as well as being faster to use. Hard disk capacities range from some 5 to 200 Mb, and they are faster and cheaper per byte of data stored. They are not only to be preferred for stand-alone systems, but are a necessity for local-area networks. Their cost has fallen so rapidly in recent years that they are available at very little cost.

Floppy disks are now available in two sizes, $5\frac{1}{4}$ and $3\frac{1}{2}$ inches. The former can hold between 100 000 and 1 500 000 characters (depending on the system), and if floppies of this size are used, obviously it will be necessary to assess if this is adequate for any one file: a rule of thumb is to allow 1 Mb of storage for each 1000 bibliographic records, which will usually allow enough space for indexes, etc., which can occupy as much space as the records. Spreading larger files over two or more disks can be inconvenient and may, in fact, not be practical.

The physically smaller $3\frac{1}{2}$ inch disks used in the Apple Macintosh and IBM PS/2, for example, have capacities of some 800 K, and capacities of 1.5 Mb are possible. Such disks have a further advantage in that the hard plastic 'envelope' in which they are encased makes them less susceptible to damage and bad handling.

An important consideration is the ability to back-up data files held on disk, whether floppy or hard. Making copies from which files can be restored should anything happen to them is vital (see section 10.2.1). Backing-up floppy disks is straightforward: one simply makes a copy onto another disk. Since it would hardly be economical to back-up a hard disk with another hard disk or with a large number of floppies, the normal practice is to use a tape streamer, an enclosed reel of high quality magnetic tape which can be built in to the hard disk unit (making backing-up almost automatic) or as a peripheral.

9.2.3 Care of disks

One of the advantages of the microcomputer over larger systems is the fact that it does not have to be housed in a special environment which can be expensive to provide and maintain. Microcomputers can sit on a desk in a normal environment and function perfectly well.

This does not mean, however, that proper care is not needed, and this applies particularly to disks and disk drives. Some thought must be given before the equipment arrives to protecting disks from the worst excesses of the office. They should never be exposed to magnetic fields – which can be generated by a variety of devices, including fluorescent desk lights and fans. Some commentators have even suggested that they be kept away from telephones. Library security systems, it appears, do not affect disks that are taken through in the normal way, though the disks should not be left in or near the checkout unit or close to exit barriers.

A major source of trouble is airborne contamination such as dust and smoke. This can be trapped on the surface of disks, breaking the contact of the reading head in the case of floppy disks: even smoke particles can be larger than the gap between the head of a hard disk unit and the disk surface. When not in use, floppies should be kept within the paper envelope and in a closed container: drives should be located away from dusty areas – they should not be placed below or in front of air and central heating ducts or windows. As with all electrical equipment, liquids should be kept well away: the usual culprit here is the cup of coffee carelessly placed on the desk!

Disk drive head-cleaning kits can be obtained from computer supply companies: when used as instructed they will ensure that the reading head is kept free of contaminants which could cause data loss.

For a dramatic but comprehensive description of the potential for disaster, the reader is referred to the article by Miller [4].

9.2.4 Printers

Most LIS microcomputer systems will be expected to provide paper-based output at some time, and there is now a range of printers available for microcomputer systems to suit almost every budget [5].

Printers are the slowest element in a microcomputer system: even the fastest cannot compete with the data transfer rates and operational speeds of the CPU. Thus, the computer may have completed a task in seconds, but the operator must then wait for several minutes for the results to be printed. The commonest answer to this is the provision of a print buffer in the printer, which will accept characters from the computer at its speed and then allow these characters to flow through to the printer at the printer's speed. Meanwhile, to the microcomputer, the job is done, and it can do the next task. The size of the buffer provided varies with the printer: cheaper machines will not provide much buffer space, and it is worth the effort to select a printer with as large a buffer as possible.

Laser and ink jet printers will normally accept single sheets of paper for printing, while dot-matrix printers are usually set up for continuous stationery with a **tractor feed** mechanism: some, however, may take single sheet feed as well.

Section 2.5 in Chapter 2 also deals with printers.

9.2.5 Hardware suppliers

Most of the comments made below about hardware suppliers are self-evident, though it has to be said that these are often the points which are missed in the rush to buy.

It will obviously be most convenient if a local supplier can be used, since maintenance calls, etc., will be (or should be) attended to more quickly, but wherever he is located, it is necessary to establish his reputation, as with software. Contact with existing customers once again can be useful. The fact that a supplier is an appointed agent is normally an additional point in his favour, and lists of approved suppliers can be obtained from the manufacturers or from advertisements.

Suppliers should also be able to give comprehensive instruction in the use of the hardware following its installation: complex systems (e.g. with a LAN) may include a training course. It will be preferable if such training can be given on-site, with relevant data on hand. This will also allow more staff to receive training.

The level of after-sales service and maintenance must be established at the outset, together with costs. Maintenance contracts required after the annual guarantee expires will vary considerably and generally one pays for what one gets: maintenance contracts can be as much as 10% of the purchase price. A parent authority may have negotiated a special contract, which will at least relieve some of the burden. On the other hand, maintenance may be provided in-house, in which case the LIS manager should ensure that the service provided is acceptable: the LIS may not rank very high in the maintenance engineer's priorities!

Study of the technical manual which should be provided with the system will ensure familiarity with the basic day-to-day maintenance required and will make it easier to discuss faults, modifications, etc., with the supplier when the time comes.

Implementation and system management | 10

In this chapter we will discuss the main points of an automation project, and look at various aspects of the day-to-day and long-term management of an automated system. In an introductory book such as this, it is not possible to go into the fine detail of systems analysis: the reader can be referred to standard textbooks on the subject (such as that by Daniels and Yeates [1]). In this chapter, however, we do look at the importance of staff participation and involvement in the design and implementation of automation, since current thinking places a great deal of emphasis on this as a means to effectiveness and efficiency. We will also consider some of the effects upon staff of the implementation of an automated system, in the light of speculation and reported research on the subject of the effects of IT in general.

As we have said, before any software or hardware is purchased, it is necessary to investigate very carefully the applications to be automated. Only then is it possible to have a clear idea of what the software and hardware must do, and thus armed to look critically at the available programs and makes of microcomputer. In many ways, the development of a *de facto* standard in MS-DOS (whatever its future) and the number of systems which will run MS-DOS software have eased this problem, as was suggested in the last chapter: however, it has also placed an even greater value on the need for staff involvement. When hardware and software were limited in what they could do, they were the critical and determining factor in systems development: now that this constraint has been largely removed, other factors must be taken into account.

Even though the purchase of a microcomputer system costing a few hundreds of pounds may not appear to justify the setting up of a large project team, the investment in time to design a system is proportional to the complexity of the application: in some cases, a project team will be a necessity.

10.1 PROJECT MANAGEMENT

The first task is to define the project in terms of the ultimate objectives to be achieved. By defining projects in terms of goals, it is possible to organize all developments and phases of the project into manageable pieces, and a project can therefore be defined as an organized effort to reach a single predefined goal or set of goals.

Often a single person is assigned to lead a project and is given responsibility for ensuring that a project is completed according to requirements, within costs and on time. The project leader has to be provided with the resources necessary to carry out the project, and this implies a measure of sympathetic understanding on the part of the parent organization. This may be assumed if it is the parent organization that sets up the project in the first place. It may, however, be necessary to convince higher authority that the proposed automation is worthy of a formal investigation, and so a certain amount of preliminary work will be required. Such preliminary work will normally include details of:

1. estimates of time to be saved;
2. estimates of money to be saved;
3. extension to the service made possible;
4. approximate costs of capital equipment;
5. approximate running costs;
6. overall reasons for automating (e.g. present system can no longer cope).

These need not be presented in precise detail, but an indication will help to convince the parent body of the need to set up the project and to begin to consider the provision of resources.

The purchase of a single microcomputer system, together with software to carry out a particular function, could be regarded as a small project with limited demands on the expertise of qualified staff. If, on the other hand, the proposal is for a local-area network of some size, the project would immediately grow in size and would require greater resources, both human and financial. The implications for project management, resources allocation, etc., are correspondingly greater.

The use of appropriate personnel and their expertise for project development is advisable, and if such expertise is not available within the organization, consultants can be brought in, though at a cost. The choice of project staff, including consultants, can be critical, and any increase in the complexity of the project puts greater demands on project management.

'Appropriate personnel' in this case must include those staff who will ultimately operate the new system and who will be called upon, on occasion, to explain it to users. They or their representatives must be involved at an early stage in discussions and investigations, so that their views on actual operating practice can be taken into account. In addition, their involvement in the planning process will go a long way towards allaying any fears over automation and will ensure that staff are aware of the reasons behind the decision to automate.

This **participative approach** to the development of computer systems may well require a change in management attitudes towards staff (which in itself may be considered a good thing) but which may be difficult to bring about. It requires management to recognize that the staff who will be working on a daily basis with the system have a valuable input to the project and have the ability to contribute usefully. Of course, it also requires staff to accept the responsibility that goes with system design and implementation, and it must be acknowledged that not all staff will be willing to accept that responsibility.

Such an approach, which has been advocated by Enid Mumford for some years [2], has had a number of notable successes, in that effective systems have been designed by the personnel most involved, on the basis of their expert knowledge of particular aspects of the task(s). It is also an approach which takes into account the human and social aspects of designing effective automated systems, rather than concentrating on the purely technical and administrative [3].

10.1.1 The phased approach

Normally it is necessary to move from the initial idea towards a realization of that idea, and one method that has been used successfully in data processing applications is the phased approach. Individual techniques may differ, but the approach described below has been successful in the past. The main phases of the project include the following aspects.

10.1.1.1 The initial study

This is a fairly rapid look at the whole project to consider the overall requirements, how the system might work, any staffing implications, time-scales, and the costs and benefits. It will result in a plan for the rest of the project being drawn up, plus a detailed plan for the next phase. The final decision will be made on whether or not to carry on: if it is decided to drop the project at this stage (because, for example, the benefits are insufficient), the minimum of resources have been used, with minimal waste of time.

10.1.1.2 Analysis of requirements

The definition of requirements will vary in detail depending on the application. Much detail will be required of very complex or large-scale applications, for example, and this definition will be used to build the system. If the application is less complicated, the definition may be a more loosely constructed document. In either case, the planning process will be updated at the end of this phase to provide a detailed plan for the next phase and for the rest of the project. A specification of requirements will be agreed and a decision taken on whether to continue the project.

10.1.1.3 Design

At this stage, a decision will be made on how to construct the system. Theoretically, the possible approaches are:

1. a custom-built system;
2. in-house development;
3. a *turnkey* system (a complete package of hardware and software designed to operate together);
4. off-the-shelf hardware and software.

Using off-the-shelf software is the only realistic choice in most cases, although turnkey systems are a viable alternative.

It is possible that some modifications to the earlier definition of requirements will now have to be made, perhaps because of design constraints or because a particular software package seems to satisfy most, but not all, of the requirements. This feedback process may be repeated several times before a final conclusion on the best design is reached. At this stage, the planning for the project can be updated and a detailed plan for the construction phase drawn up.

The design specification, costings and forward planning will ideally be considered by a committee representing the interested parties, including those involved in maintenance and operation, and those who may require information from the system, such as auditors. Even at this stage, a decision can be made to abandon the project, based on the best available information, before committing resources to building the system itself.

10.1.1.4 Construction

Once construction has begun, it is unlikely (and largely undesirable) that **major** changes will be made to the requirements: any important ones will have to be made through a formal procedure. The complexity of this phase will depend on the size of the project, and particularly on whether a specific software system has to be implemented. Since we are suggesting that off-the-shelf software is the most appropriate route, this stage may be rather simple: the software will be implemented on the hardware acquired for the task. Precisely how simple this is will depend to a large extent on the previous planning, analysis and design phases.

The system will then have to be thoroughly tested and proved to be acceptable, while maintenance procedures will be investigated. There are two possible types of maintenance: that which deals with any required changes as soon as possible in order to keep the system operational, and that which simply makes necessary changes which are not, however, time-critical.

In many applications, of course, acquisition and successful installation of hardware and software is only the first stage: the development of a database, for example, requires further work in the design of a record structure which contains all the appropriate fields, ensures that the necessary terms are indexed, and so on. A successful approach to this aspect is **prototyping**, in which an initial suggestion is rapidly implemented, tested, revised in the light of feedback and then tested again [4]. With prototyping, the original model may be successively modified until acceptable, or the original may eventually be thrown out in favour of a better design: the purpose of prototyping is to be flexible in order to achieve the most effective application. Prototyping also has the advantage that a suggested implementation is produced very quickly, so that all concerned can see results and see that progress is being made: it also gives staff the opportunity to comment further on the development of the project and to be intimately involved in its design.

10.1.2 Implementation

There are two ways in which the new automated system can be implemented, and the choice is dependent largely on the application itself. In some cases, it may be necessary to switch over to the new system completely and in one move, since to try to operate a partially automated and partially manual system will prove to be confusing and error-prone.

The alternative is to convert important or major areas of the application and to work on the remaining areas as and when it is convenient, albeit to a planned programme. Two systems will then operate in tandem, with the manual element gradually decreasing: this is a common method of implementing an online catalogue, and is suitable for such applications, i.e. those that can be conveniently divided in this way. An automated catalogue, for example, could be implemented for the most used items, as identified from a study of the circulation system. Alternatively, the division could be chronological, in that from a given date all new items will be added to the online catalogue and not to the old card catalogue. This could be augmented by a retrospective programme to include the records for in-demand items or some other suitable category of records [5].

Certain applications, however, will not be amenable to this approach. Intuitively at least, it seems that circulation control would be a cumbersome system if it were only partly automated, and this appears as a case for a complete 'switch over' at a predetermined date, once the appropriate data files for bibliographic and user records had been completed.

The size of the task, i.e. the quantity of material to be converted, will often be a major factor in any decisions at this point. The need to run two systems in parallel (possibly for some time) will have to be balanced against the time taken to prepare all records and materials for a once-only conversion. In addition, it will be necessary to arrange and implement staff training and to prepare operations manuals (see below).

In the foregoing, of course, we have only considered implementation from the standpoint of the new user who is converting manual systems to a system operated by microcomputer. However, in the ten years or so in which microcomputers have been used in LIS, many have had to face the prospect of converting existing files in order to use more up-to-date hardware or software. This may have been a particular problem for anyone who began microcomputer-based systems before the advent of MS-DOS, for example. These pioneers, having spent considerable time in developing their systems, have had to consider 'migrating' to the industry standard and in the process converting existing files. This may not always have been easy, since earlier software may not have created ASCII files, which make data transfer considerably easier, since such files can normally be read by modern software. There is no easy answer to this problem: in some instances it may not be possible, and all files will have to be re-keyed. The advice and assistance of a computer department or centre within the parent authority may be the only solution which can be suggested, since much will depend on the original software and hardware [6].

10.2 DATA SECURITY

Data security, in our context, has two aspects, namely the physical means by which damage to, and loss of, data can be minimized, and the control of access to data or parts of data files.

10.2.1 Physical security

As we have already suggested, it is axiomatic that regular back-up copies of data files are made, to ensure that data are not accidentally lost, and some of the appropriate techniques were considered in section 9.2.2. However, it is also important to develop a **policy** for making back-up copies and to ensure that this policy is adhered to.

Generally speaking, a data file should be copied to a back-up file whenever new data are entered or existing data are amended in any way. Therefore, circulation control records should be backed-up every day: databases, online catalogues and similar files, if they are not amended daily, do not require such frequent copying. Whether this is always feasible may depend on how quickly and easily it can be done, but it is the ideal which should be aimed for, and a set time should be set aside for the procedure. It should be a matter of policy that both master and back-up are clearly marked as such, and both should be kept securely when not in use, preferably in different locations. Both locations, however, should be conveniently accessible to the operator or whoever is responsible for starting up the system. As a rule, everything possible should be done to make it easy to make **authorized** back-up copies of data files and thus to encourage adherence to the policy.

Storage locations for both master and back-up copies should be fireproof metal containers, sited away from sources of electromagnetic fields. Master copies of programs can be labelled as only for use in providing working copies, and it is advisable to restrict access to master copies to individuals who can authorize the making of copies as required – and who are familiar with the relevant process: it is not unknown for master copies to be overwritten with the wrong files!

It must be emphasized, however, that security should not be so complex and time-consuming as to discourage the making of back-up files: if it is, they will not be made, with disastrous results when the system crashes, as it certainly will one day.

10.2.2 Security of access

It may be necessary to restrict access to files or parts of records for various reasons, depending largely on the nature of the file. Some information will be obviously confidential (personnel records, for example), in which case access must be restricted to those whose job it is to administer those records. At the other extreme are publicly available records which everyone may **access**, but where it is necessary to restrict unauthorized **amendments**. The online catalogue is an obvious example of the latter: users and staff alike must be able to consult entries, but only staff (and possibly only cataloguing staff) will be authorized to make amendments to the records.

There will also be records of which only part of the data could be regarded as confidential (or not for public access). An accessions file is of interest to users, informing them of titles on order or recently received, but it may be thought necessary to prevent access to ordering details such as supplier, order number, budget heading, etc.

It must also be remembered that certain files (including circulation control records) are covered by the Data Protection Act in the UK, and it will be necessary to have clear policies on who is authorized to consult these records and to make changes to them.

Unfortunately, adequate security is not always possible with many inexpensive programs: often the only control will be a password which, once known, provides access to the entire file. Provided that passwords are kept confidential and changed regularly (which is good policy) this may be sufficient. The library-specific software discussed earlier normally takes this problem into account and in general the security provided is appropriate to the files.

Passwords, when used, should be chosen with care, in order to avoid obvious words or numbers which could easily be deduced by those with a desire to beat the system, and they must not be of a type which could be keyed accidentally. The best choice may be a totally random one, though one which operators can remember without having it pasted up on the wall beside the terminal!

It is perhaps easy to become over-conscious of security, but these files represent a considerable investment in time and money, and it is not difficult to picture the chaos which would arise if users were free to amend catalogue entries or issue system records, quite apart from the question of confidential files such as personnel records. The major problems will be with accidental access and the malicious attempt to cause confusion: the first can be prevented with little difficulty and some care, while the latter can be deterred sufficiently with standard methods which do not make life difficult to authorized personnel.

Policies to control access have also taken on additional importance with the spread of computer viruses, discussed in Chapter 7.

10.3 DOCUMENTATION OF OPERATIONS

While both the software and the hardware will come with appropriate documentation (i.e. manuals on their operation), it will be necessary to draw up operating instructions for the staff who will be using the new automated system. These instructions do not have to duplicate the supplier's or manufacturer's documentation, except where absolutely necessary, but they do have to cover all day-to-day operations as they relate to the specific library or information service.

Ideally, these operating instructions should be drawn up as far in advance as possible and distributed to all the relevant staff *before* the new system is operational. This will give staff time to assimilate the instructions, to clarify points of uncertainty and to gain at least an impression of the changes the new system will bring about. This last point is also an important factor in staff training: as we suggested above, involvement of staff from the start is a significant aid to successful implementation.

One important function of the operating instructions will be to clarify any new terms and jargon which the system introduces, and to ensure that everyone concerned is clear about their meanings.

Operating instructions will apply the system documentation to specific operations. Naturally, relevant examples from daily practice should be used, and these examples should be detailed. They should proceed in a step-by-step manner through each operation or routine, so that staff can follow the routine easily. No doubt, in time, experienced staff will be able to dispense with large parts of the instructions, but they must be retained, not only for new staff, but also for reference by experienced personnel.

While the operating instructions must be seen as authoritative, they should not be seen as sacrosanct tablets of stone. Once the system is up and running, day-to-day experience will rapidly find any faults that might exist, and may indicate a better way of doing things. While there is a fine line between a genuine improvement and non-constructive criticism stemming from an undesirable dislike or fear of the system, there should be a feedback mechanism whereby improvements and constructive comment can be assessed and implemented – and, of course, incorporated in the operating instructions. This ability to gain useful feedback is a key feature of the prototyping design method outlined earlier.

In order that this feedback can operate effectively, it is useful to define an introductory period during which the new system may be regarded as settling in (the **shake-down** period). During this time, operations will be carefully monitored, and improvements made through the feedback system will be adopted. It will, therefore, be a disturbing time for all concerned, as practices may change at intervals, just as staff are getting used to them. The shake-down period must therefore be clearly defined, and staff should be encouraged not simply to accept the new system 'warts and all', but actively to study what they are doing. They will then be playing a constructive part in the development of the system, and will be aware that their opinions are regarded as valuable.

The LIS manager must also accept that during this period, productivity (however it is measured) will decline: hopefully, this decline will not last too long, but it will cause concern among staff.

The whole process of drawing up the operating instructions and modifying parts of them may be the responsibility of one person or a number of section heads, depending on the size of the application(s). In the latter case, there should be a clear line of communication between staff operating the system and those above them, so that comments and instructions flow freely. Ideally, it should be the responsibility of one person to prepare and distribute operating instructions and any amendments, since this will ensure a standard presentation which will make instructions easier to follow. Equally, it means that there is a single individual to whom feedback should be addressed, though it will be that person's responsibility to ensure that comments, etc., are passed to the appropriate individual. Properly handled, this should not lead to any undue delay, though the individual will have to be given both the time and the authority necessary for the position.

Whilst smaller services, or those implementing only one or two applications, may not need to go to such lengths, the general principle remains valid: clear documentation with a feedback mechanism for the adoption of constructive suggestions. We can only emphasize that the prototyping approach incorporates mechanisms to ensure that this is the case.

An over-riding concern must be to prevent any outbreak of the well-known syndrome of 'blaming it on the computer', 'it' being any fault, mistake or delay that occurs. Other than mechanical breakdown, faults and errors in computers are usually caused by human beings. Outbreaks of the syndrome are best prevented by open communications and the active involvement of all concerned, together with a clear presentation of day-to-day procedures.

10.4 STAFF TRAINING

One way to prevent outbreaks of this syndrome is through proper training of staff. Obviously, staff will have to be instructed in the use of the new system, be it word processing or a full-scale online catalogue, but the training should extend to developing an understanding of why things are done this way and how they will contribute to greater effectiveness and efficiency, time-saving and an improved service. Research from commerce and industry indicates that a Taylorian approach to automation, in which staff are reduced to pushing buttons because that is what they are told they should do, generally results in less effective and efficient systems, reduced productivity, etc. In contrast to this approach, the same research suggests that, where staff are able to see 'the whole picture', and their part within it (and have been involved in its design and implementation), the gains to be made are considerable [7].

Training given by the software and hardware suppliers will tend, by its very nature, to be at a general level, and in-house training will have to cover all the specific relevant aspects. The precise approach may vary, depending on the application. A word processing program is best learned in use, once the basic procedures have been mastered. Staff using it should be encouraged to experiment and practise with it, and all due allowance should be made for mistakes (in the early days, at least!).

This approach will not be suitable for large-scale routines such as circulation control or an online catalogue. Since staff must be fully acquainted with the operation of such systems before they are implemented, this will mean (a) that those carrying out the training must be well-versed in its operation beforehand, and (b) that some time will have to be set aside for regular training sessions – with all that that entails for the continued operation of the service.

A change-over date must be established, but this should not be regarded as fixed, since the progress of training may indicate that it should be put back or brought forward.

Training must cover all the relevant operations in a logical order, and there should be opportunity for staff to practise each operation as it is taught or demonstrated. The training period will also provide a further and early opportunity to assess the new system and its operation, and any feedback from staff should be studied carefully before preparing the operating instructions.

It will be useful if practical training can be preceded by a consideration of why it was felt necessary to automate. This need not be lengthy, since staff should have been involved from an early stage in the investigations, etc. Some time may have elapsed between the initial investigation and the arrival of the hardware and software, however, and a repetition of the 'philosophy' will be a useful reminder, as well as necessary background for new staff. It will also help to focus attention on the training and to provide a basis from which useful comment can be made.

Software for information retrieval and library applications

This is a list of the software available at the time of writing for information retrieval and for various library routines. It should not be regarded as definitive, since new software is being developed and introduced at regular intervals, and some programs may have been missed (the authors would be happy to learn of any software not included here). The list does not include the innumerable business programs which can also be used in libraries and which are considered in Chapters 3–6, but further details of such software can be obtained from the sources discussed in Chapter 8.

Each entry contains, as far as possible, details of the hardware on which the program runs, the name and address of a supplier and an indication of the cost. Where they are given, prices do not include VAT or the cost of carriage, postage, etc., and the full price should obviously be checked with the supplier at the time of investigation.

Further details of software for library and information retrieval applications can be found in Hilary Gates' directory of microcomputer software, and the directory of text retrieval software published by the Institute of Information Scientists, both of which are listed in the Bibliography.

A.1 INTEGRATED SYSTEMS

Bookshelf
Specialist Computer Systems and Software Ltd, Goodson Street, Henley, ST1 2AT. PICK operating system. Suite of five modules for library housekeeping, available in various configurations for 1–3 users up to 250 users.

CALM (Computer Aided Library Management)
Pyramid Computer Systems Ltd, 9 Church Street, Reading RG1 2SB. From £750 per module. IBM XT and AT and compatibles, Televideo PM-16. Integrated software packages with six modules, including thesaurus development.

CARS/CLASS
(See entries under Cataloguing and Circulation control, sections A.4 and A.5)

LICON Library Control System
Floyd Radcliffe, 2 The Crescent, Leatherhead KT22 8EE. Five modules. IBM and compatibles.

SAILS (Swets Automated Independent Library System)
Swets (UK) Ltd, Cranbook House, 287–291 Banbury Road, Oxford OX2 2JQ. Integrated set of modules (acquisitions, cataloguing, serials control, circulation control) designed for mainframe operation, but can be used with microcomputers as front-end terminals.

Sydney System
Soutron Ltd, Plessey Business Park, Technology Drive, Beeston, Nottingham NG9 2ND. Base price £1500. IBM PC and PS/2. Seven modules.

A.2 INFORMATION RETRIEVAL

Aquila
Kent Barlow Information Associates, 250 Kings Road, London SW3 5UE. £310. Can also be interfaced with some commercial databases; interface modules are extra.

ASSASSIN-PC
MGS Computing Services, 132/133 Fairlie Road, Slough SL1 4PY. IBM PC. Program derived from ASSASSIN minicomputer software; price includes all hardware.

BRS Search
BRS Europe, 26 Little Portland Street, London W1N 5AF. 16-bit systems with Unix.

Eagle
Kent Barlow Information Associates, 250 Kings Road, London SW3 5UE. RM 380Z, Apple II, CP/M, 16-bit systems. Uses the Common Command Language for searching.

i
Information Systems Design, 23 Arthur Road, Erdington, Birmingham B24 9EX. Apricot range of microcomputers. £295. Can be bought integrated with Circ (see section A.5, Circulation control).

InMagic
Head Computers Ltd, Oxted Mill, Spring Lane, Oxted RH8 9PB. From £790. MS-DOS.

MicroCAIRS
RTZ Computer Services Ltd, 1 Redcliff Street, Bristol BS99 7JS. Many 16-bit microcomputers with minimum 10 Mb hard disk.

Micro-STATUS
AERE, Marketing and Sales, Building 329, Harwell OX11 0RA. Fortune 32: 16, IBM PC.

Mirabilis
Central Information Services, University of London, Senate House, Malet Street, London WC1E 7HU. £250. A development of the FIRS program.

PRIMATE

Institute for Scientific Information, 132 High St, Uxbridge, Middlesex UB8 1DP. A complete hardware/software system, also capable of word processing and accessing online data bases.

SCIMATE

CITECH Ltd, PO Box 5, Ickenham, Middlesex UB10 8AF.

Strix

Delta Design and Graphics, The Old Stud Farm House, Ossington Lane, Sutton on Trent, Newark. Southwest Technical Products S/09; £950 (£1045 with retrieval software for microfilm reader). Includes facilities for retrieval of documents stored on microfilm.

A.3 ACQUISITIONS

(See also Integrated systems (section A.1) for packages with acquisitions module)

Bookline

Blackwell's Technical Services, Beaver House, Hythe Bridge Street, Oxford OX1 2ET. DEC Professional 350; £13 857 (£16 857 with PEARL: see Serials control, section A.7). Hardware software package with 5 Mb hard disk. Can interface with Blackwell's Bookfile, though user is not required to use Blackwell as supplier.

A.4 CATALOGUING

(See also Integrated systems (section A.1) for packages with cataloguing module)

CARS

G + G Software, Old Cider House, Golant, Fowey, Cornwall. System in use at Mid-Cornwall College of FE.

A.5 CIRCULATION CONTROL

(See also Integrated systems (section A.1) for packages with circulation control module)

Circ

Information Systems Design, 23 Arthur Road, Erdington, Birmingham B24 9EX. Apricot range of microcomputers. £995. Can be bought in integrated system with 'i' package for information retrieval (see Information retrieval, section A.2).

CLASS

G + G Software, Old Cider House, Golant, Fowey, Cornwall.

A.6 ONLINE SEARCH ASSISTANCE

Connect
Learned Information (Europe) Ltd, Besselsleigh Road, Abingdon, Oxford OX13 6LG. MS-DOS, PC-DOS.

CORTEX
British Library Bibliographic Services Division, 2 Sheraton Street, London WC1V 0BE. Used to down-load records from MARC files for local editing.

DataLink
CL Systems Inc., 81 Norwood Avenue, Newtonville, Massachusetts 02160. Offers assistance in accessing both CLSI-based files and selected IAC databases, using the latter's SEARCH HELPER. Searches are formulated on a microcomputer.

HeadForm
Head Computers, Oxted Mill, Spring Lane, Oxted, Surrey RH8 9PB. £125. MS-DOS systems. Format conversion software for copy data from one program to another. Will also handle down-loaded records from online databases.

Headline
Head Computers, Oxted Mill, Spring Lane, Oxted, Surrey RH8 9PB. MS-DOS; £120.

Liaison
CAPTEC Ltd, 3 St James' Terrace, Malahide, Co. Dublin. IBM PC, Sanyo 555 and other MS-DOS microcomputers. £280.

Micro Search
ERIC Clearing House, 130 Huntingdon Hall, Syracuse University, Syracuse, NY 13210. A subscription includes floppy disks with subsets of the ERIC database.

OL'SAM (Online Search Assistance Machine)
Franklin Institute Research Laboratory, 20th and Race Streets, Philadelphia, PA 19103. Complete hardware/software package available at $7500.

Sci-Mate
ISI, 3501 Market Street, University Science Center, Philadelphia, PA 19104. IBM PC. Search assistance for Dialog, BRS, ISI and Medline. Optional Personal Data Manager allows user to set up own database of retrieved references.

Swift
Kent Barlow Information Associates, 250 Kings Road, London SW3 5UE.

Userlink
Userlink Systems Ltd, Mansion House Chambers, High Street, Stockport SK1 1EG. MS-DOS, PC-DOS. Range of programs includes Assist, Information Transfer (uses artificial intelligence techniques) and Userlink Junior (for log-on procedure).

A.7 SERIALS CONTROL

(See also Integrated systems (section A.1) for packages with serials control module)

MicroLinx Check-in
Faxon Company Inc., 15 Southwest Park, Westwood, MA 02090. IBM XT or AT. Pricing options available. Also has bar-code check-in facilities and a CD-ROM player and disk available.

OCLC SC350 Serials Control Module
OCLC Europe Ltd, Lloyds Bank Chambers, 75 Edmund Street, Birmingham B3 3HA. IBM PC and M300 Workstation. Links with OCLC online serials database.

PC-SMS (Serials Management System)
Dawson Serials Management Services, Cannon House, Folkestone CT19 5EE. IBM PC or compatibles. Online option also available. Single- and multi-user options.

PEARL
Blackwell Technical Services, Beaver House, Hythe Bridge Street, Oxford OX1 2ET. Hardware/software package including 5 Mb hard disk. Can be interfaced with Blackwell's periodicals network.

Organizations

This is a list of the principal organizations involved in the use of microcomputers for information retrieval and in libraries. Further information is also available from the Library Association's Bibliographic and Information Systems Officer.

Advisory Unit for Computer Based Education (AUCBE)
19 St Albans Road, Hatfield, Herts AL10 0HU. AUCBE was initially responsible for the development of the program MicroQUERY. It is also investigating the use of the microcomputer in school libraries in the region.

Aslib (The Association for Information Management)
20–24 Old Street, London EC1V 9AP. Aslib's library has details of software suitable for information retrieval etc.

British Computer Society
Information Officer, IEEE Library, Savoy Place, London. The Librarian offers an information service to BCS members.

Council for Educational Technology
3 Devonshire Street, London W1N 2BA. CET is closely involved in the development of telesoftware using PRESTEL.

Institute of Information Scientists
Organizes regular meetings, workshops, etc., on word processing and microcomputers, many of which are later reported in its newsletter.

Library and Information Technology Centre
Polytechnic of Central London, High Holborn, London WC1V 7DN. The Centre was opened in November 1982. Provides demonstrations and advice.

Library Association
Bibliographic and Information Systems Officer, 7 Ridgmount Street, London WC1E 7AE. The Officer is responsible for, among other things, activities connected with microcomputers, and maintains a list of contacts. There is also a New Technology Group of the Library Association.

National Computing Centre
Oxford Road, Manchester M1 7ED (Microcomputer Centre, 11 New Fetter Lane, London EC4A 1PU). NCC has investigated many aspects of micros and publishes a number of relevant books. The Microcomputer Centre offers advice and consultancy on the selection of hardware.

Scottish Council for Educational Technology
Dowan Hill, 74 Victoria Crescent Road, Glasgow G12 9JN. Like CET, SCET is involved in the development of telesoftware, and computers in schools.

An example of information retrieval using the FIRS system

The example of a microcomputer information retrieval system shown below uses the FIRS system from the University of London Central Information Service.

Each request for an online search is entered into the microcomputer and can be stored for future use. It is valuable to see, for example, if similar searches have been carried out in the past. A number of other questions can be put to the system to provide management information. The mode of operation of the system is essentially the same as a mainframe information retrieval system.

The FIRS system is now superseded, but the example serves to show the operation of a simple microcomputer information retrieval system.

C.1 CREATION OF A DATABASE

A) **FCREATE**   (*bold terms are entered at keyboard*)
         ** FIRS ** file creation and compaction program

Copyright © 1980, 1981 CIS, University of London.
Unauthorized copying is illegal.

** FIRS ** system serial number: CF 042

CREATE or COMPACT : **CREATE**
                    ** FIRS ** file creation program

Insert disk to receive new file in drive B – press 'return' when ready, (or <ESC> to abort):
Is it a new disk? – Y/N : **N**
The FIRS files on the disk in drive B are:

SLOG   .FRS LOG   .FRS   (*other existing files on disk*)

Do not use an existing FIRS file name

A file name consists of up to eight letters and/or digits.
The system will insert the appropriate suffixes (.FRS, .KEY, etc).

File name : **USERS**   *(database to be called 'USERS')*
Number of fields per record (1–15) : **13**

Field names:

Maximum length is 16 characters. They may contain any characters, including spaces. Any or all fields may be nameless (just key <RTN>).
If a field has a name, the name must be at least two characters in length.

Name of field 1 : **SRCH. NO.**
Name of field 2 : **STATUS**
Name of field 3 : **DATE**   *(fields in the database)*
Name of field 4 : **REQUESTOR**
Name of field 5 : **ADDRESS**
Name of field 6 : **TELEPHONE**
Name of field 7 : **TYPE OF ENQUIRER**
Name of field 8 : **AUTHORIZED BY**
Name of field 9 : **ALTERNATIVE ADDR**
Name of field 10 : **PAYMENT METHOD**
Name of field 11 : **SEARCH STRATEGY**
Name of field 12 : **HOSTS:DATABASES**
Name of field 13 : **NOTES**

Please confirm –

Field 1 is SRCH. NO.
Field 2 is STATUS
Field 3 is DATE
Field 4 is REQUESTOR
Field 5 is ADDRESS
Field 6 is TELEPHONE
Field 7 is TYPE OF ENQUIRER
Field 8 is AUTHORIZED BY
Field 9 is ALTERNATIVE ADDR
Field 10 is PAYMENT METHOD
Field 11 is SEARCH STRATEGY
Field 12 is HOSTS:DATABASES
Field 13 is NOTES

Please confirm – Y/N : **Y**   *(enter details of how fields are to be indexed)*

Which fields are to be indexed?

For each field which is to be indexed you will be asked whether it is to be indexed as NAME, as ENTRY or by TEXT WORDS.

Refer to manual for further details – if in doubt choose TEXT WORDS

Is field 1 SRCH. NO. to be indexed? – Y/N : **Y**
Is this field to be indexed as 'NAME' (N), 'ENTRY' (E) or by TEXT WORDS (W) : **E**
Is field 2 STATUS to be indexed? – Y/N : **Y**
Is this field to be indexed as 'NAME' (N), 'ENTRY' (E) or by TEXT WORDS (W) : **E**

Is field 3 DATE to be indexed? – Y/N : **Y**

Is this field to be indexed as 'NAME' (N), 'ENTRY' (E) or by TEXT WORDS (W) : **E**

Is field 4 REQUESTOR to be indexed? – Y/N : **Y**

Is this field to be indexed as 'NAME' (N), 'ENTRY' (E) or by TEXT WORDS (W) : **E**

Is field 5 ADDRESS to be indexed? – Y/N : **Y**

Is this field to be indexed as 'NAME' (N), 'ENTRY' (E) or by TEXT WORDS (W) : **W**

Is field 6 TELEPHONE to be indexed? – Y/N : **N**

Is field 7 TYPE OF ENQUIRER to be indexed? – Y/N : **Y**

Is this field to be indexed as 'NAME' (N), 'ENTRY' (E) or by TEXT WORDS (W) : **E**

Is field 8 AUTHORIZED BY to be indexed? – Y/N : **Y**

Is this field to be indexed as 'NAME' (N), 'ENTRY' (E) or by TEXT WORDS (W) : **E**

Is field 9 ALTERNATIVE ADDR to be indexed? – Y/N : **Y**

Is this field to be indexed as 'NAME' (N), 'ENTRY' (E) or by TEXT WORDS (W) : **W**

Is field 10 PAYMENT METHOD to be indexed? – Y/N : **Y**

Is this field to be indexed as 'NAME' (N), 'ENTRY' (E) or by TEXT WORDS (W) : **E**

Is field 11 SEARCH STRATEGY to be indexed? – Y/N : **Y**

Is this field to be indexed as 'NAME' (N), 'ENTRY' (E) or by TEXT WORDS (W) : **W**

Is field 12 HOSTS:DATABASES to be indexed? – Y/N : **Y**

Is this field to be indexed as 'NAME' (N), 'ENTRY' (E) or by TEXT WORDS (W) : **W**

Is field 13 NOTES to be indexed? – Y/N : **N**

Please confirm –

Field 1 SRCH. NO. is to be indexed as ENTRY
Field 2 STATUS is to be indexed as ENTRY
Field 3 DATE is to be indexed as ENTRY
Field 4 REQUESTOR is to be indexed as ENTRY
Field 5 ADDRESS is to be indexed as TEXT WORDS
Field 6 TELEPHONE is not indexed
Field 7 TYPE OF ENQUIRER is to be indexed as ENTRY
Field 8 AUTHORIZED BY is to be indexed as ENTRY
Field 9 ALTERNATIVE ADDR is to be indexed as TEXT WORDS
Field 10 PAYMENT METHOD is to be indexed as ENTRY
Field 11 SEARCH STRATEGY is to be indexed as TEXT WORDS
Field 12 HOSTS:DATABASES is to be indexed as TEXT WORDS
Field 13 NOTES not indexed

C.2 ENTER DATA RECORDS INTO DATABASE

A) **FTEXT**   *(enter database maintenance program)*
      ** FIRS ** Information retrieval system

** FIRS ** system serial number : CF 042

Data entry and editing program

Which disk drive are the files on – A or B : **B**

The FIRS files on this disk are –   *(This is the new database)*

SLOG   .FRS LOG   .FRS USERS   .FRS

File name (or (ESC)) : USERS

File USERS found

>   Field 1 is 'SRCH. NO.'
>   Field 2 is 'STATUS'
>   Field 3 is 'DATE'
>   Field 4 is 'REQUESTOR'
>   Field 5 is 'ADDRESS'
>   Field 6 is 'TELEPHONE'
>   Field 7 is 'TYPE OF ENQUIRER'
>   Field 8 is 'AUTHORIZED BY'
>   Field 9 is 'ALTERNATIVE ADDR'
>   Field 10 is 'PAYMENT METHOD'
>   Field 11 is 'SEARCH STRATEGY'
>   Field 12 is 'HOSTS:DATABASES'
>   Field 13 is 'NOTES'

There are 0 records in the file
Length of file : 3 blocks

(any key to continue)

Options –   Read   R
            Write   W
            Edit   E
            Change files   C
            Index   I
            Search   S
            Append   A
            Exit the system   X

Choice : **W**
*Write – please confirm ? – Y/N : **Y**

Type H for help, or <RETURN> to continue :   *(Enter first record)*
*(1)
SRCH. NO. : 0001
STATUS : 0   *(0 = ongoing)*
DATE : 830823
REQUESTOR : **BLOGGS, A**
ADDRESS : **PHYSICS**
TELEPHONE : 2378
TYPE OF ENQUIRER : **PG**   *(PG = postgraduate)*

AUTHORIZED BY : SMITH, DR B
ALTERNATIVE ADDR :
PAYMENT METHOD : DE
SEARCH STRATEGY : LASERS INFRA RED RAMAN
HOSTS:DATABASES : DIALOG INSPEC INFOLINE CHEMICAL ABSTRACTS
NOTES : SEND ACCOUNT TO SUPERVISOR
   ('R' for rewrite, <ESC>, any other key to continue)
*(2)
SRCH. NO. : 0002
STATUS : C   *(C = complete)*
DATE : 830825
REQUESTOR : JONES, E. F.
ADDRESS : ECONOMICS
TELEPHONE : 2856
TYPE OF ENQUIRER : ST   *(ST = Staff)*
AUTHORIZED BY : WHITE, PROF. E. F.
ALTERNATIVE ADDR : POLITICS
PAYMENT : RG
SEARCH STRATEGY : RELATIONS UNITED KINGDOM ARGENTINA FALK-
LAND ISLANDS
HOSTS:DATABASES : DATASTAR ECONOMIC ABSTRACTS INTERNATIONAL
DIALOG PAIS
NOTES : 75 ONLINE P OFFLINE PRINTS AWAITED   *(typing error)*
   ('R' for rewrite, <ESC>, any other key to continue)
**(2)
SRCH. NO. : 0002   *(Go through record to correct 'NOTES' field)*
STATUS : C
DATE : 830825
REQUESTOR : JONES, E. F.
ADDRESS : ECONOMICS
TELEPHONE : 2856
TYPE OF ENQUIRER : ST
AUTHORIZED BY : WHITE, PROF. E. F.
ALTERNATIVE ADDR : POLITICS
PAYMENT METHOD : RG
SEARCH STRATEGY : RELATIONS UNITED KINGDOM ARGENTINA
FALKLAND ISLANDS
HOSTS:DATABASES : DATASTAR ECONOMIC ABSTRACTS INTER-
NATIONAL DIALOG PAIS
NOTES : 75 OFFLINE PRINTS AWAITED, INVOICE TO RESEARCH
GRANT 123456   *(correct field)*
   ('R' for rewrite, <ESC>, any other key to continue)
*(3)
SRCH. NO. : 0003
STATUS : B   *(new record)*
DATE : 830821
REQUESTOR : JONES, E. F.
ADDRESS : ECONOMICS
TELEPHONE : 2856
TYPE OF ENQUIRER : ST
AUTHORIZED BY : HARRIS, PROF. D

ALTERNATIVE ADDR : **ECONOMICS**
PAYMENT METHOD : **DE**
SEARCH STRATEGY : **MONETARY POLICY INFLATION UNEMPLOYMENT**
HOSTS:DATABASES : **DATASTAR ECONOMICS ABSTRACTS INTERNATIONAL**
NOTES : **COST £25.23**
   ('R' for rewrite, <**ESC**>, any other key to continue)

   Options –   Read   R
                    Write   W
                    Edit   E
                    Change files   C
                    Index   I
                    Search   S
                    Append   A
                    Exit the system   X

   Choice : I
*Index – please confirm – Y/N : **Y**   *(now index records, i.e. create inverted index)*

Loading indexing program

                  ** FIRS ** Indexing program

Copyright © 1980, 1981, 1982 CIS, University of London.
Unauthorized copying is illegal.

** FIRS ** system serial number : CF 042

Please indicate diagnostic display required – full, partial or none
Enter F, P or N : **P**
Which disk drive is the file on – A or B : **B**
Remove system disk from drive A, insert spare disk
Press (return) when ready

The FIRS files on this disk are –

SLOG   .FRS LOG   .FRS   USERS   .FRS

FILENAME : **USERS**

File USERS found

There are 3 records in the file.

Records edited since last index run :   0
Records deleted since last index run :   0

New records written :   3

Generate complete index – please confirm – Y/N : **Y**
   (memory 16996 bytes.)

* (B)
* Sorting (55 words).
* Sorted.

* Merging – pass 1
   (memory 13248 bytes.)

* 1 0001 (1)
* 2 0002 (1)
* 3 0003 (1)
* 4 830821 (1)
* 5 830823 (1)
* 6 830825 (1)
* 7 ABSTRACTS (3)
* 8 ARGENTINA (1)
* 9 B (1)
* 10 BLOGGS A (1)
* 11 C (1)
* 12 CHEMICAL (1)
* 13 DATASTAR (2)
* 14 DE (2)
* 15 DIALOG (2)
* 16 ECONOMIC O (1)
* 17 ECONOMICS (3)
* 18 FALKLAND (1)
* 19 HARRIS PROF D (1)
* 20 INFLATION (1)
* 21 INFOLINE (1)
* 22 INFRA (1)
* 23 INSPEC (1)
* 24 INTERNATIONAL (2)
* 25 ISLANDS (1)
* 26 JONES E F (2)
* 27 KINGDOM (1)
* 28 LASERS (1)
* 29 MONETARY (1)
* 30 O (1)
* 31 PAIS (1)
* 32 PG (1)
* 33 PHYSICS (1)
* 34 POLICY (1)
* 35 POLITICS (1)
* 36 RAMAN (1)
* 37 RED (1)
* 38 RELATIONS (1)
* 39 RG (1)
* 40 SMITH DR B (1)
* 41 ST (2)
* 42 UNEMPLOYMENT (1)
* 43 UNITED (1)
* 44 WHITE PROF E F (1)
* End of merge. 4 words in index.

* Copying main index
* Copy complete
* Copying postings file
  (1 blocks)

Output postings : 53
* Copy complete

Indexing complete

C.3 SEARCHING THE DATABASE

A) **FSEARCH**   *(enter this to call up search program)*

       ** FIRS ** Search program

Copyright (C) 1980, 1981, 1982 CIS, University of London
Unauthorized copying is illegal.

Which disk drive is the file on – A or B : **B**

The FIRS files on this disk are –

SLOG   .FRS LOG   .FRS USERS   .FRS

FILENAME (or <ESC>) : **USERS**

File USERS found

Field 1 SRCH. NO. is indexed as 'entry'.'
Field 2 STATUS is indexed as 'entry'.
Field 3 DATE is indexed as 'entry'.
Field 4 REQUESTOR is indexed as 'entry'.
Field 5 ADDRESS is indexed as text words.
Field 6 TELEPHONE is not indexed.
Field 7 TYPE OF ENQUIRER is indexed as 'entry'.
Field 8 AUTHORIZED BY is indexed as 'entry'.
Field 9 ALTERNATIVE ADDR is indexed as text words.
Field 10 PAYMENT METHOD is indexed as 'entry'.
Field 11 SEARCH STRATEGY is indexed as text words.
Field 12 HOSTS:DATABASES is indexed as test words.
Field 13 NOTES is not indexed.
There are 3 records in the file

Index contains 45 terms

* **S LASER:**   *(search for the word 'LASER' but truncated on the right, colon is the truncation symbol)*

* Searching

LASERS (1)   *(one record found)*

* Total LASER :   1

Total : S1 : LASER : (1)

* **P**   *(Enter 'P' to see the record)*
Set number : 1
The options are Print All (P) or Display (D)

'P' will print postings, in reverse order.
'D' will display one record at a time and await a further command.

Enter 'P' or 'D' : **D**
*(1)
0001
0
830823

BLOGGS, A   *(record displayed)*
PHYSICS
2378
PG
SMITH, DR B
DE

LASERS INFRA RED RAMAN
DIALOG INSPEC INFOLINE CHEMICAL ABSTRACTS
SEND ACCOUNT TO SUPERVISOR
   ('K' to keep, <ESC>, or any **other key** to continue)

* **S JONES-E-F\RE**   *(searching for 'E.F.JONES' as a 'REQUESTOR')*

* *Searching*

JONES E F   (2)

(Total : S8 : JONES-E-F\RE (2)   *(2 records found)*

* **P**
Set number : **8**
The options are Print All (P) or Display (D)
'P' will print postings, in reverse order.
'D' will display one record at a time and await a further command.

Enter 'P' or 'D' : **D**
* (3)
0003
B
830821
JONES, E.F.
ECONOMICS
2856
ST
HARRIS, PROF. D
ECONOMICS
DE
MONETARY POLICY INFLATION UNEMPLOYMENT
DATASTAR ECONOMICS ABSTRACTS INTERNATIONAL
COST #25.23
   ('K' to keep, <ESC>, or any other key to continue)
* (2)
0002
C
830825
JONES, E.F.
ECONOMICS
2856

ST
WHITE, PROF. E.F.
POLITICS
RG
RELATIONS UNITED KINGDOM ARGENTINA FALKLAND ISLANDS
DATASTAR ECONOMIC ABSTRACTS INTERNATIONAL DIALOG PAIS
75 OFFLINE PRINTS AWAITED, INVOICE TO RESEARCH GRANT 123456
  ('K' to keep, <ESC>, or any other key to continue)

* **S C** \ ST   *(searching for all 'completed' searches)*
                                       ('C' in the 'ST' or 'STATUS' field)

* Searching

C   (1)

Total : S9 : C \ ST   (1)

* P
Set number : 9
The options are Print All (P) or Display (D)

'P' will print postings, in reverse order.
'D' will display one record at a time and await a further command.

Enter 'P' or 'D' : D
*(2)
0002
C
830825
JONES, E.F.
ECONOMICS
2856
ST
WHITE, PROF. E.F.
POLITICS
RG
RELATIONS UNITED KINGDOM ARGENTINA FALKLAND ISLANDS
DATASTAR ECONOMIC ABSTRACTS INTERNATIONAL DIALOG PAIS
75 OFFLINE PRINTS AWAITED, INVOICE TO RESEARCH GRANT 123456
  ('K' to keep, <EXC>, or any other key to continue)

* **S FALKLAND AND ISLANDS** *(search for 'FALKLAND' together with 'ISLANDS')*
* Searching

FALKLAND   (1)
ISLANDS   (1)

Total : S10 : FALKLAND and ISLANDS (1)
* **P**
Set number : 10
The options are 'Print All (P) or Display (D)

'P' will print postings, in reverse order.
'D' will display one record at a time and await a further command.

Enter 'P' or 'D' : D

*(2)
0002
C
830825
JONES, E.F.
ECONOMICS
2856
ST
WHITE, PROF. E.F.
POLITICS
RG
RELATIONS UNITED KINGDOM ARGENTINA FALKLAND ISLANDS
DATASTAR ECONOMIC ABSTRACTS INTERNATIONAL DIALOG PAIS
75 OFFLINE PRINTS AWAITED, INVOICE TO RESEARCH GRANT 123456
 ('K' to keep, <ESC>, or any other key to continue)

* **C**   *(enter 'C' to exit from the retrieval program)*
Close – please confirm – Y/N : **Y**

References

Chapter 5

1. Malmberg, H.-E. (1987) PERCICO, a new user-friendly system for periodicals control and circulation. In *The Application of Micro-computers in Information, Documentation and Libraries* (eds K.-D. Lehmann and H. Strohl-Goebel), North-Holland, Amsterdam, pp. 131–3.
2. Satyanarayana, V. V. V. (1987) Microcomputer based union catalogue of periodical holdings: BHEL experience. In *The Application of Micro-computers in Information, Documentation and Libraries* (eds K.-D. Lehmann and H. Strohl-Goebel), North-Holland, Amsterdam, pp. 117–19.
3. Atton, C. F. (1987) The SPRIG union catalogue of periodicals on dBase III. *Program*, **21** (4), 376–8.
4. Williams, T. (1987) Serials control and the microcomputer in the library. In *The Application of Micro-computers in Information Documentation and Libraries* (eds K.-D. Lehmann and H. Strohl-Goebel), North-Holland, Amsterdam, pp. 690–4.
5. Rees, H. (1989) CLASS and CARS: the CFE Plymouth experience. In *MS-DOS Software for Library and Information Applications* (ed. P. F. Burton), Gower, Aldershot, pp. 61–77.
6. Taylor, D. (1985) Progress with G&G software: an update on Harper Adams Agricultural College library's computerisation program. *Library Micromation News*, **8**, 3–6.
7. Mitev, N., Venner, G. M. and Walker, S. (1985) *Designing an Online Public Access Catalogue*, LIR Report No. 39, British Library, London.
8. Walker, S. (1988) Improving subject access painlessly: recent work on the Okapi online catalogue projects. *Program*, **22** (1), 21–31.
9. Cochrane, P. A. (1985) *Redesign of Catalogs and Indexes for Improved Online Subject Access: Selected Papers of Pauline A. Cochrane*, Oryx Press, Phoenix, Arizona.
10. Powne, C. (1987) First experiences with Bookshelf at Fife Health Board. *Program*, **21** (3), 260–72.
11. Lancaster, F. W. (ed.) (1987) *What is User Friendly?*, University of Illinois Graduate School of Library and Information Science (Clinic on Library Applications of Data Processing, 1986).
12. Findlay, A. and Motherwell, S. (1987) Cataloguing to UK MARC records for the uninitiated using dBase III. *Program*, **21** (2), 124–33.

13. Sippings, G., Ramsden, H. and Turpie, G. (1987) *The Use of Information Technology by Information Services*, Aslib, London.
14. Miskin, C. (1989) Micro-CAIRS for a legal database service. In *MS-DOS Software for Library and Information Applications* (ed. P. F. Burton), Gower, Aldershot.
15. Manson, P. (1989) Integrated automated systems for cataloguing, circulation and acquisitions on microcomputers: an overview of functions and products on the UK market. *Program*, **23** (1), 1–12.
16. Beaumont, J. and Cox, J. P. (1989) *Retrospective Conversion: A Practical Guide for Libraries*, Meckler, London.
17. Kosa, G. A. (1987) Retrospective data conversion with or without the use of micro-computers. In *The Application of Micro-computers in Information, Documentation and Libraries* (eds K.-D. Lehmann and H. Strohl-Goebel), North-Holland, Amsterdam, pp. 229–36.
18. Rees, H. (1989) CLASS and CARS: the CFE Plymouth exprience. In *MS-DOS Software for Library and Information Applications* (ed. P. F. Burton), Gower, Aldershot, pp. 61–77.
19. Hays, K. M. (1987) Microcomputer support for retrospective conversion. In *The Application of Micro-computers in Information, Documentation and Libraries*, (eds K.-D. Lehmann and H. Strohl-Goebel), North-Holland, Amsterdam, pp. 643–8.
20. Miskin, C. (1989) Micro-CAIRS for a legal database service. In *MS-DOS Software for Library and Information Applications* (ed. P. F. Burton), Gower, Aldershot, pp. 39–57.
21. Batty, D. (1984) Microcomputers in index language design and development. *Microcomputers for Information Management*, **1** (4), 303–12.
22. Ashford, J. and Willett, P. (1988) *Text Retrieval and Document Databases*, Chartwell-Bratt, Bromley.
23. (Anon.) Play it again, Adonis. *Information Market*, **59**, 8 (1989).
24. Callow, M. (1985) Producing an index to legal periodicals in the Foreign and Commonwealth Office library using Cardbox. *Program*, **19** (3), 251–61.
25. Johnson, J. (1988) INFO: a Cardbox-plus index to sources of computer and telecommunications information. *Program*, **22** (2), 177–81.
26. Davies, J. (1989) Fangwel: a program to generate complex author bibliographies from a Cardbox-plus database. *Program*, **23** (2), 189–96.
27. Gallimore, A. (1988) Developing a microcomputer database for local company information. *Program*, **22** (3), 262–7.
28. Gadsden, S. R. and Adams, R. (1984) *The Administration of Interlending by Microcomputer*, LIR Report No. 30, British Library, London.
29. Noel-Lambot, F. and Somville, A. (1987) Using a microcomputer for the administration of the interlibrary loan, mainly requests for photocopies. In *The Application of Micro-computers in Information Documentation and Libraries* (eds K.-D. Lehmann and H. Strohl-Goebel), North-Holland, Amsterdam, pp. 200–8.
30. Marmion, D. (1989) *Essential Guide to the Library IBM PC. Volume 9: The OCLC Workstation*, Meckler, London, pp. 131–48.
31. Snell, M. J. and Duggua, H. (1985) Microtext: electronic blackboard, expert system or teaching package. *Library Micromation News*, **8**, 9–10.
32. Binkley, R. D. and Parrott, J. R. (1987) A reference-librarian model for

computer-aided library instruction. In *The Application of Micro-computers in Information Documentation and Libraries* (eds K.-D. Lehmann and H. Strohl-Goebel), North-Holland, Amsterdam, pp. 190–6.

Chapter 6

1. Rush, J. E. (1987) Automation support for the management function in libraries and information centres. In *The Application of Micro-computers in Information, Documentation and Libraries* (eds K.-D. Lehmann and H. Strohl-Goebel), North-Holland, Amsterdam, pp. 339–46.
2. Saye, J. D. and Wilt, C. C. (1986) Database management programs and decision making in libraries and information centres. In *Microcomputers for Library Decision Making: Issues, Trends and Applications* (eds P. Hernon and C. R. McClure), Ablex, Norwood, New Jersey, pp.118–29.
3. Devadason, F. J. (1987) Manpower planning for a library or an information centre: a microcomputer based operational and instructional system. In *The Application of Micro-computers in Information, Documentation and Libraries*, (eds K.-D. Lehmann and H. Strohl-Goebel), North-Holland, Amsterdam, pp. 354–61.
4. Jackson, L. S. and Aluri, R. (1987) Using dBase III to manage continuations. In *The Application of Micro-computers in Information, Documentation and Libraries* (eds K.-D. Lehmann and H. Strohl-Goebel), North-Holland, Amsterdam, pp.723–30.
5. Simpson, I. S. (1988) *Basic Statistics for Librarians*, 3rd ed., Bingley, London.
6. Hernon, P. (1986) Microcomputers for in-house data collection and research. In *Microcomputers for Library Decision Making: Issues, Trends and Applications* (eds P. Hernon and C. R. McClure), Ablex, Norwood, New Jersey, pp. 198–220.
7. Smith, N. R. (1987) Using the MULTIPLAN spreadsheet package to model online search costs. *Program*, **21** (2), 146–59.

Chapter 7

1. Burton, P. F. (1987) *Microcomputer Applications in Academic Libraries II*, LIR Report No. 60, British Library, London.
2. Shoolbred, M. (1986) Microcomputers for student use in academic libraries. *British Journal of Academic Librarianship*, **1** (3), 207–14.
3. Dodd, S. A. and Sanberg-Fox, A. M. (1985) *Cataloging Microcomputer Software Files: A Manual of Interpretation for AACR2*, American Library Association, Washington, DC.
4. *Anglo-American Cataloguing Rules* (1988) 2nd ed., 1988 revision. Library Association, London.

Chapter 8

1. Burton, P. F. (1987) *Microcomputer Applications in Academic Libraries II*, LIR Report No. 60, British Library, London.

2. Batt, C. (1988) *Information Technology in Public Libraries 1987*, Public Libraries Research Group, Winchester.
3. Sippings, G., Ramsden, H. and Turpie, G. (1987) *The Use of Information Technology by Information Services*, Aslib, London.
4. Trevelyan, A. and Rowat, M. (1983) *An Investigation of the Use of Systems Programs in Library Applications of Microcomputers*, LIR Report No. 12, British Library, London.
5. Hunter, E. (1982) *The ABC of BASIC: An Introduction to Programming for Librarians*, Bingley, London.
6. Davis, C. (1988) *Pascal Programming for Librarians*, Greenwood, London.
7. Burton, P. F. (1987) Microcomputers as innovation: policies for implementation in libraries and information services. *The Electronic Library*, **5** (4), 210–20.

Chapter 9

1. Eyre, J. (1989) A review of some significant developments in microcomputer hardware and software: their implications for selection. *Program*, **23** (2), 127–39.
2. MacMorrow, N. (1987) Do VDUs make you sick? *Aslib Proceedings*, **39** (3), 65–74; MacMorrow, N. (1987) Are you sitting comfortably. *Aslib Proceedings*, **39** (4), 97–105; Dyer, H. (1989) *Human Aspects of Library Automation*, Gower, Aldershot.
3. Buschman, J., Reilly, R. and Andrich, E. (1988) Smart barcoding in a small academic library. *Information Technology and Libraries*, **7** (3), 263–70.
4. Miller, R. B. (1988) Libraries and computers: disaster prevention and recovery. *Information Technology and Libraries*, **7** (4), 349–58.
5. Rouse, R. C. (1989) Printers for libraries: recent developments and selection criteria. *Program*, **23** (3), 269–75.

Chapter 10

1. Daniels, A. and Yeates, D. (1988) *Basic Systems Analysis*, 3rd edn, Pitman, London.
2. Mumford, E. (1983) Participative systems design: practice and theory. *Journal of Occupational Behaviour*, **4**, 47–57.
3. Burton, P. F. (1987) Microcomputers as innovation: policies for implementation in libraries and information services. *The Electronic Library*, **5** (4), 210–20.
4. Lazinger, S. S. and Shoval, P. (1987) *Prototyping a Microcomputer-based Online Library Catalog*, Occasional Papers No. 177, Graduate School of Library and Information Science, University of Illinois.
5. Beaumont, J. and Cox, J. P. (1989) *Retrospective Conversion: A Practical Guide for Libraries*, Meckler, London.
6. Vratny-Watts, J. and Valuaskas, E. J. (1989) Prospective conversion: data transfer between fossil and new microcomputer technologies in libraries. *Information Technology and Libraries*, **8** (1), 34–41.

7. Zuboff, S. (1988) *In the Age of the Smart Machine: the Future of Work and Power*, Heinemann, London.

Bibliography

Adams, R. (1986) *Information Technology and Libraries: A Future for Academic Libraries*, Chapman and Hall, London.

Adams, R. (1989) *Communication and Delivery Systems for Librarians*, Gower, Aldershot.

Anglo-American Cataloguing Rules (1988) 2nd ed., Library Association, London.

Ashford, J. and Willett, P. (1988) *Text Retrieval and Document Databases*, Chartwell-Bratt, Bromley.

Atton, C. F. (1987) The SPRIG union catalogue of periodicals on dBase III. *Program*, **21** (4), 376–8.

Batt, C. (1988) *Information Technology in Public Libraries 1987*, Public Libraries Research Group, Winchester.

Batty, D. (1984) Microcomputers in index language design and development. *Microcomputers for Information Management*, **1** (4), 303–12.

Beaumont, J. and Cox, J. P. (1989) *Retrospective Conversion: A Practical Guide for Libraries*, Meckler, London.

Beiser, K. (1987) *Essential Guide to dBase III+ in Libraries*, Meckler, London.

Bergen, C. (1988) *Instruments to Plague Us? Human Factors in the Management of Library Automation*, MCB, Bradford.

Binkley, R. D. and Parrott, J. R. (1987) A reference-librarian model for computer-aided library instruction. In *The Application of Micro-computers in Information, Documentation and Libraries* (eds K.-D. Lehmann and H. Strohl-Goebel), North-Holland, Amsterdam, pp. 190–6.

Burton, P. F. (1987) *Microcomputer Applications in Academic Libraries II*, LIR Report No. 60, British Library, London.

Burton, P. F. (1987) Microcomputers as innovation: policies for implementation in libraries and information services. *The Electronic Library*, **5** (4), 210–20.

Burton, P. F. (ed.) (1989) *MS-DOS Software for Library and Information Applications*, Gower, Aldershot.

Buschman, J., Reilly, R. and Andrich, E. (1988) Smart barcoding in a small academic library. *Information Technology and Libraries*, **7** (3), 263–70.

Callow, M. (1985) Producing an index to legal periodicals in the Foreign and Commonwealth Office library using Cardbox. *Program*, **19** (3), 251–61.

Clegg, C., Warr, P., Green, T., Mark, A., Kemp, N., Allison, G. and Langdalls, N. (1988) *People and Computers: How to Evaluate Your Company's New Technology*, Ellis Horwood, Chichester.

Cochrane, P. A. (1985) *Redesign of Catalogs and Indexes for Improved Online*

Subject Access: Selected Papers of Pauline A. Cochrane, Oryx Press, Phoenix, Arizona.

Daniels, A. and Yeates, D. (1987) *Basic Systems Analysis*, 3rd edn, Pitman, London.

Davies, J. (1989) Fangwel: a program to generate complex author bibliographies from a Cardbox-plus database. *Program*, **23** (2), 189–96.

Davis, C. (1988) *Pascal Programming for Librarians*, Greenwood, London.

Devadason, F. J. (1987) Manpower planning for a library or an information centre: a microcomputer based operational and instructional system. In *The Application of Micro-computers in Information, Documentation and Libraries* (eds K.-D. Lehmann and H. Strohl-Goebel), North-Holland, Amsterdam, pp. 354–61.

Dodd, S. A. and Sanberg-Fox, A. M. (1985) *Cataloging Microcomputer Software Files: A Manual of Interpretation for AACR2*, American Library Association, Washington, DC.

Dyer, H. and Gunson, A. (1988) *A Directory of Library and Information Retrieval Software for Microcomputers*, 3rd edn, Gower, Aldershot.

Dyer, H. (1989) *Human Aspects of Library Automation*, Gower, Aldershot.

Eyre, J. (1989) A review of some significant developments in microcomputer hardware and software: their implications for selection. *Program*, **23** (2), 127–39.

Findlay, A. and Motherwell, S. (1987) Cataloguing to UK MARC records for the uninitiated using dBase III. *Program*, **21** (2), 124–33.

Gadsden, S. R. and Adams, R. (1984) *The Administration of Interlending by Microcomputer*, LIR Report No. 30, British Library, London.

Gallimore, A. (1988) Developing a microcomputer database for local company information. *Program*, **22** (3), 262–7.

Hays, K. M. (1987) Microcomputer support for retrospective conversion. In *The Application of Micro-computers in Information, Documentation and Libraries* (eds K.-D. Lehmann and H. Strohl-Goebel), North-Holland, Amsterdam, pp. 643–8.

Hendley, T. (1985) *Videodiscs, Compact Discs and Digital Optical Discs*, Cimtech Publications, .

Hernon, P. (1986) Microcomputers for in-house data collection and research. In *Microcomputers for Library Decision Making: Issues, Trends and Applications* (eds P. Hernon and C. R. McClure), Ablex, Norwood, New Jersey, pp. 198–220.

Hernon, P. and McClure, C. R. (eds) (1986) *Microcomputers for Library Decision Making: Issues, Trends and Applications*, Ablex, Norwood, New Jersey.

Hunter, E. (1982) *The ABC of BASIC: An Introduction to Programming for Librarians*, Bingley, London.

Hunter, E. (1985) *Computerised Cataloguing*, Bingley, London.

Jackson, L. S. and Aluri, R. (1987) Using dBase III to manage continuations. In *The Application of Micro-computers in Information, Documentation and Libraries* (eds K.-D. Lehmann and H. Strohl-Goebel), North-Holland, Amsterdam, pp. 723–30.

Johnson, J. (1988) INFO: a Cardbox-plus index to sources of computer and telecommunications information. *Program*, **22** (2), 177–81.

Kilpatrick, T. L. (1987) *Microcomputers and Libraries: A Bibliographic Sourcebook*, Scarecrow Press.

Kimberley, R. (1987) *Text Retrieval: A Directory of Software*, 2nd edn, Gower, Aldershot.

Kosa, G. A. (1987) Retrospective data conversion with or without the use of micro-computers. In *The Application of Micro-computers in Information, Documentation and Libraries* (eds K.-D. Lehmann and H. Strohl-Goebel), North-Holland, Amsterdam, pp. 229–36.

Lancaster, F. W. (ed.) (1987) *What is User Friendly?* University of Illinois Graduate School of Library and Information Science (Clinic on Library Applications of Data Processing, 1986).

(Anon.) (1988) Laser printing for a variety of library applications. *Information Technology and Libraries*, **7** (1), 41–50.

Lazinger, S. S. and Shoval, P. (1987) *Prototyping a Microcomputer-based Online Library Catalog*, Occasional Papers No. 177, Graduate School of Library and Information Science, University of Illinois.

Leeves, J. (1989) *Library Systems: A Buyer's Guide*, 2nd edn, Gower, Aldershot.

Lehmann, K.-D. and Strohl-Goebel, H. (1987) *The Application of Micro-computers in Information, Documentation and Libraries*, Contemporary Topics in Information Transfer, Volume 4, North-Holland, Amsterdam.

MacMorrow, N. (1987) Do VDUs make you sick? *Aslib Proceedings*, **39** (3), 65–74.

MacMorrow, N. (1987) Are you sitting comfortably? *Aslib Proceedings*, **39** (4), 97–105.

Malmberg, H.-E. (1987) PERCICO, a new user-friendly system for periodicals control and circulation. In *The Application of Micro-computers in Information, Documentation and Libraries* (eds K.-D. Lehmann and H. Strohl-Goebel), North-Holland, Amsterdam, pp. 131–3.

Marmion, D. (1989) *Essential Guide to the Library IBM PC. Volume 9: The OCLC Workstation*, Meckler, London.

Manson, P. (1989) Integrated automated systems for cataloguing, circulation and acquisitions on microcomputers: an overview of functions and products on the UK market. *Program*, **23** (1), 1–12.

Miller, R. B. (1988) Libraries and computers: disaster prevention and recovery. *Information Technology and Libraries*, **7** (4), 349–58.

Miskin, C. (1989) Micro-CAIRS for a legal database service. In *MS-DOS Software for Library and Information Applications* (ed. P. F. Burton), Gower, Aldershot, pp. 39–57.

Mitev, N., Venner, G. M. and Walker, S. (1985) *Designing an Online Public Access Catalogue*, LIR Report No. 39, British Library, London.

Mumford, E. (1983) Participative systems design: practice and theory. *Journal of Occupational Behaviour*, **4**, 47–57.

Noel-Lambot, F. and Somville, A. (1987) Using a microcomputer for the administration of the interlibrary loan, mainly requests for photocopies. In *The Application of Micro-computers in Information, Documentation and Libraries* (eds K.-D. Lehmann and H. Strohl-Goebel), North-Holland, Amsterdam, pp. 200–8.

Powne, C. (1987) First experiences with Bookshelf at Fife Health Board. *Program*, **21** (3), 260–72.

Rees, H. (1989) CLASS and CARS: the CFE Plymouth experience. In *MS-DOS Software for Library and Information Applications* (ed. P. F. Burton), Gower, Aldershot, pp. 61–77.

Satyanarayana, V. V. V. (1987) Microcomputer based union catalogue of periodical holdings: BHEL experience. In *The Application of Micro-computers in Information, Documentation and Libraries* (eds K.-D. Lehmann and H. Strohl-Goebel), North-Holland, Amsterdam, pp. 117–19.

Saye, J. D. and Wilt, C. C. (1986) Database management programs and decision making in libraries and information centres. In *Microcomputers for Library Decision Making: Issues, Trends and Applications* (eds P. Hernon and C. R. McClure), Ablex, Norwood, New Jersey, pp. 118–29.

Shoolbred, M. (1986) Microcomputers for student use in academic libraries. *British Journal of Academic Librarianship*, **1** (3), 207–14.

Simpson, I. S. (1988) *Basic Statistics for Librarians*, 3rd edn, Bingley, London.

Sippings, G., Ramsden, H. and Turpie, G. (1987) *The Use of Information Technology by Information Services*, Aslib, London.

Snell, M. J. and Duggua, H. (1985) Microtext: electronic blackboard, expert system or teaching package. *Library Micromation news*, **8**, 9–10.

Taylor, D. (1985) Progress with G&G software: an update on Harper Adams Agricultural College library's computerisation program. *Library Micromation News*, **8**, 3–6.

Trevelyan, A. and Rowat, M. (1983) *An Investigation of the Use of Systems Programs in Library Applications of Microcomputers*, LIR Report No. 12, British Library, London.

Vratny-Watts, J. and Valuaskas, E. J. (1989) Prospective conversion: data transfer between fossil and new microcomputer technologies in libraries. *Information Technology and Libraries*, **8** (1), 34–41.

Walker, S. (1988) Improving subject access painlessly: recent work on the Okapi online catalogue projects. *Program*, **22** (1), 21–31.

Williams, T. (1987) Serials control and the microcomputer in the library. In *The Application of Micro-computers in Information, Documentation and Libraries* (eds K.-D. Lehmann and H. Strohl-Goebel), North-Holland, Amsterdam, pp. 690–4.

Zuboff, S. (1988) *In the Age of the Smart Machine: the Future of Work and Power*, Heinemann, London.

Index